aurora metro press

Founded in 1989 to publish and promote new writing, the company has specialised in new drama and fiction, winning recognition and awards from the industry.

new drama

Six plays by Black and Asian women. ed. Kadija George
ISBN 0-9515877-2-2 £7.50

Seven plays by women, female voices, fighting lives. ed. Cheryl Robson **ISBN 0-9515877-1-4 £5.95**

Young Blood, five plays for young performers. ed. Sally Goldsworthy **ISBN 0-9515877-6-5 £9.95**

European drama

A touch of the Dutch: plays by women. ed. Cheryl Robson **ISBN 0-9515877-7-3 £9.95**

Mediterranean plays by women. ed. Marion Baraitser **ISBN 0-9515877-3-0 £9.95**

other

How Maxine learned to love her legs and other tales of growing up. ed. Sarah Le Fanu **ISBN 0-9515877-4-9 £8.95**

The Women Writers Handbook eds. Robson, Georgeson, Beck. **ISBN 0-9515877-0-6 £4.95**

Series editor   Cheryl Robson

BEST OF THE FEST

A collection of new plays celebrating
10 years of London New Play Festival

editor   Phil Setren

a m

AURORA METRO PRESS

A collection of new plays celebrating 10 years of London New Play Festival

Wild Turkey
by Joe Penhall

Everlasting Rose
by Judy Upton

Strindberg Knew My Father
by Mark Jenkins

Maison Splendide
by Laura Bridgeman

In The Fields of Aceldama
by Naomi Wallace

Two Horsemen
by 'Biyi Bandele

AURORA METRO PRESS

We gratefully acknowledge financial assistance from Stoll Moss Theatres The Peggy Ramsay and Cameron Mackintosh Foundations, London New Play Festival, The Stage and TV Today and Gardner Merchant.

Production Manager Gillian Wakeling

With thanks to: Alison Spiby, Chris Preston, Karen Gerald, David Prescott, Elizabeth Graham, Harold Finley, David Banks, Peter Allegretti, Harold Sanditen, Lisa Forrell, Chris Cooke, Jayne Rose Nelson, Gary Davy, Nica Burns, David Kinsey.

ISBN 0-9515877-8-1   Printed by Anthony Rowe, Chippenham.

Contents

Phil Setren (Editor)

Artistic Director and co-founder of London New Play Festival where he has developed scripts with some of Britain's most up-and-coming writers. He has produced the first plays of emerging playwrights like Mark Ravenhill, Judy Upton, Joe Penhall, Naomi Wallace and the early works of 'Biyi Bandele, Jessica Townsend, Bonnie Greer and Anthony Neilson. He has guided over 100 playwrights into full productions of their new plays in London at the Old Red Lion, the Gate, the Finborough and the Bush Theatres, and at the Riverside, the Lyric and the Young Vic Studios.

As a Director specialising in new work he has directed Lisa Kotin's **Temporary Girl**, Daniel Scott's **Below the Belt** (Independent Theatre Award Nominee), George Singer's **Terminal Greeks**, T. J. Edwards **Busboy**, John Doona's **Hard Shoulder**, Wendy Hammond's **Julie Johnson** and **Jersey City**, Alan Cooke's **Something in the Air**, Sara Scopp's **Lady**, Barbara Lindsay's **Free,** a commisioned trilogy about the Los Angeles Race Riots **Walking in L.A.** and the British premiere of Christopher Durang's **Beyond Therapy** which won the 1986 *London Fringe Award for Best Comedy.*

Phil is a part-time lecturer in Performing Arts at Richmond College, teaches physical theatre at the Academy Drama School and was previously the Director for Post-Graduate studies at Mountview Theatre School where he developed a Contemporary Drama programme.

Cheryl Robson (Series Editor)

Worked for the BBC, before founding Women's Theatre Workshop and Aurora Metro Press. She has developed, produced and published the work of many UK and international writers.

In 1991 she completed her MA in Playwriting Studies at Birmingham University. She has had several plays produced, winning the Croydon Warehouse's Playwriting Festival in 1990.

Introduction
by Phil Setren

The driving force

Beauty, truth and insight live behind the writer's eye. For new playwrights, productions of their plays liberate dreams. A writer may dedicate months of thought and commitment to craft a story worthy of the stage for an evening's entertainment. The opportunity of a production demonstrates the theatre company's belief that a writer has something to say to the public. The chance to have a new play produced happens rarely, and is often the inspiration a playwright needs to continue to develop.

Providing that first opportunity is the thrill of producing London New Play Festival, and the driving force behind our perseverance, building one of London's most prolific 'grass roots' institutions for contemporary playwriting. As London's rich tradition of classical production develops, few companies have been able to make a commitment to the long-term development of new plays and new writers for theatre. Many theatres rely on popular revivals or classics because they can be less risky propositions at the box office. London New Play Festival develops the writers who can create classics of tomorrow through the development of bold, progressive, immediate and contemporary new plays.

Programming

London New Play Festival has produced ten annual Festivals of premiere productions of new plays. A diverse reading panel evaluates plays on originality in form, style, language, content, entertainment value and contemporary relevance to an audience today. As some Festivals have involved up to 14 productions, a variety of styles and lengths of plays are chosen. Raw, progressive plays that challenge conventional playwriting are as prominent to the programme as plays that are modern advancements to traditional forms. Genres like mystery or farce are as important to develop as are less traditional forms, both of which push and redefine the boundaries of modern theatre. London New Play Festival has included plays for children, plays for teenagers, commissioned plays on current topics such as racial tension, prison censorship, and gay marriage. There's been a futuristic horror play about mad cow disease and, even a programmed full season of 17 plays dealing with the themes 'Healing, Spirituality and the Afterlife.'

Artistic policy

Choosing to break through the conventional 2 hour play with interval, London New Play Festival selects plays that are complete journeys' rather than plays conforming to what most theatres in Britain consider 'commercial length.' Where some London literary managers will condemn a writer for anything but 'full length' work, London New Play Festival regularly encourages one-act plays, short plays, 10 and 15 minute plays (sometimes theme based) as well as 90 minute and 2 hour plays, without limiting the creativity of the playwrights participating. This approach has provided young playwrights with a chance to experience production without length pressure, and given many writers the confidence to take risks and, above all, to keep writing. Playwriting, like many art forms, can only grow and thrive by continually extending its boundaries.

This policy has proved successful, having produced the formative plays of writers now considered to be some of the most important new voices of the 90's. Festival alumni include Mark Ravenhill (**Close to You**) 1993, who went on to write the successfully shocking **Shopping and Fucking**, Naomi Wallace (**In the Fields of Aceldama**) 1993, who later wrote the moving West End adaptation **Birdy** and the RSC's graphic **Slaughter City,** Bonnie Greer (**A Few White Boys Talking**) 1993 and Judy Upton (**Everlasting Rose**) 1991 both Verity Bargate Award winners, Joe Penhall (**Wild Turkey**) 1993, who later wrote the Bush Theatre's warm-hearted and convincing **Love and Understanding** and 'Biyi Bandele (**Two Horsemen**) 1994, writing the chilling **Death Catches the Hunter** which toured nationally. Through successful collaborations with these writers and many more, London New Play Festival has clearly given a start to, and provided a career launch for many of London's most up-and-coming dramatists.

Best of the Fest : 10 year collection

This collection represents a variety of playwright styles from a few of the many strong dramatists to have their work produced in London New Play Festival. The book can be used by theatre companies, drama schools, youth theatre companies and commercial theatre companies. In addition, the plays can be read for pleasure as well as performance.

Along with the six plays, a brief history of each Festival is included to give a flavour of the event. Practitioners in the industry often comment on the amount of work London New Play Festival has accomplished with very limited resources. We hope to communicate the great joy and sense of occasion that has come with working on each Festival, and to encourage young theatre artists interested in creating new work, that even in the most difficult of financial climates, it can be done.

The Plays

Wild Turkey by Joe Penhall (1993) Two penniless small businessmen struggle to keep their flagging hamburger bar afloat in the face of increasingly bizarre and savage forces. When a midnight break-in threatens to destroy the business, their all-male world is shattered with frightening and comic consequences. The play is loosely based on the author's experiences working in the late-night Stockwell café called 'Do the Right Thing.' A four character play and the first play from a writer of immense talent, packed with scathing realistic dialogue.

Everlasting Rose by Judy Upton (1992) A caravan Casanova is terrified of ageing. He changes wives every decade to placate his phobia until wife number four, a woman of the 90's, challenges the repetition and routine of the male ego. A slightly surreal three character exploration of modern vanity and self-perception, and a first play from the writer, who at the age of 22 would later go on to win the Verity Bargate and the George Devine Awards for playwriting.

Maison Splendide by Laura Bridgeman (1996) Honey and Moon are a pair of petty crooks house-sitting for a big time gangster, aching to 'get out of the rented room and into the maisonette.' The stability of their relationship is hilariously explored and ceremonial custom is parodied by enacting a 'let's pretend' lesbian white wedding with garden gnomes as witnesses, and Barry White music as backing for their vows. Part of the 'Gay Marriage in Suburbia' trilogy at the Young Vic, this delightful two character play commissioned by London New Play Festival reveals an up-and-coming writer with an acute ear for the nuances of modern dialogue.

Strindberg Knew My Father by Mark Jenkins (1992) A comedy where real life descends into modern farce as the Swedish playwright, on the verge of paranoid schizophrenia, loses control over his characters while writing 'Miss Julie.' After being framed for libel and the rape of a young gypsy girl, the people around him become gross exaggerations of his own making. A contemporary farce for five characters of dark humour and a touch of Magritte from a gifted humorist.

In the Fields of Aceldama by Naomi Wallace (1993) When their only child dies in an accident at seventeen, Mattie and Henry draw on her spirit to find the strength to carry on. A rural setting, travelling poetically through past memories and present time, exploring the closeness and separation experienced by two parents and the daughter they lived for. A haunting song of loss and discovery with three characters and an early play by this award-winning and prolific writer.

Two Horsemen by 'Biyi Bandele (1994) Banza and Lagbaja, two philosophical streetsweepers, trade stories of life, sex and God in a run down shack. Will their imaginations save them, or trap them in a rich world of make-believe? An enigmatic and exciting play, and winner of the 1994 Time Out Award for theatre.

Festival history
1989

Invited to manage the Café Theatre in Leicester Square for the theatre director's summer holiday, London New Play Festival began as a lunchtime theatre Festival. Plays were produced in the 20 seat venue at 12:00, 1:15, 2:00 and 3:00pm. Twelve playwrights received premiere productions of their plays for five performances including rising comedienne Julie Balloo's **Dinner and a Movie** and plays by formidable writers David Ansdele (**Tom's Gift**), Val Doulton (**The Quilt**), and Sue Aldred (**Hannah's Place**). Also featured were **Boo To The Moon** by Paul Slabolepsky, now considered one of South Africa's leading playwrights, **Written In Sickness** by Giles's Croft and **Marital AIDS** by Jack Bradley, both of whom went on to become Literary Manager of the Royal National Theatre in the 1990's.

The Festival's producer/co-founder Cathy McMahon set small budgets for the plays and found cheap rehearsal space as even modest costs would burst the budget. Technical rehearsals, usually lasting three days, were squeezed into four hours, and the four minimal sets were stored in the tiniest of cupboards. Acting as producers, production managers and publicists we organised and promoted the first season, and instituted a 'no reviews' policy which continued through the first four years of production. This encouraged journalists to write preview articles about the plays instead of elevating some writers while damaging others.

Of course, the best support we could give to playwrights was to produce their work well, which sometimes required us to cope with some extreme situations. When Val Doulton's play **The Quilt** employed two actresses of 60 and 80 years of age, our job also involved guarding the ladies' loo for required pre-show visits. The company for **Nine Night**, a Jamaican retelling of Medea in patois, requested that the set include earth, water and fire. With the demands of 10 minute set changes, the writer agreed that the elements could be accomplished with lighting changes. Some of the most popular plays packed as many as 50 people in the 20 seat Café Theatre with audience seated on the floor and practically on the stage. Richard Daug's **Miles To Go** was invited to the Samuel Beckett Theatre in New York with the original London New Play Festival cast, and four of the plays enjoyed transfer runs to fringe theatres across London.

Celebrating with a closing party upstairs at the Arts Theatre Club in Leicester Square, writers commented on the dynamism the Festival had brought to the London theatre. The energy, vitality and talent of the nearly 100 participants was certainly an inspiration, encouraging us to believe that London New Play Festival served a vital function and would continue to grow.

1990

The Festival was now hosted by the 60 seat Old Red Lion Theatre, in Islington, presenting four plays per day over a three week period. With the support of the theatre's enthusiastic Artistic Director Ken McClymont, who allowed sets to be stored on the roof of the building, 12 playwrights' premiere productions were presented to growing audiences. Highlights included Alan Cooke's cartoon farce about pollution **Something in the Air** and Julie Balloo's hilarious **Clay** about a housewife creating a clay sculpture head which comes to life and exposes the secrets of her cheating husband. A full-length version of **Clay** later transferred to the Man in the Moon Theatre, as did Jan Maloney's poetic childbirth account **Cherub** and Murray Woodfield's childhood rediscovery **Fragments** (which was later filmed starring Paul McGann and Brian Rawlinson). Sue Aldred's maternal dream journey **Jacob's Ladder** toured to the Dublin Festival, and Rebecca Ranson's southern American love triangle **Blood on Blood** played in New York after the Festival premiere with the original London New Play Festival company.

As the ladies' loo in the pub was usually the women's dressing-room, this provided the Red Lion regulars with an intriguing topic of conversation when seven women emerged in nuns' habits for Nicola Davies' **After Eeyore** and then walked up the fire escape to the roof to set scenery before performing. With only a tiny grant from Islington Arts and Entertainment, company stage manager Areta

Breeze created stage-craft miracles, including a realistic working prop heart monitor, made out of a cardboard box (for less than £5). Company associate director Madeleine Wynne led script reader meetings assessing over 200 plays, and producer Cathy McMahon continued to build the Festival by embracing the challenges of the job with verve and optimism, moving from photocopying programmes to changing sets to asking a mortician to borrow a coffin for a stage set. He quickly agreed as no-one had ever asked him to borrow one before.

1991

Shattered Peace by Claire Booker shocked audiences with the story of a grief-stricken Irish woman employing horrifying revenge methods when her husband is killed in Northern Ireland. Acid house novelist Trevor Miller's first play **The Heart of Saturday Night** dramatised three Soho prostitutes' desperate need to escape their lifestyle, and Norman King Lloyd's absurdist **Seringapatham**, which interpreted suburban life from the inside of a giant birdcage. Perhaps one of the Festival's most stylistically diverse seasons, also included were Barbara Lindsay's Drama League Award-winning comedy **Free** about a carnival show baffling a small town's inhabitants with a man who can actually float, and Tim Newton's verse melodrama about Victorian London **Ballad Of The Limehouse Rat** which went on to tour nationally and won the 1991 London Fringe Award for Best One-Person play.

The Old Red Lion became the confirmed home of the Festival. The supportive atmosphere created by pub owners Pauline and Tony Sherrif-Geary, and Joanne and Paul Parrish (now a successful playwright) combined with the flexibility of the theatre space allowed a wide variety of staging possibilities for the plays. The family dog Heidi occasionally contributed new lines to the plays and Ken's Sunday barbecues in the garden gave casts and writers a warm farewell before the plays changed the following week. New audiences developed and endured the heat of the Old Red Lion. Producer Cathy McMahon found rehearsal spaces in numerous available rooms throughout the community, organising up to 8 plays in rehearsal at a time. The Motley and St Martin's design programmes provided up and coming stage designers interested in new writing, with design opportunities on the festival. Student stage managers were trained in lighting and sound-board operation and learned to crew the set changes and quick turnarounds. The Float Space, a flotation tank business, provided a small sponsorship for **Free** as the play was about metaphysical floating, which was matched financially by The Association for Business Sponsorship of the Arts. Robert Peckham's **It Never Rains** featured a Marilyn Monroe look-alike in the cast. As the women's dressing room was still the ladies' loo in the pub, when the actress Tamsin Hollo emerged in her white 'Marilyn' dress, wig and full make-up, the pub locals commented that since the seven nuns of the previous year, the Festival was certainly looking up.

1992

How up to the minute can playwriting be? Can plays be more immediate than journalism? After the 15 plays of Festival '92 were chosen, three of the playwrights were individually all directly affected by the Los Angeles race riots in April of that year. Tim Blackwell had just left London for a screenwriting career in Hollywood, and Brandyn Artis and Mark Williams were L.A. residents who came to London for the rehearsals of their Festival plays. The responses all three writers had to the racial explosions were so raw, emotional and diverse that we decided to commission a 20 minute piece from each titled **Walking in L.A.**, which we presented at 10pm at the Old Red Lion. Pages of writing were flying in and out of the production in response to current news items and rehearsal feelings, a full rap was choreographed by Donna King for the middle of the piece, and the racially diverse cast, featured artists who would later become significant actors and writers in modern British theatre (Harold Finley, Bonnie Greer, Scott Gilmore).

New plays for children and young people were also programmed, opening with Louise Warren's moving **Night, Night** about a deaf child who learned to chase away nightmares caused by the mockery of other children. Claire Booker's **Gone Fishing** was a play aimed at teenagers' first experiences of employment. Other highlights included Ruth Worrall's **Asking For It** about the chemical castration of rapists, and Oscar Watson's bold **Coming Home**, dealing with black homosexuality, adjustment and individual acceptance, which later played at the Lillian Bayliss Theatre. Alan McMurtrie's moving **The Prisoner's Pumpkin** dealt with a South African political prisoner's return to Britain, and went on to run at the Chelsea Centre Theatre. Mark Jenkins' hilarious farce **Strindberg Knew My Father** went on to be presented at the Sherman Theatre in Cardiff. Three contrasting styles of Canadian drama were also presented with John Lazarus' warm-hearted father/son comedy **Homework For Men**, Don Hannah's hard-hitting portrait of a teenage mother **Rubber Dolly**, and Quebecois Normandy Cancan-Marquis' memory drama about the emotional cause of a car crash (**The Cézanne Syndrome**) which the Festival produced at the Finborough Theatre with the support of Quebec House and The Canadian High Commission.

1993
Mark Ravenhill's comedy about gay 'outing' **Close to You** outraged script readers and packed in audiences for his first play about a group of gay men and lesbians, who accidentally kill a Member of Parliament they are trying to 'out' at a 70's theme party. Ravenhill's next play earned significant commercial success (**Shopping and Fucking**) as did Naomi Wallace (**In the Fields of Aceldama**) and Joe Penhall (**Wild Turkey**), further proof of the Festival's role as a seedbed for emerging playwriting talent. Other highlights included Andrew Rattenbury's moving **Soundings**, Wendy Hammond's graphic **Jersey City** and Bernard Padden's outrageous farce **Normality**. Graeme Holmes' comedy with video **Fleshing Out** centred on a cartoonist's relationship with his characters, including vibrantly visual elements like a toothless shark, a female cactus, a pink ball of fluff and a killer iron, that flattens its victims.

With the support of the London Borough Grants Unit, a small office on the top floor of Sadlers Wells Theatre was hired allowing the Festival office proper work space. Directors Kate Valentine and Jessica Dromgoole joined the Festival team as Literary Manager and

Co-Producer, and Casting Director John Cannon took on the daunting task of casting 80 roles. Numerous senior and celebrated playwrights gave their endorsement by agreeing to be patrons of the company including Edward Bond, Caryl Churchill, David Hare and Arnold Wesker. Bonnie Greer, whose play **A Few White Boys Talking** was based on video-taped interviews with young white men across the country, was commissioned with funding from a 25th anniversary sponsorship from Time Out magazine.

Scottish writer Brian Devlin's 'bicycle race' play for children **The Freewheel Armada** was programmed. Unfortunately the play-wright's archaic typewriter lacked the letters 's' and 'l' – so London New Play Festival word processed the script so that the actors could read it. Production demands increased with larger budgets. Some set changes had to be completed in 15 minutes. This meant a production line of 8 were needed to empty a bathtub used in **Soundings**, and then mop up before loading stacks of hay into the theatre for **In the Fields Of Aceldama**. Production Managers Mark Rainbow and Jayne Rose Nelson had to help one cast member from City Farm up the fire escape daily. It was the title character for Scott Frank's zany comedy **Butter's Goat** (who was often found eating the scenery).

1994

LNPF expanded to two venues for this 10 play Festival, with International plays presented at the Gate Theatre in Notting Hill, and British new plays at the Old Red Lion. Highlights included David Bridel's **Shreads And Fancies** about new age travellers pitching tents on a posh family's farmland. Wendy Hammond's love story **Julie Johnson** explored the love between women and Noelle Jana-scewshka's play with film **The History Of Water** explored the relationship between Asia and Australia. Naomi Wallace and Bruce McLeod's children's play **The Girl Who Fell Through A Hole In Her Jumper** encouraged audience participation from very lively Islington children's groups. 'Biyi Bandele's **Two Horsemen** kept audiences laughing while the last two remaining horsemen of the apocalypse sank into a flood of surreal doomed oblivion. **Two**

Horsemen won a Time Out award for theatre and later transferred to the Bush Theatre for a three week run.

While the company was continuing to improve the quality and standard of writing under the Literary Management of Christine Harmar-Brown, extending the Festival's limited resources to two venues created a deficit for the first time. A disappointing response from a funding scheme we were depending on meant it could have been the end of the company without careful and stressful financial management. How difficult to be winning awards, prestigious transfers and public praise while suffering internally with little help from the funding bodies. A kind note from playwright and Festival patron David Hare arrived, suggesting we send a package to the Peggy Ramsay Foundation for support. The Foundation provided vital support which has continued over the past five years, without which London New Play Festival could not exist. The dedicated support of Trustees Lawrence Harbottle, John Tidyman, Simon Callow, John Welch, Michael Codron and David Hare acting on behalf of the Peggy Ramsay Foundation has liberated over 50 playwrights to production.

1995

'Healing, Spirituality and the Afterlife' were the central themes of this 17 play event at the Finborough Theatre. Two main productions included the theatrical AIDS drama **Zero Positive** by Harry Kondoleon and collaborative commissioned play **Three Tides Turning** by Louise Warren. Staged readings included Nick Sutton's futuristic rave play **Bioluminescence on the 22nd Floor**, Judy Upton's intrigue about a man with a toothache and a vampiric dentist **Stealing Souls** later produced by The Red Room, and the controversial Peter Quint's solo of a man attempting to recreate the spirit of Veronica Lake in a bedsit, **Pornography of the Infinite.**

A commissioned programme of late-night shorts, invited playwrights including Aidan Healy, Phil Wilmott and Gary Swing to explore healing, spirituality and the afterlife in a 15 minute format, which was especially popular with audiences. This season, although smaller in terms of production due to finance constraints, still served the creative and developmental needs of 17 playwrights. In addition, the writing explored spiritual concerns and matters of the soul at a time when the theatre field seemed intent on new work of a shocking and hard sell 'Trainspotting' variety.

1996

With productions at the Young Vic Studios and readings at the Lyric Studio, this season marked a transition for the Festival moving out of pub venues and into three Off-West End theatres. Highlights included Anthony Neilson's futuristic mad cow disease horror play **Hoover Bag**, Sara Clifford's play with film **Tongue Tied** dealing with the persecution of imprisoned writers, and Anita Sullivan's savage comedy about HRH trading places with a rural Scotswoman in **An Audience with Queen.** John Doona's **Hard Shoulder** explored the topical issues of road rage and capitalism, while the trilogy **Gay Marriage in Suburbia** commissioned three writers to explore modern relationships and commitment. The 22 year old Rhiannan Tise's **Where the Devils Dwell** explored the private lives of city dwellers, and James Waddington's **The Cricket Test** was a fictional retelling of African woman Desire Ntolo's story – she was forbidden to build an African hut in her garden by the local council. Ms Ntolo attended the first night performance to meet the actors and writer and to share the experiences of living the story with a slightly shocked response to the play. She enjoyed a conversation with the writer who explained how he created the story from a newspaper article about her, imagining what her real story might be.

A series of discussions was also presented in association with New Playwrights Trust, inviting points of view from leading practitioners, on topics like mixed-form theatre, children's theatre and notions of identity. Festival patron and celebrated playwright Arnold Wesker was commissioned by *The Observer* to write a piece about the Festival, which resulted in Wesker spending time and providing guidance to many young writers in and around the season.

After months of advanced planning with producer Karen Gerald, and with our deficit under control, thanks to new support from the Foundation for Sport and the Arts and the continued support from The Peggy Ramsay Foundation, the Festival took new offices at the Diorama Arts Centre. Increased rehearsal space was available to us to develop plays, and casting director Gary Davy used the empty artists' studios to cast the 65 roles. Writers' workshops were offered on topics like alleviating writer's block, settings and new approaches to collaborating.

This season featured some particularly bold literary imaginations with specific requirements. When the playwright Anita Sullivan required that rabbit meat be sliced on stage, we listened to the ethical arguments in the office, and then continued with our job of facilitating a writer's requirements for production to the best of our ability. I remember standing at the box office at Riverside Studios having a discussion with the literary agent Mel Kenyon, while this play was being performed. We watched a ranting man run out of the theatre and yell at the box office staff that he was a vegetarian and he was disgusted by the scene. As Artistic Director I'm always willing to discuss plays with the audience. But on this one occasion at the end of a very long day, and bearing in mind that this was the playwright's desired effect, I decided that this might be a good time for me to walk Mel to her motorcycle in the car park.

1997

A short season at the Lyric Studio featured readings of Gillian Plowman's **Try a Pair of Baggy Trousers** dealing with two sisters raising a handicapped daughter together and Kevin McGee's **Flow Like Honey** and **A Somewhat Indecent Situation**, revealing a young Irish writer of great wit and promise. John Doona's daring **Linger** full of epic imagery and Tom Minter's poetic **Dahlias and Moonshine,** were presented alongside of Sally Wainwrights' comedy **The Wrong Parents** and the Spanish Paloma Pedrero's **A Night Divided** about the chance meeting of a bible salesman and an actress. To close the season, the Festival invited pieces of new

writing in poetry, music, film and performance in an evening titled
The Steam Basin.

For the second year, Festival Education Director Chris Preston co-
ordinated writing workshops to provide skills training for
playwrights. The importance of these workshops is especially
significant as there is little opportunity for the training of
playwrights in London and no structure for writers to progress
through, particularly in comparison with other regions like the
Northwest. One-day workshops also provided Festival staff with the
opportunity to meet new writers in a skills development forum, and
allowed the writers an opportunity to work with the company. This is
the kind of valuable contact a writer misses out on in the larger
theatre companies. The success of our education work meant that we
could expand the writers workshops to a full Writers School in the
next season.

1998

A generous sponsorship from Stoll Moss Theatres for this tenth
anniversary season enables the Festival's first presentation of new
work in the West End. By providing the Apollo Theatre on
Shaftesbury Avenue with four 6:00pm 'platform' events, London
New Play Festival will give nine new writers the opportunity to see
their plays on a West End stage for the first time. And, with four
premiere productions and a reading series at Riverside Studios and
two premiere productions at the Diorama Theatre, London New Play
Festival is finally able to achieve one of its long-term goals – to
reach audiences across the spectrum of London theatre by presenting
new plays in the West End, Off-West End and in Fringe theatres. In
addition, an expanded Writing School provides learning
opportunities for more than 200 emerging playwrights to participate
in one-day skills workshops on topics ranging from play structure, to
dialogue, to the popular 'write a play in a day' workshop.

For the tenth anniversary party at the Diorama, London New Play
Festival will invite the hundreds of past participants to celebrate, see
old friends and accept our thanks for their work over the years. The

high artistic standards of the Festival have been achieved through the dedication and hard work of so many actors, directors, designers and technicians who collaborate in support of the playwrights. These practitioners have subsidised the Festival through their support, patiently accepting the lack of funding and their tiny expenses honorariums, looking forward to a time when the company will have the necessary resources to compensate them in line with their expertise.

Production highlights at Riverside Studios include David Bridel's powerful drama, **The Last Girl** about the pornographic boundaries of artistic inspiration, Helen Cooper's disturbing memory fuelled thriller **The House of Ruby Moon** and the premiere play from the wildly futuristic imagination of Finneas Edwards, whose **TV Tots Meet Bomb Boy**, explores media damaged youth searching for a future. Judy Upton's surreal comedy about vanity and fear of ageing **Everlasting Rose**, which had three workshop performances in 1992, receives a full production run and is also included in this anthology.

A writers' group of five new playwrights has been formed to create a collaborative play titled **Underbelly** which looks under the skin and peers into the guts of the real vulnerability of late 1990's life. **Underbelly** plays at the Diorama Theatre along with US performance artist Tim Miller's fiercely committed **Shirts and Skins** charting one gay man's journey through the challenges of the last two decades of the millennium. Miller will host a post-show discussion with the author Martin Sherman and a debate between playwrights David Hare and Mark Ravenhill opens the West End season, discussing the success of new writing in the commercial theatre.

In the autumn when the idea of this publication started to take shape, we wrote to a few West End producers asking if we could read scenes from the plays in the foyers of West End theatres. Stoll Moss' production director Nica Burns invited us for a meeting to tell us that she felt readings would get lost in the foyers, but they'd like to put London New Play Festival on the stage for four platform events that they would sponsor. Some weeks later, David Kinsey from Stoll Moss took us on a walk around four West End Theatres on Shaftesbury Avenue. For a company used to working on tiny stages, this was certainly an exceptional series of events, and we found working with people who understand the need to develop new writers an energising experience, in contrast to the painful funding cuts by two-thirds, due to the dissolving in 1998 of the London Borough Grants Unit's Festival Fund programme for the capital.

New creative topics are now discussed in the Festival office, like: What makes a play work on a West End stage? How does the size and scale of the space affect the writing? How quickly do characters and situations have to be established in a larger theatre? What is the West End expectation of a new play as an entertainment? How can playwrights get the feel of a large theatre unless they have the opportunity to see their work performed in one?

The publication of this anthology, our first, gives the selected playwrights a chance to receive second and subsequent productions of their work by theatre companies and drama education institutions nationally and internationally. Publishing a new play gives the writing a permanence and makes new work available to practitioners who are hungry for new ideas. As London New Play Festival continues to grow and when the public funding bodies finally validate the Festival's vital contribution with annual revenue funding, that support can be channelled into regular new play publication alongside of productions and playwriting skills education. With this necessary support London New Play Festival will emerge to become an institution of permanence, existing beyond the energy of its founding staff.

Wild Turkey

by Joe Penhall

Wild Turkey

by Joe Penhall

First performed at The Old Red Lion Theatre, Islington in 1993.
Directed by Kath Mattock.
Designed by Guiseppe Belli

Stu, in his late twenties a   Sean Patterson
small-time restaurateur
Ben, same age, Stu's friend   Peter Helmer
and employee
Danny, a petty thief   Tim Gallagher
Hank, a thug   Chris Adamson

*The action takes place at Stu's burger bar and steakhouse over a
period of roughly twelve hours.*

SCENE 1

*Midnight. A small, licensed steakhouse / burger bar in South
London. The stage is the restaurant part, with a door leading to the
burger bar and shop front, right, and a door leading to a bathroom
and the upstairs flat, left. Running the length of the stage, left to
right, a few yards from the backdrop is a bar with shelving behind it.
On the shelves there is a small and poor selection of bottles and on
the bar top there is an ancient till. Facing the audience, is a new and
expensive-looking colour TV, flashing disparate static images and
the occasional picture. It looks distinctly out of place. Centre stage
is a small round table with a couple of chairs.*

*Stu is at the centre table, counting money – coins – and placing it in
a shoebox in front of him. Ben is leaning against the bar, facing Stu
and smoking a cigarette. There is a wallphone to the right.*

BEN   Yes or no?

STU *(counting)* Ninety, ninety-one, ninety . . . two . . .

BEN   Or yes, that's all I'm asking.

STU *(looking up)* You're asking?

BEN   I'm just saying phone them. Why not?

STU *(regarding the cash)* This is very depressing.

BEN   A simple phonecall.

STU   I'm depressed.

BEN *(crosses to wallphone right and picks it up as if to dial)*
Tomorrow, you pick up the phone, you go: 'Hello, this is' –

STU *(interrupting)* Ben do you have any idea how much these things
cost?

BEN   Same as I say – phone them.

STU   A fortune.

BEN   So does a brick through the window. *(he returns to
centre. Stu puts the lid on the shoebox, pushes it away and rests
his chin on his hands)* The police said – this is *the police* Stu – if
we get licensed at this point, we'll need a grill, shutters, something to –

STU *(interrupting)* Balls to the police. What the fuck do they know?

BEN   They're the –

STU   They know about crime? Is this what you're saying?
(shaking his head) The police, Ben – very over-rated.

BEN *(sits opposite Stu)* Listen –

STU *(interrupting)* What's got into you Ben? Why you getting so
uptight about this?

BEN   I'm not uptight.

STU   You are. You're uptight. On edge. *(leaning closer)*
Ants in your pants and it's driving me up the wall. *(pause)* You
still upset about that feller?

BEN   No.

STU   Is that what it is?

BEN   No. I'm over that.

STU   You can't lie to me Ben.

BEN	. . . but that was a good example.
STU	. . . because I know you're upset.
BEN	Yes and I'm saying, I'm suggesting . . .
STU	Ben listen, that was a one off.

BEN   That was the tip of the iceberg. *(pause)* He pulls a knife and he has it in my guts.

STU   Near your guts Ben. Very near without actually inserting.

BEN   He said: 'I want money'. Is that reasonable? Who doesn't?

STU	And he didn't pull a knife, he picked one up.
BEN	OK, he picked up a knife . . .
STU	A vegetable paring knife.
BEN	That is a sharp knife!
STU	The vegetable paring knife?
BEN	Yes.
STU	With the . . . with the serrated edge?
BEN	Yeah, and the black handle.
STU	That knife is blunt. Blunt as a baby's arse.
BEN	It was a hold-up. He held me up!

STU *(slight pause)* Listen Ben. Hold-ups, they go with the territory. If you can't stand the heat, get out of the kitchen.

BEN   We don't have a kitchen.

STU *(standing)* Well . . . when we get one. *(he goes to the bar, fetches a rag, crosses to a front table, wipes it down, wipes the other front table down, returns to centre, picks up shoebox and hands it to Ben)* Take this upstairs and put it under the bed. *(he takes the box, looks at it then looks at Stu)*

BEN   It's time we got a safe.

(Stu says nothing, gives him a 'look')
Why not? Splash out. Live a bit.

STU	Take the box upstairs. Please.
BEN	Or get a better box.
STU	Ben.

BEN   A piggy bank.
(Stu takes the box back, glares at Ben)
You can't be too mean to buy a piggy bank, Stu.

STU   Mean? What do you mean *mean*?

BEN *(takes the box off Stu)* I'm sorry. I didn't mean that.

STU *(snatches the box back)* You saying I'm greedy or something?

BEN *(snatches the box back and turns toward door, left)* No. I'm
saying the money is becoming . . . you are becoming ruled by the
money side of things. By business.

STU   I am sorry for being a capitalist . . .
(Ben heads towards door left. Stu follows)

BEN *(pausing)* You seem to care less about –

STU   Do I now?

BEN   . . . about looking after –

STU   What are you so upset about? You got a room, you
got a job, you don't pay any rent.

BEN   I earn my keep.

STU   You're set up.

BEN   It's no picnic living here.

STU   It's better than a bloody box under a bridge.

BEN   . . . all day, all night. You can't put a price on the
value of me being here at night. Looking after the place. I am the
security measures.

STU *(relenting)* OK.

BEN   No safe, no grill, I am the security measures.

STU   Yes, you –

BEN   I am them.

STU   I'm agreeing with you.

BEN   As long as you know that.

STU   I do. I appreciate it.

BEN *(pause)*   Well, good.
(slight pause. He opens the door and is about to exit, when)

STU   And, and, and so we don't actually need a grill now.
Or a safe. *(pause)* And when we get them, you'll go.

BEN *(pause)*   What do you mean?

STU   There'd be no point in you being here. I'll take the room back. When we get the things.

BEN *(pause)*   Oh.

STU   See what I mean?

BEN   No.

STU   It's in your best interests for us not to get security. *(slight pause)* And it's in your favour that we are at risk, twenty-four hours a day. Seven days a week. We need you.
(Ben shakes his head and puts box down. Stu throws his rag over bar, then walks around and behind bar, retrieves a baseball bat, then wanders back to centre, swinging bat idly)
Here. I bought you a present.
(Ben glances at the bat, then turns his attention to the TV on the bar, fiddles with a knob, murmuring)

BEN   Just what I've always wanted.

STU   They're all the rage. Everybody's got 'em. Danny brought it 'round. Security measures.

BEN *(facing Stu)* Stu, I don't like this.

STU   What?

BEN *(indicating bat)* This . . . this, the way you're operating now. You've become an operator.

STU   I don't like it. Nobody does. Who do you know that likes anything in this world? But we all have a job of work to do.

BEN   Maybe you should get Danny to move in here.

STU   Danny wouldn't move in here.

BEN   Well someone else.

STU *(pause)*   Who else am I gonna get to move in here?

BEN   I dunno. They'd have to be mad.

STU   No.

BEN   Yes.

STU   No, they wouldn't.

BEN   Completely bonkers.

STU   No.

BEN   Yes!

STU *(beat)*   OK but, but you see also I'd have to be able to trust them. This is the main thing.

BEN   OK.

STU   And, and how can you trust a person who is bonkers?

BEN   You can't.

STU   Precisely. But I can trust you, you see. You are the only person I can trust in this life. You are a friend instead of just another nutpot employee.

BEN   OK.

STU   . . . some thieving imbecile with nothing better to do than swallow drugs and grow boils.

BEN   Yeah alright.

STU   . . . poke birds . . . steal cars . . . that's what these kids do. And grown men too. Most people, see, they live their lives without gravity. They are in a void of trivia. We are doing something good here.

BEN   Something good, right.

STU   We are doing something important.

BEN   Yes.

STU   We cook hamburgers.

BEN   Hamburgers, yes.

STU   We are entrepreneurs.

BEN   Mm-hm.

STU   It's the new thing. *(pause)* Now let's sort this TV out, open a bottle and watch the fights. Eh?

BEN   OK.

STU   Relax a bit. Get slaughtered. Balls to the lot of them. *(he goes behind bar, dumps the bat, grabs three shot glasses and a bottle from the shelf, brings them to table centre while Ben attempts to get a picture on the TV. Stu holds up the bottle and admires it as if it were a golden chalice. He opens it, takes a slug and gasps happily)*

BEN *(to TV)*   Bastard. What's the matter with this thing Stu?

STU   You gotta wiggle the thing.

BEN *(wiggling aerial)* I am wiggling the thing. It's a dud.

STU *(to bottle)* What a baby. True bourbon. The very last bottle.

BEN *(looking up)* What is it?

STU   *Wild Turkey.* An honest hard-working drink for an honest hard-working man. *(he pours two shots and sits)*

BEN *(of TV)*   This is a lemon. Danny's lumbered us with a lemon.

STU   It's not his fault.

BEN   We're gonna miss the fight. If we miss the fight I shall be very upset with Danny.

STU   We won't miss the fight. He'll fix it. He likes fixing things. *(pause. He lights a cigarette)* Did you know he fixed the lock on the front door?

BEN   No. I didn't know that.

STU   I didn't know it either. But he did. *(sips his drink)* It kept slipping. People could just walk in and take their pick, unless we had the mortis on. He fixed the car as well. Amazing. I say to him: 'Listen, I don't know if you can help me with this one but I think it's the mix. Air-fuel whatever. It chugs. Like a tractor. When I drive it I'm on the farm. This car is not well. Help me Danny.' So in other words, I just tell him the symptoms of my problem and he says 'I can fix that.' Just like a doctor or something.

BEN   Yeah, he's alright – Danny.

STU   Fixed the fridge.

BEN   Yes. And the heater.

STU   My shoes.

BEN   My shoes too.

STU   I like him.

BEN   I like him too. Yes, because you, you get a doctor in –

STU *(correcting him)* Repair man.

BEN   . . . yes and he'll charge the earth and he still won't do it.

STU   They don't fix it. They are out for themselves.

BEN   Absolutely.

STU   Then things fuck up for you. And we, and they say: 'This is the free world. We have fought long and hard for the right to fuck things up. There is no communism so fuck you brother!'

BEN   No-one cares anymore.

STU   They don't give two squirts of shit. Anymore.

BEN   Too busy minding their own business when –

STU   Yes . . . when the shit hits the fan. It's the English way.

BEN *(stands and heads for door right, talking)* And you want to know why?

STU   Why? Where are you going?

BEN   Seeing where Danny's got to.

Ben exits right. Stu reaches for Ben's drink, downs it, downs his own and refills both. Enter Ben.

BEN   . . . because we are scared.

STU *(drinking)* What do you think of this stuff?

BEN   The whisky?

STU   Bourbon.

BEN   I like it. *(he sits for a moment and sips his drink. Then he stands, goes to door, peeps out again, then returns to centre. He fidgets. Stu watches him bemused)*

STU   It's the heavyweights tonight, isn't it?

BEN   Super-middleweight.

STU   Remember when you were a kid watching the heavyweights from Las Vegas? Best bit was the girls in between rounds. It's not the same anymore. They have to wear clothes. What is the matter Ben?

BEN   I just saw this guy out there.

STU *(gets to his feet)* Is it Danny?

BEN   No. Some feller completely off his head. Just screaming into the night. *(Stu crosses to door right. Ben follows)* Don't go out there. *(Stu halts)* Just some nutcase.

(They pause. Ben takes a peek out the door) I can see him through the glass. He's doing karate kicks now.

Stu pushes past and exits right. He returns.

STU   You're right. Just abusing the world in general. *(he peeks through the door)* He's vomiting now. *(he returns and sits with a sigh)* Look at it, out there. Not the same as Battersea. Half a mile south and we're in the swamps. *(pause)* We had it all, didn't we? *The Clam Bake* – nice little restaurant. Friendly clientele. Happy people. *(pause. He goes to TV, fiddles)* Yes . . . We just got to be extremely philosophical.

BEN   Yes.

STU   You can try and understand it all . . .

BEN   Yeah.

STU   You can get intellectual about it . . .

BEN   Nope.

STU   Blame somebody . . .

BEN   Pointless.

STU   Exactly, there is no point . . .

BEN   Yes . . .

STU   . . . because . . .

BEN   . . . it's silly.

STU   . . . no, yes and . . .

BEN   . . . not real.

STU   . . . yes and . . .

BEN   Surreal . . .

STU   And we may be dead tomorrow.

BEN   Yesterday even.

STU   But this – *(indicates TV)* . . . this is real. The fights.

BEN·   This is what men do, captured up there on the
               screen.

STU   This is reality . . . life.

BEN   This is a good thing.

The door right bursts open and Danny enters, his hands cupped to his chest. He lunges across the stage to the other side, murmuring.

DANNY   Fucking fucking, fucking, fucking shit.

He exits left. Stu and Ben look puzzled but say nothing. A moment passes, Danny enters left, crosses to table, pours and drinks three shots in a row.

STU   Everything alright Danny?

DANNY   Yeah, I'm fine. Fuck.

STU   You score?

DANNY   No.

BEN   What was up with your hands?

DANNY   Just a bit of blood.

STU   Who's blood?

DANNY   This cunt up the junction. He was pissed as a newt. I was walking up the road and he was heading straight for me in a car. I knew he was going to hit me but I didn't have anywhere to run. I got behind a post-box and the bastard drove straight into it.

BEN   Jesus!

STU   So what'd you do?

DANNY   Well I was just standing there, pinned by these blazing headlights – cunt was on high beam, I hate people who drive on high beam – so suddenly I got this instinct and I bolted towards this mess of light and this guy and I leaned in the window and grabbed him. Then I hit him about . . . two or three good, clean blows to the head – a hook, a cross, a vicious little cut, and another hook for luck – lovely punch that one. By this time there's claret streaming down his ugly face and he's weeping, begging for me to let him go. So I get his head and I crack it against the door frame a few times which is when I notice that he's managed to get the door open a little way! So I slam the door on his hand for a bit, yank him out of the car, give a quick boot in the guts just to be on the safe side and then I leg it back here. *(slight pause)* Well, I didn't actually. After a few yards I think: why worry? So I stop off at Dean's and get a quick pint down, cool off. Then I trot back.

BEN   I don't believe it!

STU *(chuckling)* Always fighting . . . that's Danny for you!

BEN   Where's the guy now?

DANNY   Probably still there. *(he crosses to TV and fidgets)* Fuck it . . . he nearly killed me. You don't wanna let somebody get away with something like that or he'll do it again. Gotta show some discipline. What's the matter with this TV?

BEN   That is so dangerous.

STU *(answering simultaneously)* Can't get a picture.
(Danny examines TV, Stu pours more drink. Ben regards Danny)
It's a dud, Dan. We need a new TV.

BEN *(to Danny)* Just because this man accidentally –

DANNY *(to Stu)* This is a new TV.

STU   A different one then . . . can you get one?

BEN   . . . crashes his car . . .

DANNY   Not tonight, I can't.

STU   But we wanna watch the fight! It's the big fight tonight!

BEN *(to himself by now)* . . . I mean, what is this country coming to?

DANNY   TVs don't grow on trees you know.

STU   Well I'm placing an order for, as soon as you can . . .

DANNY   You can't order it mate. When I go into someone's house I gotta take whatever they've got. I'm a burglar. I just gotta take pot luck.

STU   Alright, I understand but this TV is no good, is it?

DANNY   No.

STU   No. So we are entitled to a new one.

DANNY *(slight pause)* Alright give us a ten.

STU   This isn't a car boot sale, this isn't the free market, we're friends.

DANNY   OK.

STU   I want a new TV. Teddy's got one. And a satellite
dish. Now don't fuck me about. I pay my taxes.

DANNY   Alright.

*Suddenly a loud hammering is heard offstage. It persists for a
moment then stops. Silence. Stu, Ben and Danny look from one to
another in alarm.*

BEN   What the fuck was that?

DANNY   Shh . . . listen.

Hammering is heard again, louder and longer.

STU   Ben, get the bat.
(Ben stands and the hammering stops)
Probably some cunt doesn't know what time it is.
(Ben is frozen, half-standing, half-sitting)

STU   They've gone.

BEN   Maybe they're picking the lock. Maybe they think
there's no-one in now.

DANNY   They can't pick that lock – not after I fixed it.

BEN   They're trying to get in.

DANNY   They're not coming in. Nobody's coming in here. I
defy anybody to –
*(he breaks off as they hear a loud thump, then the door creaking
open and footsteps inside the shop)*

BEN   They're coming in.

DANNY   Fuck me.

STU   OK, I'll sort this out.

*All three stand. Stu puts down his drink and crosses to the door
right. Danny follows. Stu is about to open the door when it opens
seemingly by itself. Stu looks into the darkness, then looks upwards
as if regarding a giant. He backs up.*

Enter an immensely tall man (Hank), large around the chest and girth too, unshaven. He glares at Stu and flashes a glance at the others who, like Stu, take a step back instinctively. Stu finally gets up the courage to speak.

STU Can I help you?
(Hank says nothing. After a pause Stu tries again)
Alright?
(Finally Hank speaks. He is a little drunk so he slurs his words and sneers as he does so. He appears to ooze menace)

HANK Do I look alright?

STU *(slight pause)* You look OK to me.

HANK *(stands still and grinds his teeth)* I want a drink.

STU Well, we're closed at the moment. See it's after midnight.

HANK I know what time it is. Are you saying I'm stupid or something?

STU No.

HANK What time do you think I think it is?

STU I don't know.

HANK Well don't ask funny questions. And don't get funny either. I don't need any funny stuff from anyone.

STU OK.

DANNY Now listen here pal, my friend was only –

HANK *(cutting him off)* You. Shut up. *(to all)* I don't need anymore shit . . .

STU No. OK.

HANK . . . tonight.

STU *(pause)* No.

HANK No. OK. Now, can I have a drink or not?

STU Well we can probably find you something . . .

HANK That's right you can.

STU What would you like?

HANK You're fucking right you can. Because I used to work for a living. *(he glares at each of them in turn)* Workers not shirkers. *(shouts)* Workers not shirkers.

STU *(pause)* Of course. What would you like to drink?

HANK *(spying their bottle)* Bourbon.

STU OK. Which bourbon would you like?

HANK *(points to bottle)* That.

STU This one ?

HANK *Wild Turkey.*

STU Sure, sure it's a great drink isn't it?

HANK True bourbon.

STU It certainly is. I'll just go and see if – *(he heads for the door right and Hank springs to attention)*

HANK *(shouts)* Where do you think you're going?

STU To, to, to get the bourbon. The *Wild Turkey.*

HANK *(grinding his teeth)* An honest hard-working drink for an honest hard-working man.

STU *(pause)* It's out the back, there's more out the back. I'll get it.

BEN I thought you said –

STU What? *(he makes another move for the door)*

HANK *(tenses)* No funny stuff.

STU No I'm just –

HANK Back off!

STU I'm getting you the drink.

HANK *(eyes Stu, then Ben, then Stu again)* Wait a minute, wait a minute. What are you fuckers up to?

STU Nothing.

HANK *(indicating Ben)* What's wrong with him?

STU Nothing.

HANK Is he happy?

STU I, yes . . . he's alright.

HANK *(shouts)* Well what are you fucking talking about then? You and him. You going to take me on?

STU   No, no, no. Of course not. No. I just said I'm going
to —

HANK   What. You're going to what?

STU   Get the whisky.

HANK   Bourbon, yes.

STU   Bourbon.

HANK   True bourbon — an honest hard-working drink for an
honest hard-working man.

BEN   We've run out.

STU *(pause)*   That's right. I made a mistake. There's no more *Wild
Turkey.*

HANK *(eyes him suspiciously but says nothing)* What do you mean?

STU   No *Wild Turkey.*

HANK *(shouts)* You've either got it or you haven't.

STU   We haven't.

HANK   What does that mean?

STU   It means . . .

HANK   You're either going to serve me or you're not.
What's the matter, aren't I good enough? Eh?

STU   No. Yes.

HANK *(shouts)* Salt of the fucking earth, I am! Salt of the fucking
. . . earth! *(beat)* What's the matter? Are you frit?

STU   What?

HANK   It's an old expression. Means frightened.

STU *(looks at Ben. Ben looks at Stu)* Maybe, maybe not.

HANK *(looks at all three)* Are you two taking the piss out of me?

STU   No.

BEN   No.

HANK *(shouts)* Well get me the fucking drink!

STU   Listen, we're just saying this is all we've got. Half a
bottle. You can have it. It's yours *(offers the bottle).*

HANK *(refusing)* What do you mean, it's mine. What's mine is
mine. No-one can take that away. No-one.

STU   Please . . .

HANK *(stepping back, shouts)* Don't insult me!

DANNY   Look pal, we want to give you the bottle.

HANK *(shouts)* You're fucking right you wanna give me the bottle. *(normal tones)* Because I fucking deserve it. And I don't need to be fucked about by any fucking fuckers like you! Or maybe I'll just come back later and do your front windows.

DANNY   OK mate, there isn't any need for that kind of talk. The man's just told you he hasn't got it.

HANK   Oh hasn't he? Who are you? *(glares at Danny, then scrutinises his face)*

DANNY   He's offered this.

HANK   Oh well, maybe I'll just take this. *(snatches bottle)*

DANNY   Take it then but –

HANK   Wait a minute. Wait a minute. *(studying Danny carefully. Danny looks away then looks at Ben and Stu)* What's the matter?

DANNY *(facing him)* Nothing.

HANK   What are you looking at?

DANNY   Nothing.

HANK   You wanna take me on?

DANNY   Look mate –

HANK *(in a flash he pulls a knife and carves it through the air elaborately)* Yeah . . . yeah . . . I'm looking. I'm looking.

DANNY *(ready for him)* Come on then . . . what are you going to do?

HANK *(shouts)* I'm going to cut you to fucking pieces, that's what I'm going to do.

DANNY   Because my friend here ran out of whisky?

HANK *(shouts)* I've fucking run out of whisky! I'm always running out of whisky! *(suddenly grabs Danny by the throat, holds the knife to it)* I know you! I know you. Did you think I was stupid or something? I fucking know who you are. You wanna kick a man when he's down? When he's had a bit to drink? Think he's easy game?

STU *(inches to the phone, picks it up)* Let him go or I call the police.

HANK *(shouting)* The police? The police? Why – am I breaking the
    law?

STU   Well . . .

HANK   We're below the law, boy. They're not concerned
    with you and me.

DANNY   Stu don't –

HANK *(to Danny)* And that's what it's about isn't it? You and me.

DANNY   Yes . . .

HANK   Who's bigger than who?

DANNY   Yeah . . .

HANK   I'm bigger than all of you!

DANNY   Yes, you're right . . .

HANK *(shaking Danny)* Don't you fucking contradict me! Don't tell
    me what's right and wrong! Don't tell me . . . what side of the
    road I'm on! Lick my boots. *(he forces Danny to his knees and
    pushes his head to the floor, shouting)* Lick them! *(Danny licks
    them)* What kind of man are you? Licking the piss off my boots.
    *(he kicks Danny violently. Danny groans. He picks Danny up by
    the lapels and flings him into the tables, which scatter and one
    breaks. Silence)* I could kill you as easy as this. *(snaps fingers)*.
    All of you. Snap you between my fingers. Then you'll be sorry.

STU   We're sorry now.

HANK   You're lucky.

STU   Yes.

HANK   I'm in a good mood.

STU   Yes.

HANK   It won't last.

STU   OK.

HANK   Never does.

*Exit Hank, grabbing the Wild Turkey on the way. We hear the front
door slam as he leaves. Silence for a moment. No-one moves. Then
Danny slowly gets up.*

DANNY   Arsehole.

BEN   Do you think he's gone?

Stu and Danny exit right.

DANNY *(offstage, shouts)* Cocksucker!

Stu and Danny enter right, arguing.

STU   What the fuck did you say that for?

DANNY   Because he is one.

STU   You want him to turn 'round and come back?

DANNY   He wouldn't dare.

BEN   Has he gone?

STU   He's gone.

DANNY   Fucking, fucking, fuck! You see that knife? We
should have shoved it up his arse.

BEN   What . . . what did he want?

DANNY   He wanted that knife shoved up his arse. We should
have taken him out! You weren't any help. Why didn't you back
me up?

STU *(pause)*   This was the guy you bashed –

DANNY   I didn't bash him.

STU   Oh, what then?

DANNY   I hardly touched him. You saw him – he didn't have
a mark on him.

STU   But he's the one you met up the junction?

DANNY   Yeah.

STU   So you didn't bash him.

DANNY   I slapped him 'round a bit.

STU   He left in a car. Did he really crash his car?

DANNY   He crashed his car. I told you he nearly ran me
down.

STU *(pause)*   What's the truth here Danny?

DANNY   Look I . . . I went over and I gave him a slap.

STU	A slap. What kind of slap?
DANNY	You want me to show you?
BEN	Come on Danny.
STU	Did you stop at Dean's or did he follow you back here?

DANNY *(beat)* I don't know.

| STU | Did you go to the hatch or not? |

DANNY *(beat)* No.

STU *(with a snort)* Fuck me.

DANNY *(pause)* What are you saying? *(slight pause)* You saying I caused this?

STU	No.
DANNY	I made that guy come in?
STU	I didn't say that.
DANNY	I made him pull that knife?
STU	Did I say that?
DANNY	You –
STU	I don't know why the fuck he came in! I don't know! *(pause)* I just don't want him coming back.
DANNY	He's not coming back.
BEN	He said he was.
DANNY	He hasn't got the guts.
STU	What?
BEN	. . . to do the windows. He said he'd come back and smash the front windows.
DANNY	He won't be back.

(long pause)

STU	If he comes back tonight and smashes this place up, my place, my livelihood . . . you're dead.
DANNY	I'm dead, am I?
STU	I'll kill you.
BEN	If he comes back –
DANNY	Really?
STU	Yes.

DANNY   I don't think so.

STU   I think so . . .

BEN   I'm the one who's dead. That guy goes crazy and takes this place apart I go with it! *(pause)*

STU   Nothing's going to happen, Ben. You'll be alright.

DANNY   I suppose I'm responsible for that too?

STU   Danny . . .

DANNY   Just what exactly are you scared of?

STU   Let's just call it a night.

DANNY   You people are women.

STU *(pointing to the door)* Shall we?. . .

DANNY   You throwing me out?

STU   No, I'm saying –

DANNY   Thanks, mate. I save your lives you're throw –

STU   I'm not throwing you –

DANNY *(at the door)* That's rude pal.

STU   Look I didn't, wait, I'm . . . where are you going?

DANNY   I'm going.

STU   Danny.

DANNY   I don't care where.

STU   You gonna see your mother?

DANNY   Maybe. Maybe my brother.

STU   Which brother?

DANNY   Dunno. Ives maybe.

STU   I thought he was inside.

DANNY   He escaped. *(pause)* We fought together tonight. Side by side. Doesn't that mean anything to you?

STU *(puzzled)* No.

BEN   No.

DANNY   You don't know what that means?

STU   No.

DANNY *(slight pause)* I don't either . . . but believe me it's meaningful.

Exit Danny. We hear the front door bang.

STU   I wish he wouldn't do that.
BEN   Why did he go? I don't understand.
STU   Got the hump, hasn't he?
BEN   Why has everybody got the hump these days? What
is going on?
(they sit at the table, light up cigarettes)
STU *(pause)* I'll tell you something. That big bonehead would have
left us alone if Danny hadn't come over all macho. One drink and
he thinks he's Batman.
BEN   That guy. Jesus! Jee-sus!
STU   He should have kept his mouth shut.
BEN   Yeah.
STU   That was the wrong thing to do.
BEN   Not advisable.
STU   Completely wrong.
BEN   . . . under any circumstances.
STU   . . . shouldn't have got involved.
BEN   . . . shouldn't have argued with the man.
STU   No.
BEN   He was right to speak up, yes, these things shouldn't
go unnoticed but –
STU   No, he shouldn't have even –
BEN   . . . he just said all the wrong things.
STU   He shouldn't have said anything.
BEN   Yes.
STU   In this situation, say nothing, do nothing.
BEN   . . . because you cannot argue with people like that.
It annoys them. Puts them on the defensive.
STU   Yes.
BEN   They don't listen anyway.
STU   No.
BEN   . . . could not be persuaded we'd run out of whisky.

STU	No.
BEN	He *wanted* us to be out of whisky.
STU	How'd you mean?
BEN	He wanted a reason to do what he did.
STU	Pull the knife.
BEN	Yes.
STU	Vent spleen.
BEN	Exactly. Precisely. This is what he wanted to do.

Vent spleen.

STU	Insane.
BEN	Yes.
STU	Insanity – it's everywhere.
BEN	. . . and we gave him a reason.
STU	What d'you mean?
BEN	We gave him a reason to crack.
STU *(pause)*	Danny gave him a reason.
BEN	Danny is not happy.
STU	Danny is upset.
BEN	I'm not happy.
STU	How many people are happy?
BEN	How many people are not unhappy . . . in the face of

things.

STU   Very few Ben. We just have to stick together and do the best we can.

BEN	Yeah. Stick together. Are you going home tonight?
STU	'Course I am.
BEN	You're not going to wait around in case something

happens?

STU	I've told you Ben, he's not coming back.
BEN	I know, I just thought . . .
STU	. . . OK?
BEN	You'd want to . . .
STU	What, what can I do?

BEN	. . . make sure.
STU	. . . there is nothing we can do.
BEN	No . . .
STU	⸱And when there's nothing you can do . . .
BEN	But –
STU	Do nothing. *(pause)* Relax. Get some sleep.
BEN	I'll try Stu, I'll try. *(pause.)*

STU *(gets to his feet, pats Ben on the shoulder)* So . . . I'll lock the door behind me.

He gets out his keys and exits. Ben sits forlorn, smoking a cigarette for a moment. Suddenly Stu enters right, highly agitated.

STU	Someone's stolen my fucking car!
BEN	What?
STU	It was parked right outside and it's gone. Jesus fucking Christ! I don't believe it.
BEN	Maybe it got towed away.
STU	At one in the fucking morning?
BEN	They don't give a shit. They work on commission.
STU	Fuckin' barbarians! Fuck that! Fuck it! That is not civilised. *(pause)* Wait a minute. It was on a fucking meter! They couldn't have taken it! It's been fuckin' stolen right from under my nose! *(pause)* Lend us a fiver. I'll get a cab.

BEN *(hands over a fiver)* They still open down there?

STU They're open all night. *(heads for the door right)* I'll see ya tomorrow.

BEN Yeah, see you.

Exit Stu right. Lights down.

SCENE 2

Morning. Ben is seated at the table centre, barefoot and half-dressed. Enter Stu right with broom and dustbin full of glass.

STU   I didn't believe he'd do it. I just didn't believe he'd really do it.

BEN *(pause)*   I did.

STU   But the box as well! He swiped the fucking' box! Ninety-five quid!

BEN   Opportunist.

STU   That really takes the cake. I mean if he'd said he was gonna . . .

BEN   He said he was gonna do the windows. He said: 'Why don't I just –'

STU   I know, I know . . . but the box. I'm talking about money.

BEN *(pause)*   Well I did say –

STU   What? What did you say?

BEN   I said something is going to happen. I had an instinct.

STU   Why didn't you do something about it?

BEN   What was I supposed to do?

STU   You were here. You were here while this was happening. Why didn't you come down?

BEN   And do what Stu?

STU   Use your initiative Ben. That's what you're here for, so you can look after the place. Do I have to do everything myself?

BEN   Use my initiative?

STU   Something like that, yes! *(pause)* Where was the bat? Why didn't you use the bat?

BEN *(pause)*   I don't know how to use the bat.

STU   What do you mean: 'I don't know how to use the bat'? You just hit him with it!

BEN   I couldn't just hit him with it. There's an art to braining someone with a baseball bat. Anything could happen.

STU   Like what for Christsake?

BEN *(pause)* You could miss.

STU   Jesus . . . *(pause)* And, and why didn't you take the box upstairs when I told you to?

BEN   Why didn't you get a safe when I told you to?

STU   I don't believe I'm hearing this.

BEN   The . . . the shutters, what about the shutters?

STU *(pause)*   You know what I think ?

BEN   What?

STU   I think you didn't come down –

BEN   Why?

STU   . . . because . . .

BEN   What's your theory, tell me?

STU   . . . because you are too lazy.

BEN *(pause)*   Lazy?

STU   Yeah. Yes. Because . . . because . . . *(pause)* Look, I don't know what you were thinking, I'm not a, a mind-reader . . . you might be, but I'm –

BEN *(on his feet)* Wait a minute . . . what?

STU   I don't want to argue about this. *(he makes a move towards door right, Ben halts him)*

BEN   Well, we are, aren't we? Arguing about it.

STU *(faces him with a sigh)* All I'm saying is . . . why, why pay you to be here to do something . . . give you a room, whatever – when you don't do it?

BEN   But you don't pay me.

STU   Alright . . . when I do pay you.

BEN   When, next Christmas?

STU   Don't start about that Ben. I'm not in the mood. I pay you when I can pay you.

BEN *(pause)* Stu you gotta understand that if you want somebody to work properly you gotta pay 'em properly. That's how you run a business. And that doesn't mean paying Danny for toot and TVs.

STU   I would have thought you could be a bit flexible about this. I mean isn't that what we agreed at the beginning?

BEN   Yes, yes and I –

STU   Because we're friends.

BEN   And I am flexible –

STU   And we make sacrifices for the good of the cause.

BEN   And it's a great cause but I'm saying I become less flexible when the shit hits the fan. *(pause)* Because maybe I just won't want to do it anymore.

STU *(beat)*   Really?

BEN   Maybe. I think so.

STU   Well maybe I just think you will do it.

BEN   And why is that?

STU   Because I need you to do it and I say that you should do it and I am the boss.

BEN   You're the boss now.

STU   I always have been.

BEN   First you're my friend and now you're the boss and I'm what, working for you? An employee?

STU   No you're Mary fucking Poppins – don't try it Ben. Don't try any of your smart-arse morality with me, alright? I'm trying to run a business here. *(beat)* You're damn right I'm the boss. Somebody's gotta be the fuckin' boss. Somebody's gotta do the job of work without actually thinking about it the whole time.

BEN   Fuck you.

STU   'It's not my business, it's Stu's business. I'm just along for the free ride.'
(Ben launches himself at Stu and grabs him by the shirt, sending the broom and dustbin flying. Stu grabs him back and they struggle silently for a minute)
Come on then, come on.

BEN   Shut up Stu! Just –

STU   Get . . . off me!

BEN   I'll do you! I swear I'll –

STU *(shoves Ben away)* Don't threaten me. *(pause)* *(they catch their breath)* What the fuck's got into you Ben? What is it?

Danny enters right.

DANNY *(slight pause)* Hello Stu . . . Ben. Alright?

STU   No, we're not alright. Do we look alright? Does that . . . does this . . . look alright to you?

DANNY   He came back.

STU   Yes, Danny. He came back.

DANNY   Stu, you wanna come outside a minute?

STU *(pause)*   Why?

DANNY   I got something to show you.

STU   Whatever it is Danny, I don't wanna know.

DANNY *(pause)* Well it's just . . . I went to see my brother last night. Ives. And on the way . . . it's weird. I saw your car.

STU   My car? Where was it?

DANNY   It was just sort of . . . abandoned . . . in this alleyway.

STU   Which alleyway?

DANNY   I dunno . . . it was . . . what's that one? . . .

STU   Well where is it? D'you get it back?

DANNY   Yeah. Yeah I drove it back. It's outside.

Stu exits right, followed by Danny. Ben goes behind the bar, pours a whisky, lights a fag, then after a pause, exits left. As the door shuts behind him, Stu and Danny enter right.

STU   I'll kill 'em . . . If I ever catch 'em, I'll kill 'em.

DANNY   Don't worry about it, Stu. I'll fix it.

STU   It's mangled. They fuckin' mangled it. Why've they gotta to do that?

DANNY   Ah you know . . . joyriders.

STU   What . . . what the fuck is going on? Everything's falling apart. First the shop, now this . . . What's the point? *(beat)* Is there one?

DANNY   We should get some boards on those windows.

STU   Yeah . . . yeah. *(he lights a cigarette)*

DANNY   D'you call the cops?

STU   Yeah, Ben called 'em.

DANNY   How's Ben?

STU   Ah fuck . . . you know *(gestures with his hand 'Yak, Yak, Yak')*

DANNY   Yeah . . . right.

STU   'I told you so' . . . blah, blah.

DANNY   So what'd he do about it?

Ben enters left, dressed, Danny doesn't see but Stu does.

DANNY   Come on – what'd he say?
          (Stu signals to Danny to keep schtum. Danny turns and sees Ben) Hey Ben, what'd the cops say?

BEN   Nothing much. Said they'd be 'watching the place'.

DANNY   Yeah watching it go up in flames.

BEN   I told them about the guy with the knife. They said it sounds like this guy, Hank or something.

DANNY   So they know who it was?

BEN   They said if he does it again to let them know.

STU   Great.

DANNY   Did you see him do it?

BEN   No I –

STU   He was upstairs.

DANNY   But you didn't tell the cops that?

BEN   Yeah . . . I said –

DANNY   You actually said you didn't see him?

BEN   Yeah. Yes . . .

DANNY   Shouldn't have said that mate. Should have said yes – you witnessed it.

STU   He was upstairs the whole time. He didn't come down.

BEN   Jesus.

DANNY   Really?

STU   He didn't even come down. Guy makes off with the day's takings.

DANNY   Why didn't you come down? *(pause)* Come down and taken the fucker out, that's what I would have done.

STU   No, see Ben's up there waiting for the heavens to open up . . .

BEN   For Christsake I was –

STU   Playing with his whisky . . .

DANNY   Why didn't you come down? *(to Stu)* How much d'he get?

BEN   I was –

STU   Don't tell me, you had a bird up there ! *(to Dan)* The bloody lot.

BEN   Christ, I –

STU   A fella. *(to Dan)* Cleaned us out.

DANNY   Where was the bat?

BEN   For fuck's sake I was –

STU   What?

BEN *(pause)*   I was scared.

Stu snorts and exits left.

DANNY   You don't wanna be scared, mate. Life's too short to be scared. You wanna get out there, show 'em what you're made of. You wanna keep a big lump of four by two by your bed and if there's any trouble you take it down and show 'em the business end.

BEN   It's OK, I've got the bat.

DANNY   Nah, forget the bat, pal. Bats are for kids. You want something that's gonna do some damage. What've you got in the basement?

BEN   Just junk.

DANNY   I'll go and have a look. See if I can find you a nice weapon.

BEN   No . . . really . . .

DANNY   It's no trouble.

Enter Stu left, carrying boards, as Danny crosses left.

STU   You gonna give us a hand Danny?

DANNY   In a minute.

Danny exits left.

STU *(to Ben)* What's he up to?

BEN   He's getting me a suitably sized plank with which to defend myself.

STU   Well, what've you been talking about?

BEN   This is what I'll be doing from now on. Cooking beefburgers and warding off evil with a lump of four by two.

STU   If you don't like it you know what you can do.

Danny enters left carrying a four by two.

DANNY   Here, this is what you need.

BEN   What can I do ?

          (Danny moves to centre, trying to look busy with his piece of wood)

STU   You can piss off.

DANNY *(demonstrating)* You see, you grab it here *(he cups one hand over an end)* and here *(clasps the wood in the middle)* and you put all your weight behind it and you run at the bastard as hard as you can. Here, Stu, you be the guy . . . Hank.

STU No thanks . . .

DANNY Charge at him . . . stay there Stu . . . *(he takes a step back and charges at Stu)* Like this . . . *(he halts)* And always, always aim for the ribs. *(he thrusts the bat dangerously at Stu to give the idea. Stu doesn't flinch but looks unamused)*

BEN OK, I see.

DANNY 'Cos you wanna break his ribs, see? Get his vital organs. His lungs. That's how you disarm him. See? See the grip? *(he demonstrates the grip)*

STU Listen Danny . . .

DANNY *(to Ben)* You have a go.
(Ben gets up and takes the four by two from Danny gingerly)
See you hold it here . . .

STU Can we do this some other time?

DANNY No, you watch this too. It's my favourite technique. But you gotta have gloves on or else you'll get splinters.

STU OK I'll make sure I get some gloves.

DANNY Leather gloves.

STU And when Hank comes back I'll just ask him to wait while he gets his gloves on.

DANNY Whatever . . . *(helping Ben)* . . . like this, see? So long as you're ready for him. Then next time he –
(Stu seizes the four by two and flings it to the floor)

STU *(angrily)* You bloody fools! What do you think you're doing? *(pause)* There isn't going to be a next time.

DANNY *(pause)* Well how do you know that?

BEN Yeah, how do you know that? *(pause)* How can we be sure he's not coming back tonight?

STU *(pause)* Look. He's had his fun, got it out of his system. Let's just get on with it.

DANNY No chance. He's probably just starting to have fun. *(pause)* My guess is he's in protection.

STU   Protection?

DANNY   See the bulges under his jacket?

BEN   No. Yeah. I did.

DANNY   He had bulges under his jacket.

STU   Maybe it was his wallet.

DANNY   Yeah, stuffed with protection money. *(pause)*
Happens all the time. You get a big bloke, packs a knife,
probably packs a shooter as well. Probably came in to suss the
place out.

STU *(to Danny)* He came in because of you.

DANNY   Why did he come back after that? *(pause)* He came
in to calculate the turnover.

BEN   How's he going to calculate the turnover when we're
shut?

DANNY *(pause)* I dunno. Probably counted the tables or something.

STU   He came in because he saw you come in.

DANNY   Maybe he saw me come out.

STU   What?

DANNY   In the first place. Maybe he'd been, been watching
me. Watching us.
(long pause)

BEN   I think he's right. *(pause)* I've got an instinct.

DANNY   You're damn right, I'm right.

BEN   I think he's coming back.

STU   Don't be paranoid Ben.

BEN   Was I being paranoid last night?

STU *(pause)*   Alright. Let me think.

BEN *(more to himself)* I'm not paranoid. *(pause)* What's paranoid
about –

STU   Will you please go and do some work? *(hands Ben
the broom)*

BEN   I was just saying – *(Stu glares)* If you want my
advice –

STU   Do you want to run the shop?

BEN . . . no.

STU You want some of my advice? *(pause)* Try and relax a bit more. Before you lose your marbles.

BEN *(pause)* Okay.

STU And I lose mine.

BEN Mm-hm.

STU And we end up killing each other.

Exit Ben carrying broom.

DANNY He's right you know.

STU Is he?

DANNY Yes, he is.

STU First he's saying you're right and now you say he's right. What is this a mutual appreciation society?

DANNY Well, I just think –

STU What?

DANNY I think –

STU Do tell me, what do you think? *(pause)* He can't help it. *(pause)* It's no crime . . . to be afraid.

STU No. You're right.

DANNY You should have a little . . . sympathy. He's caught in the crossfire. He's in the thick of it and he's not cut out to deal with it. He's a bit . . . sensitive.

STU What are you getting at?

DANNY Well I mean . . . I don't mean this in any bad way . . . don't tell him this but . . . he's a berk. He don't know what he's doing.

STU Yes. Yes Danny, I'd say that's a fairly fair assessment.

DANNY I mean . . . I don't mean this personally but . . . he's a bit cracked. He's not doing the job.

STU Really?

DANNY   He's taking the piss. *(pause)* You've given him the room and everything and he don't appreciate it. Maybe he should find somewhere else. Somewhere more suited to his nature. Find a nice squat somewhere. *(pause)* I mean I can always help you out. Till this blows over.

STU   I think you should talk to Ben about that.

DANNY *(pause)* What if he doesn't wanna go?

STU   Well then he'll stay.

DANNY   Yeah but what about this guy – Hank. What happens when he comes back? *(he picks up the bat and wields it)* Well I'll tell you. If he comes back and I'm here, I'll make him wish he never clapped eyes on the place.

STU   Will you?

DANNY   Yes. I can do this for you. Make him wish he'd never been born.

STU   I don't think so.

DANNY   I'll rip his fucking heart out.

STU   Look –

DANNY   I'll break his legs. Drag him off somewhere quiet and slit his fuckin' throat. Teach him a lesson.

STU   I think you've done enough for the moment.

DANNY   What does that mean?

STU   You come 'round last night saying you're gonna score. The big one. Then you get in some stupid fight –

DANNY   I was trying to –

STU   Then this place gets done.

DANNY   I'm trying to help you out.

STU   Then the car gets smashed up.

DANNY   So is that my fault?

STU   Don't you think I've got enough on my plate? *(pause)* Why don't you just try and stay out of trouble for a bit?

DANNY   I'm not in trouble. You're in trouble. *(pause)* You're losing the plot.

STU   Look man, I'm just trying to run a business.

DANNY   And that's all that matters is it? Your business.

STU *(pause)*   Yes.

(They glare at each other. Then Stu goes to the phone on the wall right and dials)

DANNY   What are you doing?

STU   I'm using the telephone.

DANNY   What for?

STU   To telephone somebody.

DANNY   Well who?

STU   I'm phoning Teddy so I can get some glass so we can get on with things.

DANNY   For the windows?

STU   Yes . . . yes this is what glass is usually for . . .

DANNY   So, so Hank can come and smash 'em again.

STU   Hello Teddy . . . Stu . . . I'm alright, yeah, you? I'm fine, yeah. Yeah, it's a beautiful day. Yeah, I've seen it . . . beautiful.

DANNY   Fuckin' . . .

STU   I need some glass . . .

DANNY   He likes you mate.

STU   Really? I didn't know about that . . . terrible . . . no this is a different thing . . . I don't know anything about Ravi's place . . . Listen, listen Teddy this is quite urgent . . . yes fifteen by thirty.

DANNY   You're wasting your time.

STU   Thank you Teddy. You're a gentleman Teddy . . . that's nice of you . . . I'm concerned too . . . *(he hangs up)* Nosey cunt.

DANNY   What's he say?

STU   Says Ravi's place got done too. *(pause)*

DANNY   Yeah? Who's Ravi.

STU   Some cocksucker. Runs the hi-fi shop or something.

DANNY   Fuck. Lucky Teddy.

STU   Maybe.

DANNY   He's laughing all the way to the bank.

STU   Yeah OK, OK.

DANNY   Sees you idiots coming.

STU   Will you kindly shut it?

DANNY   I'm only trying to –

STU   Yes you're trying to *help* – I don't need your help.

DANNY   No you do because –

STU   I'm getting a bit tired of this.

DANNY   Because you won't help yourself.

STU   Just leave it! If you wanna help go and help Ben
clean –

DANNY   Ben's not helping you –

STU   . . . clean up.

DANNY   The cops aren't exactly contorting themselves.
(Stu holds the door right open for Danny.) Clean up? You wanna
do something? Clean up the streets. It's a . . . a . . .

STU   Danny . . .

DANNY   Poisonous, vicious, stinking jungle out there.

STU   What do you know about the streets?

DANNY   I live on the streets, mate! *(Stu snorts)* I'm a fucking
expert. All I know! And I'm telling you, Stu, you've got something here and there's people out there who want it. That's why
you're in the shit now.

STU *(pause)* I'm only going to say this once Danny. My philosophy.
One word – things happen.

*Pause. Danny doesn't move. Stu holds the door. Ben enters right,
carrying a board. He looks distracted. He passes Stu and goes
behind the bar, forages about, emerges and heads left, whistling. He
notices the other two watching and halts.*

BEN   Street's crawling with cops.

STU   Really, is it?

DANNY   What?

BEN   A whole van-load. Getting out of the van, asking
people questions, getting back in the van, arguing, getting back
out of the van again . . .

DANNY   What do you mean? What are they doing?

BEN   Checking cars.

STU   What do you want?

BEN   I need the hammer.

STU   What do you want the hammer for?
*(Ben's nosing about for the hammer, Danny has crossed right
and is peeking out the door)*

BEN   Fix the windows.

STU   You're fixing the windows now?

BEN   Mm-hm . . .

STU   He's dancing about like a tit and you're fixing the
windows? *(pause)* It's out the front. I took it out the front.

Ben exits right and Danny returns centre.

STU *(to Danny)* What's up your arse?

DANNY   Nothing . . . nothing up with me. *(pause. He paces)*
Sky's falling on our fuckin' heads and he's taken up carpentry
and you're all fuckin' . . . how, 'things happen'. Marvellous.

STU   Yeah. That's right.

DANNY   I'm going.

STU   What d'ya mean?

DANNY   See you. Bye bye. I'm finished. I don't wanna know.
(he crosses to exit left)

STU   Wait, wait, wait. Where are you going?

DANNY   I can't be dealing with this crap.

STU   What crap?

DANNY   These things happen . . .

STU   Yeah. Yes!

DANNY   By themselves? No . . . I'm off.
(Danny opens door left, Stu steps towards him)

How do they happen all of a sudden – the fairies? They come up from the garden and say: 'Let's piss the humans off, let's knock off a burger bar!' They just happen?

STU   No.

DANNY   No, exactly, no they don't just happen. We invite them to happen by being too . . . too soft in the head, by not taking precautions.

STU   So where are you going now?

DANNY *(pause)* I dunno. *(pause)* I'm just going . . . have a look 'round.

STU *(shakes head)* I don't want you to do that.

DANNY   Oh no? Well that's where I'm going. To do that. *(he crosses to the bar, retrieves baseball bat, returns to door left)*

STU   I think you should stay here.

DANNY   I'm gone. Some guy tears your fuckin' life apart, wrecks your business, your livelihood, insults you to your face. . . do you just sit here and do nothing?

STU   Danny . . .

DANNY   Wait for it to happen again? No. Oh no, you don't and I really am sorry to say it but you don't let them get away with it, people like this, because next thing you know, what? They kill you. *(pause)*

Ben enters right.

BEN   The cops are here. They wanna see you.

STU   What do they want?

BEN   I dunno. They've been nosing 'round the car.

STU   This is all I need . . .

DANNY   What are they doing with the car?

BEN   Inspecting.

DANNY   What, are they inspecting the tyres or what?

STU   Great. Magilla Gorilla's on the loose and they're checking my tyres are safe. *(he crosses right. Danny halts him)*

DANNY   Wait. *(pause)* Did you report it? Last night.

STU What d'you mean?

DANNY Did you report it stolen?

STU Yeah, 'course.

DANNY Well . . . that's not going to look good, is it? You reported it stolen and the bloody thing's outside!

STU So I got it back!

DANNY No. No chance. They'll do you for –

STU What?

DANNY False pretences. Filing a false report. Wasting police time.

STU Danny, it *was* stolen. *You* got it back for me. You found it. In some street somewhere. *(pause)* Which street?

BEN *(peeking out the door)* They're crawling all over it. Like little blue flies.

STU Which street Danny?

BEN You'd better get out there.

STU Where did you find it?

DANNY *(pause)* As far as the cops are concerned, I didn't find it. I don't know anything about it.

STU But you *said* you found it.

DANNY No I didn't. I'm not even here.

STU Where did you find it Dan?

DANNY What does it matter?

STU *(pause)* Where?

DANNY *(pause)* Just down the road.

STU Which road?

DANNY What?

STU Which road?

DANNY *(nods right)* Out there. That one out there. *(pause)* 'Round the corner. Down a lane.

STU Which lane. What's the name of the lane Danny?

DANNY *(pause)* I told you before.

STU Remind me. I may have forgotten.

BEN I think someone should get out there.

STU *(to Dan)*   Well?

BEN   They're getting frisky.

STU *(pause)*   You stole my car, didn't you? *(pause)*

DANNY   I borrowed it.

STU   You took it and you fucked it up.

DANNY   Look I had to –

STU   What have you been up to?

DANNY   I had to see Ives.

STU   All this time . . . all this time you've been –

DANNY   My brother . . . Ives, he was –

STU   How d'you fuck up the front?

DANNY   He's in trouble.

STU   What did you hit?

DANNY   He's got no-one to turn to.

STU *(advances on Danny who backs up a little)* You've landed me
   in the shit again.

DANNY   Our mother . . . she got beaten up.

STU   What last night? You run her down or something?

DANNY   I hit a post.

STU   Oh . . . you sure it wasn't a postbox?

DANNY   No . . . why?
   (Stu halts, pause)
   It could have been a fire-hydrant.

STU   You fucking cretin! *(he grabs Danny by the collar
   and backs him against the bar)* What was it? What did you hit?
   What have you done in my car? What do they want?

DANNY   Get off me!

STU   Tell me!

DANNY   I've told you! *(they struggle)* Now don't . . . push
   me! *(he throws Stu off and seizes the bat off the counter)* I'm
   warning you pal. If I say I hit a fire hydrant then I hit a fire
   hydrant. And you'll tell the cops it happened last week and that
   the car wasn't stolen and that you were mistaken and you won't
   fuck with me.

STU   And why is that?
(There is a loud hammering on the door offstage)
DANNY   Because I say so. And because if you don't, I will
tear this place apart myself and I will do you with it.
STU *(snorts)* I don't think you're going to do that.
DANNY   No?
STU *(glares at him)* No.

*They glare at each other, then Stu exits right. Danny looks at Ben.
Uneasy pause.*

BEN   You've made him cross now. I can tell.

*Danny exits left. We hear brief crashes and rattling on a door. Ben
lights a cigarette and waits. Danny enters left.*

DANNY   Where's the key?
BEN   What key?
DANNY   The back door key. Fucker's locked.
BEN   Stu's got it.
DANNY   Go and get it.
BEN   Why?
DANNY *(annoyed)* What?
BEN   Watcha doing?
DANNY   I'm going mate. I'm finished. I'm outta here.
BEN   Calm down for Christsake. He's not gonna grass
you.
DANNY   Oh no? What makes you so sure?
BEN   Because I know him. *(pause)*
DANNY   Oh yeah?
BEN   Yeah. Yes.
DANNY *(crosses to door right, peeks out, returns to centre, paces a
little and stops)* You know he wants you out of here, don't you?
BEN *(slight pause)* What?

DANNY   That's right. He just offered me your bloody job.

BEN   What d'ya mean?

DANNY   He asked me to move in. Take the room, take over. Says you're not pulling your weight. Said, none of this would have happened if it weren't for you.

BEN   What?

DANNY   Pathetic, isn't it? He's blaming them windows on you. He said . . . his exact words: 'I'm trying to run a business . . . and I can't – 'cos of Ben.'

BEN   He said that?

DANNY   My word of honour.

BEN   You're not just . . . winding me up or something?

DANNY   Stinks doesn't it? *(pause, he moves close to Ben, puts a hand on his shoulder)* Which is why I want out. Preferably before the cops drag me out. And if you got any brains you'll split too – before things really get nasty.

BEN *(pause)*   I'm gonna go and talk to him. *(he makes a move right)*

DANNY *(catches him by the arm)* You don't wanna talk to him about it. You wanna do something about it.

BEN   I'm going to. I'm gonna kill him. I've had enough of this. *(he breaks away again and Danny catches him again)*

DANNY   Ben, Ben, Ben . . . no. Let me give you some advice. Walk away.

BEN   Look, me and Stu, we –

DANNY   Ignore him.

BEN   He owes me Danny. I helped him build this place up from scratch. I've known him since I was a nipper. I put my balls into this place . . . and he's done nothing but fuck me about!

DANNY *(as Ben struggles)* So, that's life mate. That's what people do to you. That's what the rest of the world is there for – to fuck us about.

(pause. Ben calms down a little, looks confused)

Now – as a friend – will you please do this for me? Go get the key.

Ben crosses to door right and is about to open it when it bursts open and Stu enters. Stu halts, Ben halts. Stu eyes Danny. Ben eyes Stu.

STU *(to Danny)* I want a word with you. *(to Ben)* What are you looking at?

(Ben and Stu eye each other. Pause)

DANNY *(to Stu)* What did you tell 'em?

STU   What do you think I told 'em?

DANNY   Don't be fuckin' funny with me pal!

STU   That you stole the car?

DANNY *(advancing)* But I didn't steal the car.

STU   That's funny. They think you did.

DANNY *(face to face with Stu)* So what did you say?

STU *(pause)*   I told them it was a mistake.

DANNY *(pause)* And . . . and what did they say?

STU   They told me about last night. Their investigation.

DANNY   What investigation? What about last night?

STU   About how somebody did Ravi's windows as well as mine.

DANNY   What are you trying to say?

STU   They nicked his TVs.

DANNY   Don't make me laugh. What about the cops then? Eh? *(he looks from Stu to the door and to Ben and back to Stu)* Why haven't you been arrested? Why haven't I been arrested, smart-arse?

STU *(pause)*   Because I wanted to give you a chance.

DANNY   What the fuck does that mean?

STU   To tell me why you're still here. After fucking with us for so long.

DANNY   I beg your pardon?

STU   Why did you do this to us Dan?

(Suddenly Danny swings the bat and hits Stu viciously in the head. Stu falls)

BEN *(on his feet)* Jesus Danny!

DANNY   Are you saying I did this? You saying I did that out
there?

STU   I didn't tell them anything.

DANNY   Tell them what? What didn't you tell them?

STU   I wanted to ask you? . . .

DANNY   Ask me what? *(kicks Stu)* What do you want to
know?

STU   I know you did it.

DANNY *(kicks again)* You fuck! What did I do?

BEN   For Christsake Danny – what?

DANNY   I fucked up the shop. I'm the big bad wolf. I'm the
culprit! I smashed up your burger bar! It wasn't Hank, it was me!
I stormed out in a mood and I took the car and came and fucked
you over! Say it, go on, say it! Because I am evil! Because I do
not *like* you anymore! Because I'm a peasant! *(pause)* Because I
resent you? *(laughs. Pause)* It doesn't fucking wash! There is no
evidence! What did I take then? A till full of coppers. Luncheon
vouchers? *(pause. Turns to Ben and Stu)* You people are
parasites. You and your business. You don't deserve this . . . all
this . . . you don't deserve anything.
*(Silence. Stu is motionless on the floor. Danny regards him. Ben
comes over and peers down at Stu)*

BEN   You've . . . you've killed him. *(he squats beside Stu,
tries to revive him)* Stu? Stu . . . can you hear me? *(he cradles
Stu's head, then holds his hand up and sees blood on it)* Christ
he's bleeding like a bastard. What have you done Danny?

DANNY   He betrayed us.

BEN   What are you talking about? You mad, fucking –
you're insane. You've gone off your screw!

DANNY   He betrayed his friends.
(Stu regains consciousness, groans. Ben comforts him)
Thinks he's above us. Thinks 'cos he's got a bit of paper . . . a
thing saying he's in charge, saying he owns a thing, it makes him
alright. Better than us.

BEN   Danny . . .

DANNY   Well you know what that is?
  (Stu's groaning)
BEN   He needs a doctor.
DANNY   I said, you know what that is?
BEN *(to Stu)*   Can you hear me?
DANNY   Fascism. A fascist.
BEN   How many fingers am I holding up? *(he holds up five fingers to Stu)*
STU   Piss off.
BEN   It's his eyesight. Call an ambulance.
DANNY   I've met people like you before.
  (Ben gets up to go to the phone right but halts as Danny says:)
  Fuckin' ninety-five quid . . . a pissy ninety-five quid and he accuses me.
BEN   What did you say?
DANNY   What?
BEN   What did you just say?
DANNY   I'm saying how dare you fuckin' accuse me. *(pause)* When there's no evidence. *(pause)* And nothing even worth taking.
BEN *(pause)*   So you didn't have anything to do with this?
DANNY   Fuckin' right I didn't.
BEN   It was Hank, right?
DANNY   Well it certainly looks like it.
BEN   So how come you knew about the ninety-five in the box?
DANNY   What?
BEN   The ninety-five quid. How did you know about it?
DANNY *(pause)* I saw you cashing up. *(pause)* Last night.
BEN   You saw me cashing up?
DANNY   Yes I did Ben, now have you got a problem with that?
BEN *(pause)*   I think you'd better go.
DANNY   What's that?

BEN   I think you better go. Before I call the cops.

DANNY   Oh yeah?

BEN   Yeah.

DANNY   You're gonna call the cops?

BEN   I didn't cash up last night Danny. And you weren't even here. *(he crosses to the phone right)*

DANNY   Ben wait, wait, wait. Hang on.
          (Ben stops)

BEN   You're a bastard Danny. I don't think I want to know you anymore.

DANNY   My mother . . . she . . . she is –

BEN   I'm sorry for you.

DANNY   A fucking cripple. She needs me.

BEN *(pause)*   Is this true?

DANNY   Yes.

STU   He's lying through his teeth.

DANNY   Christ.
          (Ben is about to dial when Danny raises the bat and brings it down on the phone. A few frenzied blows and it's on the floor in pieces) I'll fuckin' show you what it's all about . . . Fuckin' playing with me . . . fuckin' call the cops . . .
          (he brings the bat down on the till, it rings madly) Call them!
          (he hits the till a couple more times, then as he moves behind the bar, destroys the shelving bottles and finally the TV, saying:) The fire brigade . . . Batman and Robin! *(shouts)* They won't come. You don't count. This place is worthless. You are worthless. You're all worthless . . . nothing . . . nowhere . . . I am not nothing.
          (silence)

STU   Danny, look –

DANNY   Shut up. *(pause)* You people – you . . . I used to like you people. I really did. I think you've got problems. I really do. I thought we were friends. Silly me. My mistake. We weren't friends. I . . . I . . . I don't even know what that word means. I don't know what it means. How about that? I don't even . . . *(trails off. Pause. Looks around)* Look at this place. Fuckin'

disgrace . . . all this glass and rubbish . . . you want to get it
outside that's what you wanna do . . . you wanna . . . fix the place
up a bit . . . *(he bends down and picks up a piece of glass and
examines it)*

BEN   Why'd you do that Danny?

DANNY   Sorry?

BEN   Why'd you do what you just did? Smash everything
up. *(pause)* I mean you started with the outside and, and worked
your way in. It doesn't make much sense.

DANNY   What?

BEN   Why'd you do this?

DANNY   Why d'you wanna know?

BEN   I'm curious.

DANNY   Is it a problem?

BEN   Yes.

*(Danny shrugs. Stu seats himself with difficulty on a chair,
centre. Ben helps)*

STU *(to Dan)* You robbed me, you cunt.

DANNY   I know. *(pause)* I'm sorry.

STU   You smashed my place up and you robbed me.

BEN   It's OK Stu.

STU   It's bloody not OK.

DANNY   You want me to go?

STU *(to Ben)* He brains me with a fuckin' baseball bat . . . fucks up
the bar . . . TV . . .

BEN   I know.

STU   And, and what about the car? D'you see what he did
to the car?

BEN   I haven't seen the car.

STU   He fucked it up. He used to fix things now he fucks
them up. *(pause)*

DANNY   I better get going.

STU   What?

DANNY   Make a move.

STU	Are you? . . . is he kidding?
BEN	No.

(Danny crosses to door right)

STU	Now just a fuckin' minute . . .
BEN	Cool it Stu . . .
STU	Where the bloody hell you going?
DANNY	I'll be seeing you.
STU	You cunt.
DANNY	Gotta . . . you know . . . do a few things.
STU	You can't just . . . he can't just . . . Fuck . . . Fuck . . . Fuck you.

Danny exits right.

BEN *(pause)*	You OK?
STU	I don't believe that guy. I just don't believe it.
BEN	No.
STU	He fucked it up for us. He fucked it all up for us.
(pause)	
BEN	You want me to get a doctor?
STU	He came here and he – no, I'm OK . . .

(Ben sits opposite Stu. Pause) You OK?

BEN	Yeah, I'm OK.
STU	You're not . . .
BEN	No.
STU	I mean . . . I didn't know it was gonna . . .
BEN	Yeah . . .
STU	I mean I feel bad. Obviously I feel . . . you know.
BEN	I know.
STU	Things were fucking up for a while there. I mean the . . . everything was happening. It was a kick in the nuts. He was kicking me in the nuts all along. So I kicked –
BEN	Yeah, me . . .

STU   . . . in the nuts. *(pause)* I mean that's the way it goes
   isn't it? Last in line, first to whatever.

BEN   Yes.

STU *(pause)*   I mean . . . I'm sorry.

BEN   OK.

STU   I'm sorry I fucked you about.

BEN   Yeah.

STU   If there had been someone else to fuck about I would
   have.

BEN   I know.

STU   But there wasn't.

BEN   It's just us.

STU   It's just me an' you.

BEN   Yeah. *(pause)*

STU   I don't understand why we do these things.

BEN *(takes out his cigarettes, puts one in this mouth and offers one
   to Stu)* Want one of these?

STU *(taking one)* Cheers. *(they light up)* All I wanna do is my job. I
   get up in the morning, I come to work, chop the vegetables, make
   the mincemeat, I cook and I go home to sleep. Then I get up,
   come to work, make the mincemeat, put the rubbish out, I cook
   and I go home to sleep. Sometimes there's a variation. Sometimes
   some maniac tries to kill me. People lie, cheat and deceive me. It
   adds spice. But by and large I'm a simple soul. Is that, do you
   think that's such a bad thing?

BEN   It's a good thing Stu. It's alright. We cook the food.

STU   Yes.

BEN   We do the job.

STU   We do the job.

BEN   It's okay.

STU   Yeah.

Lights down slowly, leaving only the glow of their cigarettes.

The end.

Joe Penhall

His first play **Wild Turkey** was staged at the Old Red Lion and he made his screen debut with **Go Back Out** for the BBC.

His Royal Court debut was **Some Voices**, which won the 1995 John Whiting Award. For his follow-up play, **Pale Horse**, he was awarded the 1995 Thames Television Writers' Award. His screen version of **Some Voices** is currently in development with Channel Four.

Joe's next play, **Love and Understanding** was produced in 1997 at the Bush Theatre and The Living Theatre in Athens, and transferred to the Long Wharf Theatre, Connecticut. His screen version is being developed by Kismet Films.

Joe is currently associate writer at the Donmar Warehouse and his latest play, **The Bullet** is his first commission. He is also under commisssion from the Royal Court and the Royal National Theatre for new plays.

Everlasting Rose

by Judy Upton

Everlasting Rose

I don't remember where my head was when I wrote **Everlasting Rose**. At that time I was selling baskets of dried and silk flowers at car boot sales, and I think that had an influence. It was the first play I had produced, and I can clearly recall the moment when Phil Setren rang me to say it was going to be in the Festival.

I don't think I'd set out to write a play to explore any particular theme or subject, but like some other things I've done, it seems to be about fear of change, and people trapping themselves in cycles of repetitious behaviour, rather than take a step into the unknown. In this way I think it's a forerunner to **The Shorewatchers' House**, and also **Bruises.**

The shop dummies were, if I remember correctly, borrowed from an Essex police station. One of them had 'take me, take me!' scrawled across her chest. (There's another play in there somewhere.) I used the dummies to avoid too much exposition. I wanted Carney and Tricia to be haunted by his previous marriages, and the dummies provided a constant of the past, even when they weren't being alluded to.

I'm surprised that I didn't specify the setting in the original script, and I remember Phil asking me whether it was set in America (partly because of the mobile home). In fact I was trying to achieve a feeling of Southern Gothic, in the tradition of Flannery O'Connor, Carson McCullers etc. though my notion of 'The Deep South' is East and West Sussex, and the river with 'Blood On The Tide' is the Adur, in my home town of Shoreham-by-Sea.

Things didn't go particularly smoothly on the production, and I owe a debt of gratitude to the actors for their patience, support, and for rising above our difficulties.

I would like to thank Phil Setren for giving the play a second production in the 1998 Festival.

Judy Upton

Everlasting Rose

by Judy Upton

First produced by the London New Play Festival at the Old Red Lion
Theatre, Islington in 1992.
Directed by Dee Hart.
Designed by Naomi Wilkinson.

Carney	Charlie Grima
Tricia	Debbie Radcliffe
Nym	Jonathan Hansler

ACT ONE

*The present day. Carney's immaculate mobile home. There is a door
and window, back. To the right (unseen) is the bedroom and bathroom. It is daytime, though the sky outside the window has a red
tinge.*

*Carney and Nym are discovered on stage. Carney is tidying the
already tidy room. Nym, dressed only in a large grey blanket, sits
looking out of the window.*

NYM   Look! *(Carney joins Nym at the window)* The river's
red again.

CARNEY   It's only algae. Beautiful though.

NYM   Blood on the tide.

CARNEY   It's the weather. I went over there on my way to the
paper shop. I knelt on the shingle bank and put my hands under
the water, just to see what they looked like red. Have you ever
tasted the river water? It's saltier than salt. How can that be? –
saltier than salt.

NYM   Ever tasted tears?

CARNEY   Snot's saltier. Don't say you've never tasted snot. When you were a little kid . . .

NYM *(interrupting)* The tears you cry when you're alone are the saltiest.

CARNEY   Women huh! *(looks at his watch)* Think she'll come? Have I ever missed a girl this badly?
(Nym shrugs) Have you ever known me be in this state? I'm trembling. Did I make the bed?
(Nym shrugs)

Exit Carney. Nym sees something outside, stands up, looking out of the window, smiling. Enter Carney. He runs to the window.

CARNEY   Crossing the bridge! I knew it. *(goes to the mirror. He has all kinds of pots and potions on the shelf beneath. He moisturises his face and combs his hair, then re-examines his face critically.)* Pick some flowers from the daisy bank. Quick! And break a few branches of the wild rose. *(rushes back to the window)* No time! She's here. Couldn't you walk slower, you stupid cow? Nym get out! *(Nym stands up)* In the bedroom. No the bathroom. Go!

NYM   I'll have a bath . . .

CARNEY   Another? There'll be no hot water.
(There is a knock on the door. He checks the mirror again)
Coming, angel.

Only half-satisfied that he has put his appearance to rights, Carney opens the door. Tricia enters. She is young, gauche and rather boyish. Carney embraces her, engulfing her. She is uncomfortable but is tolerant.

CARNEY   Mmm, hi gorgeous.

TRICIA   What a stupid thing.

CARNEY   Forget him. We're alone.

TRICIA   In the paper. Everyone read it.

CARNEY   Your mum?

TRICIA *(disentangles herself)* Been giving me hell about you.

CARNEY Divorce or stand by your man?

TRICIA *(mimicking her mother)* Your father and I . . .

CARNEY ʹHad our ups and downs . . .

TRICIA But stuck together . . .

CARNEY Through thick and thin . . .

TRICIA In our day . . .

CARNEY Marriage was a life sentence!

TRICIA Has your mum been having words too?

CARNEY Still thinks I'm with wife mark three . . . or two maybe.

TRICIA Let's get one thing straight, right away . . .

CARNEY Tea? Coffee? You know where it is.

TRICIA I haven't come back.

CARNEY We can talk about that. But let's have a cup of tea first.

(There is the sound of water running, off. Tricia looks at Carney) Not a girl, I promise you. *(pause)* So how have things been?

(Nym appears looking round the door)

TRICIA Well, I've had some time to . . . *(she notices Nym)* Hello?

CARNEY For Christ's sake come in – stop peeking at my wife!

Enter Nym. He is still wrapped in the blanket and is not self-conscious about it. He approaches Tricia.

NYM I can't shake hands, I'm just going to have a bath.

CARNEY Tricia – my son Nym. *(sharply to Nym)* What do you want?

NYM Something clean to wear after the bath.

CARNEY The blanket is alright.

NYM It's not Carney.

CARNEY Get a clean one from your bed.

NYM They need washing.

CARNEY   Again?

NYM   I've put them in the bag. *(pause)* Your duvet's clean.

CARNEY   And we need it!

TRICIA   I'm not staying . . .

CARNEY   Can we spare it, angel? We can have it back this
evening.

TRICIA   I haven't come back.

CARNEY   You don't need to decide right now. I'm not putting
the pressure on.
(Tricia shakes her head) Aren't I a slightly more attractive
proposition than your mother? Or is it him? Three's a crowd huh?
Well he can go . . .

NYM   Where?

TRICIA   Don't be stupid. I don't mind Nym being here. I'm
pleased to meet him at last.

CARNEY   So we're all gonna get on alright then? Terrific.
Weren't you going to put that kettle on sweetheart?
(Tricia gives Carney a black look) Well alright, I'll do it.

Exit Carney.

TRICIA   So you're Rhonda's son . . .
(Nym is staring at Tricia with admiration)
You're at university . . .

NYM *(pause, engrossed in looking at Tricia)* Yeah. No, not now.

TRICIA   I get muddled. Rhonda with the black hair . . .

Enter Carney.

CARNEY   And big creole earrings. Like Cher when she was
still with Sonny.

TRICIA   Sonny?

NYM   She's too young to remember that, dad.

CARNEY *(glances at the mirror and fiddles with his hair)* Your
bath will overflow in a minute.

Exit Nym. The sound of running water stops. Carney smiles and leans on Tricia's shoulders.

CARNEY   It's good to see you.

TRICIA   Is he okay?

CARNEY   Mmmmm. *(he nuzzles her neck)*

Enter Nym carrying a shop dummy with black hair and 60's clothes. This is 'Rhonda'. Exit Carney. He returns with two cups of tea, handing one to Tricia. Exit Nym.

TRICIA   So Rhonda lives in the bathroom now?

CARNEY   Not when Nym's having a bath. He's shy.

TRICIA   And Maureen and Carol?

CARNEY   In the bedroom. *(Tricia raises her eyebrows)*

Exit Carney, re-entering a moment later carrying a shop dummy dressed in 70's clothes. This is 'Maureen'. He exits again and returns with another dummy, this time dressed in 80's fashions – 'Carol'. He lines them up, 'Rhonda', 'Maureen', 'Carol'. Tricia walks down the line and back like an army officer inspecting a line of guardsmen. She takes her place at the end of the line of 'wives', next to 'Carol'. She mimics the models' stiff pose. Carney approaches her, walks around her, strokes her face and kisses her. She remains stiff and unmoving.

CARNEY   My fourth and favourite wife. *(seeing he is having little effect on her, he moves to 'Carol', the next in the line)* Three times lucky. *(he pulls away from 'Carol')* Or maybe not. *(he goes to 'Maureen')* Twice as nice. Or double the trouble . . . *(he leaves her for 'Rhonda')* You know what they say about your first love. *(he leaves Rhonda)* I forget what it is. *(he returns to Tricia. She has dropped the pose. He stands before her, saying nothing)*

TRICIA   What?

CARNEY   I've missed you so much, babe. *(he waits expectantly)*

TRICIA   You've the most handsome face . . . *(awkwardly, she strokes his face)* The deepest, most soulful eyes . . . the cutest nose . . . the . . . the . . .*(to cover her shame and unease at this pretence, she kisses him without skill or feeling)*

CARNEY   Can't remember, huh? What did you use to say to me? What words did you use to describe me, every morning and night? Come on, Trish, come on. Tell me! Make me believe it! Trish!

TRICIA   I've forgotten. I mean I can't think of all the things you like me to say . . .

CARNEY *(moves away from her)* Perhaps I should've written them down for you.

TRICIA *(looks at the three dummies)* Were they really beautiful women?

CARNEY   Rhonda – long black hair, straight and shiny with the fragrance of dark, morello cherries. Eyes you could dance in . . . until the love light went out. Maureen – skin so soft you couldn't feel it beneath your fingers. You could've been stroking air. She was elemental, uncomplicated, free . . . too free. Carol's smile – so innocent but all-knowing. Lips which parted so sweetly, pouted bitter-sweet. Gradually more bitter.

TRICIA   Three beauties . . . and then me. An ugly duckling.

CARNEY   You're a pretty girl . . . You just need confidence, a little poise and grace. Small things like a sense of your own style . . . self-worth . . .

TRICIA   Nym's mother. *(looking at 'Rhonda')* Preserved in all her glory. She could be his sister. Still so young. *(she strokes the face of the dummy. Carney grabs hold of her hands and places them on his own face)* So fresh-faced, so smooth . . . *(Carney relaxes slightly)* They could be twins, couldn't they? She could be your daughter.

CARNEY *(distressed, he shakes Tricia)* Look! look closely! *(he forces Tricia's face close to his own)* What do you see? There! What's there?

TRICIA   You look tired, love . . .

CARNEY   Tired!

TRICIA   I noticed when I came in, I thought how weary you look. Perhaps you haven't been sleeping . . . perhaps you aren't taking proper care of yourself . . . maybe you're not eating the right things . . . Perhaps it's all that getting up at four o'clock on Saturday mornings, struggling with poles and tarpaulin in the wind and rain . . .

Nym, wrapped in a towel, is standing in the doorway, unobserved by Carney or Tricia.

CARNEY *(near panic)* What!

TRICIA   What then.

CARNEY   Where? What do you see! *(he shakes her)* Tired! What do you mean! Have I changed? What is it? Tell me! Trish, tell me!

TRICIA   Around your eyes . . .

CARNEY   What about my eyes! Tell me! *(becoming rough with Tricia)*

NYM *(concerned)* Lines, Carney!

TRICIA *(turning Carney to face her)* No love . . .

NYM   Crow's feet!
*(Carney dashes to the mirror)*Bags under the eyes.
(Carney rubs his hair up, then crams his cap on his head)

CARNEY *(shouts)* Everything 50p, anywhere you like!

TRICIA   No, love don't . . .

NYM   Wrinkles!

CARNEY   Anywhere on the stall, only 50p! Come on ladies, grab the old man's wallet, pick up all of these bargains!

TRICIA   Don't start . . . please don't start this!

CARNEY   Get your packs of Christmas cards, all different pictures, get your sellotape – 50p the big reel! Bumper packs of freezer bags, get your bargains now, only 50p while stocks last, anywhere on the stall ladies!

TRICIA   Please love!

CARNEY   Everlasting roses, two for fifty! Everything 50p anywhere you like!

TRICIA   Shut up!

CARNEY   Balls of string, your kitchen string, your garden twine . . .

TRICIA   Shut up! Shut up!

CARNEY   Anywhere you like!

TRICIA   Listen to me!

CARNEY   50p, anywhere on the stall, all your household goods, ladies!

TRICIA   You and Nym could be twins . . .

NYM   No!

CARNEY *(quieter and slower)* Anything 50p, anywhere you like! Your potato peelers, your salad bags . . .

TRICIA *(catches hold of Carney)* Look at me, you could be Nym's brother. I thought when I saw him, you were brothers . . .

NYM   No, don't lie to him!

CARNEY   Get your bargains here today ladies, be sold out by mid-morning, all at 50p, no catches, bring it back next week if you ain't satisfied!

TRICIA   My husband, I could be your sister, older sister . . .

NYM   He has to face it!

CARNEY *(hugs Tricia to himself, hard)* No, don't be shy, come right up close ladies, all the bargains for you today . . .

TRICIA   You could be my son . . .

NYM *(furious)* Shit! Could he shit!

CARNEY *(tenderly)* What've I got for 50p? Ask me! What've I got for you today, ladies?
(Tricia manages to reach a coin in her pocket. She holds it up) Ask me.

TRICIA   For 50p. What've you got?

CARNEY *(kisses her)* What did you get?

TRICIA   A bargain. A beautiful bargain.

NYM *(stands wringing his hands)* Lies and deceit, Patricia.
(Tricia steps towards him) I . . . I'm going to have a bath.

Exit Nym.

TRICIA   I thought he'd just had one.

CARNEY   There won't be any hot water left.

TRICIA   Lies and deceit. He's right isn't he? We're deceiving ourselves, you and I.

CARNEY   Sure we are, everyone is. Take his mum for instance, ravishing Rhonda, she was the worst one for spinning a tale. She used to dress up exotic. Buy her anything ethnic and she loved it, you know? Tasselled skirts, silk scarves, necklaces nearly to her waist. Told me she was Spanish on her mother's side. I took her to a Mexican restaurant and she couldn't read the menu. So what? We all do it. It's nothing to be ashamed of. Laura, a former flame, between Maureen and Carol, her ex-husband's boat grew bigger every time I heard the story. Finally, it became a yacht. And Carol and her modelling career. She talked like it was the catwalks of Paris and Milan, when actually she was working for a mail-order catalogue. We're all romantics.

TRICIA   That's a different thing, being romantic . . .

CARNEY   We're romantic aren't we? Do you remember how you used to think I was a real Romany because I live in a trailer? But I didn't lie to you. When you asked me outright, I told you the truth.

TRICIA   You'd let me believe anything which suited you.

CARNEY   I fanned the fire of your fantasies a little. There's no harm in that. That's what it's all about, angel. The very gentle art of deception and subterfuge.

NYM *(offstage)* Carney! Can I have the duvet!

CARNEY   Can he?

TRICIA   I'll take it to him.

CARNEY   I'd better, babe. He's shy.

Exit Carney. He collects the duvet then exits again. Carney and Nym enter together.

CARNEY   So what're you going to wear tomorrow?

NYM   One of your shirts?

CARNEY   You had the last clean one yesterday. You'll have to make it do. *(Nym shakes his head)* What're you going to wear tomorrow? You won't put the duvet on again. You'll say it needs washing. You'll have to go down the laundrette and get all our gear washed. Then we can dry it on the radiator overnight. You'll be able to wear real clothes again tomorrow. Clean clothes.

TRICIA   He can't go out wearing a duvet.

CARNEY   It wouldn't be the first time.

NYM   People stare.

CARNEY   Tell them you're a Hari Krishna. Shake a tin and collect us some donations. Anything to help pay your cleaning bills. I think they ought to give tokens with each wash, like you get with the petrol. We'd have enough for a couple of sets of cocktail glasses already.

NYM *(picks up his shoes)* My shoes are too dirty.

TRICIA   They look okay to me.

NYM   You can't see germs, Patricia.

CARNEY   You can always have another bath when you get back.

NYM *(looks at his feet and at the shoes for a while)* Alright. *(he puts the shoes on his bare feet)*

TRICIA   Have you no socks?

NYM   I've got to wash them.

Exit Nym.

TRICIA   Is he? . . .

CARNEY   Nutty as a fruit-cake?

TRICIA   No, I didn't mean . . .

CARNEY   He'll go out in a minute, babe. And with the amount of things, he thinks need washing, we'll have the place to ourselves for a good, long while.

NYM *(offstage)* Oh God! Oh God!

Enter Nym.

NYM *(dismayed)* It's raining!

CARNEY   Yeah, well you can wear my jacket if it'll go over the duvet.

NYM   I wore your jacket, yesterday.

CARNEY   Here we go. Look, you can wear it again.

NYM   But . . .

CARNEY   It needs washing? It won't even touch your precious, clean, baby soft skin. You've the duvet to protect you from the dirt and germs.

NYM   Can I borrow your gloves?

CARNEY   And a clean cloth to wipe the shop door handles?

(Tricia laughs)

NYM   People brush up against me, *(he shudders)* I smell them.

CARNEY   And you always walk in the road, don't you?

(Nym nods) Dog shit and spit on the pavement.

NYM *(shudders)* It's raining very hard.

CARNEY   Umbrella by the door.

NYM   It's going to be muddy.

Exit Nym.

TRICIA   He doesn't want to go.

CARNEY   He's going.

Enter Nym with a huge sack of washing. Carney gives him some money.

CARNEY   We need more soap, yeah? And bath oil. What else?

NYM   Air freshener, washing-up liquid . . .

CARNEY   He gets through it by the pint.

TRICIA   No doubt Nym gets to do all the washing and cleaning, now I'm not here.

CARNEY   If I wash up or hoover, he comes along behind me, inspects everything and then redoes it all.

NYM   You leave bits. That's where the germs collects.

CARNEY   Better get another couple of hoover bags, some bin bags, a big bottle of disinfectant . . . *(he fetches his jacket and offers it to Nym. Nym does not want to take it. He takes it finally, holding it by the corner at arm's length)*

NYM   I can't wear it.

CARNEY   Put the coat on, Nym.

NYM   I can't Dad.

TRICIA *(tries to break the tension, steps between them)* Does it matter whether he wears a coat or not? If he's going to have a bath as soon as he gets back, it won't do any harm.

CARNEY   I'm not thinking of him. I'm thinking of our duvet. *(Nym picks up the sack of washing)* You're not going out in the rain with the duvet! *(he blocks Nym's way)* Take it off. *(Nym shakes his head)* Take it off. *(seizes hold of Nym)*

TRICIA   Leave him, Carney! *(Carney starts to pull the duvet off Nym, who cringes, frightened. She stops him)* Leave him! Leave him alone!

CARNEY *(releases Nym who wraps himself up tighter, before standing, wringing his hands)* The duvet, Nym. Ten seconds. I'm counting. One . . . two . . .

TRICIA *(yells)* We don't need the bloody duvet. We can sleep on the sofa.

CARNEY *(relaxing)* You will?

TRICIA *(flatly)* It doesn't matter to me.

CARNEY   Who you're with is all that matters, eh babe? *(embraces Tricia)*

NYM   I . . . I'm going to have a bath.

Exit Nym.

CARNEY   Hey! Wait a minute . . .
(The sound of water running, offstage. He is on the point of going
after Nym, but Tricia holds on to him. He kisses her)
Perhaps, I better take the laundry.
(he puts his jacket on and picks up the huge bag of laundry)
Blankets, sheets, *all* of his gear and all the shirts and jeans I've
lent him. Guess how many times a day he changes shirt? Guess.
(Tricia shrugs) After every bath. Four to six times. Jesus!

TRICIA   It's kind of a mania . . . a compulsion . . .

CARNEY   He's loopy, yeah. *(he puts the bag down and starts*
to comb his hair in front of the mirror)
(The sound of running water stops)

TRICIA   So half of that stuff doesn't need washing ?

CARNEY *(sprays his hair liberally with hair spray)* Course it
doesn't. Does that look okay? *(he works some more moisturiser*
into his face) Life's hell when you've got combination skin.
How's that feel? *(he offers his face for stroking)*

TRICIA   Soft. You're going to be real popular down the
laundrette.

CARNEY   Mmmm. *(he splashes on aftershave extravagantly)*
Jealous. I'll try not to be too long or you'll start to wonder.

TRICIA   I mean you'll take up all the machines with a load
like that. People will be queuing down the street.
(Carney is making admiring faces at himself) Supposing you
didn't wash it all? I mean, if half of it is clean anyway?

CARNEY   You think he wouldn't notice? Everything will get a
complete inspection when he's ironing. Then he'll probably
check it all over again before he wears it. Same as with plates and
cups. He inspects them all before he puts them away, then he has
to wash them all over again before he can have anything to eat or
drink. *(mimicking Nym)* Dust, Carney, dirt, *germs*!

Carney picks up the bag of washing, takes another look at himself in
the mirror, kisses Tricia and exits. Tricia sits beside the window, her
head in her hands. Enter Nym.

NYM   The river's flowing red again.

TRICIA *(looks out of the window)* I thought you were having a bath.

NYM   I thought he was going to hit me.

TRICIA   Carney's not . . . he doesn't does he?

NYM   No. *(pause)* Blood on the tide. That's what they call it. Did you know? Lasts two or three days usually . . .

TRICIA   I've never seen it before.

NYM   Last time it happened, a woman was murdered . . .

TRICIA   Around here? *(Nym shrugs)* Are you trying to scare me, Nym?

NYM   She was murdered by her husband . . . *(rubs his hands)* Don't come in the bathroom. I'm having a bath.

TRICIA   Haven't you just had one?

NYM   No, I was cleaning the bath. I always clean the bath first. You should, you know.

TRICIA   Because of germs?

NYM   Germs and dirt.

TRICIA   You're afraid of germs and dirt? What, in case they make you ill? *(Nym shrugs)* So you have to keep washing?

NYM   I'm always washing, all the time, always washing and cleaning. There's so much to be done. It never finishes. Things get dirty so quickly. Look.

TRICIA   What?

NYM   What then? That's Carney's little game. Either you say 'what?' and he says, 'what then?' or he says 'what?' and you say 'what then?'

TRICIA   Did he do that with the others?

NYM   Others? Oh them *(indicates the dummies)* Yeah. Don't you think it's a bit of a strange thing to do?

TRICIA   The dummies?

NYM   He's nuts. I didn't ought to say that about my dad, did I? Look.

TRICIA   At what?

NYM   Specks of dust falling. Just choose one, watch it as it falls. Some fall quickly, straight down, others float to and fro, lower and lower, some of them sparkle as they catch the light . . .

TRICIA *(follows a speck of dust with her fingers)* Mine sparkled.

NYM Do you know what would happen if we didn't hoover?

TRICIA The room would get very dusty, I should think.

NYM If no-one in the world ever hoovered, or swept, or cleaned or bathed . . .

TRICIA Ugh. There'd be a hell of a mess.

NYM Things would change . . . you can't imagine, we'd become different . . .

TRICIA Smelly. *(gets up)* It's not dirt that scares you is it? It's not germs either. You're the same as your dad, exactly the same. *(walks over to the dummies)* I need a drink.

NYM There's only tea or coffee.

TRICIA Just a glass of water.

Nym exits and returns with a glass of water.

TRICIA Did you wash the glass?

NYM I could wash it again though, if you want.

TRICIA It's fine. *(lifts the glass and then deliberately drops it on the floor)*

NYM *(rushes to clear it up)* I'll get you another.

TRICIA No, it's okay.

NYM I'll get you one.
(he brings Tricia an identical glass of water)

TRICIA You've washed the glass?

NYM *(nods)* Does it look dirty? I'll wash it again.

TRICIA It's fine. *(she drops the glass on the floor)*

NYM *(rushes to clear up again)* I'll get you another.

TRICIA No.

NYM Won't be a minute.

TRICIA *(blocks his way)* I don't want another drink. I'm not thirsty anymore. You go and have your bath.

NYM I'll get you . . .

TRICIA *(takes hold of Nym)* I don't want it, love. What's so terrible about that? It's only a little change, a little harmless change. *(Nym is shaking)* You're damp, you're like a frog – amphibious. Come and sit down. *(she makes Nym sit down beside her)* You like a routine, don't you, love? You like doing the same thing, over and over. What is it you're scared of? Things changing? *(she gets up and goes over to the dummies)* So you do the same thing again and again and again.

Exit Nym. He returns with another glass of water. Tricia takes it and drinks it. She hands him the empty glass.

NYM   Another?

TRICIA   Eventually, you know what would happen? *(Nym shrugs)* We run out of glasses. *(she smiles, so does Nym)* But what happens when things don't run out? That's when you think you can stop changes happening. You can stop time passing. Water doesn't run out. You could go on bringing me water forever. And women don't run out do they?

NYM   Mum did. Maureen did and Carol did.

TRICIA   And I did. But I came back . . . again. Over and over again, I've come back. Did they? Did Rhonda come back?

NYM   And Carol and Maureen.

TRICIA   Why?

NYM   Carney put an advert in the paper.

TRICIA   Saying?

NYM   'Come back' . . .

TRICIA   'I love you' . . . but they didn't just keep on coming back, over and over, forever, did they? *(Nym nods)* Well, where are they? Where's Rhonda?

NYM   She's in Basingstoke, with my step-father and my half-sister.

TRICIA   So one day, she managed to change things. She broke the pattern, she stopped herself going back to Carney. She ignored his advert in the newspaper . . .
(Nym shakes his head) She left him. She realised that things had

to change, her life was slipping away, she was getting nowhere. She couldn't put up with his ways anymore and she left him.

NYM No. She got old. I'm going to have a bath.

Exit Nym. Tricia turns to look at herself in the mirror, then turns back to the line of dummies.

TRICIA Nym! Nym, will you be alright by yourself for a while? I'm going to my mum's to pick up my things.

Exit Tricia. Enter Nym wearing only a towel, lost.

Blackout.

ACT TWO

The next day. Carney's mobile home. There are now two vases of fresh flowers on display. Tricia and Nym are discovered on. Nym is dressed in normal clothes. Tricia is showing Nym an egg-timer.

TRICIA Time passes, the sand falls grain by grain. A change happens, it has to. There, it's finished. *(she sets the timer down. Nym turns it over immediately)*

Enter Carney. He kisses Tricia. She stares at him.

CARNEY What?

TRICIA What then?

CARNEY Why are you looking at me like that?

TRICIA You've changed.

CARNEY Nym's changed. Third shirt today.

TRICIA No, you're different somehow. Something's altered.

CARNEY What?

TRICIA What then?

CARNEY *(wearily)* How am I different?

TRICIA   It's just something about you.

(Nym is watching them closely)

CARNEY   Which has changed since when?

TRICIA   Since yesterday.

CARNEY   I've changed overnight? Must've been having you here, babe. Don't mind me shaving in here, do you? The light's better than in the bathroom. *(shaves in front of the mirror)* Did you notice the flowers? I picked them as soon as I got up.

TRICIA   They're lovely. But, I don't know, cut flowers always make me sad somehow, I don't like to watch them wither and die . . .

CARNEY *(looks round at Tricia, worried)* Neither do I angel. I can't bear seeing them when they're withering. As soon as I see the first signs, a slight fade in colour, a tiny curl at the edge of a petal, that's it, out they go.

TRICIA   Are my petals starting to curl yet?

(Carney laughs)

Are my colours fading?

CARNEY   Quite the opposite, you've a beautiful pinky-flush this morning. That's what I do for your circulation. I'm good for you, see how pretty you look. *(holds Tricia in front of the mirror)*

TRICIA   Am I in full bloom?

CARNEY   You certainly are.

TRICIA   Are you sure? Can't you detect a faint fading? My lips. Are they as rosy red as they were last night?

CARNEY   If not, I can soon put that to rights. But they look just as red to me, red as the river. Have you noticed the blood tide?

TRICIA   Nym showed me yesterday.

CARNEY   He's quite superstitious about it. It's only algae, nothing sinister.

(Tricia wanders over to the flowers. He resumes shaving) You're not really bothered by those blooms are you?

(Tricia shakes her head) Good, because you'll have to put up with them forever now. As soon as I chuck those out, Nym will

go and pick some more. Those will die and he'll bring us fresh ones. On and on and on – flowers forever.

TRICIA   Will I be here forever?

NYM   The flowers will run out.

CARNEY   I wouldn't put good money on you not leaving me again, but I *would* bet on you coming back. You'll always come back to me.

NYM   Eventually there'll be no flowers left on the daisy bank, no roses on the tree.

TRICIA   Will you always want me back?

CARNEY   Always, angel. But I won't put an advert in the paper again if that embarrasses you. You see, I've had a lot of experience of being a husband, and you haven't been a wife for more than a few months. So I know everything about marriage and you're still at the learning stage. Feel that. *(he offers his face for her to stroke)* Smooth?

TRICIA   Like silk.

CARNEY   Smoother than Nym's?

(Tricia shrugs. Nym goes to Tricia and puts her hand on his face. Surprised) Well?

TRICIA   A . . . about the same, I think. You know you two could be brothers, rather than . . .

NYM   No! Don't say it, Patricia. He has to face it, you should help him.

TRICIA   He has to face it! There's one or two things you need to understand. What if I stayed here forever, you wouldn't like that would you? Would you?

(Nym anxiously takes Tricia's hand)

NYM *(quietly)* Go away from here . . .

TRICIA   Go away and come back again, go and come back, so I don't break the routine, so nothing changes . . . Then what happens? My colours start to fade, my petals start to wither, and Carney moves on to wife number five.

CARNEY *(gasps)* No love! *(he hugs Tricia)*

NYM   I'm going to have a bath.

Exit Nym.

CARNEY *(burying his head against Tricia)* I'll never do that, never. *(Tricia moves away)* You wouldn't doubt me, if you loved me.

TRICIA *(walks along the line of dummies)* Perhaps not.

CARNEY What?

TRICIA Perhaps I don't love you. What then?

CARNEY You came back.

TRICIA And?

CARNEY I love you, you love me. Nothing's changed.

TRICIA You've changed.

CARNEY In the four days since you walked out?

TRICIA Time has moved on.

CARNEY *(looking anxiously at the mirror)* Time.

TRICIA You look tired. The shadows under your eyes look darker. I never noticed those thin lines at the corners of your mouth, perhaps they weren't there before. I don't remember those hollows in your cheeks . . . that your hair was so grey at the sides . . .

CARNEY *(puts his cap on)* Anything on the stall, anywhere you like, ladies. *(he addresses the mirror rather than Tricia)*

TRICIA But it isn't the passing of time which scares me.

CARNEY All your household goods, all your packs of Christmas cards, all different pictures . . .

TRICIA It isn't the ageing process.

CARNEY *(loudly)* Get your sellotape – 50p the big reel!

TRICIA I'm ageing at the same rate. I don't fear the inevitable.

CARNEY Get your bargains now while stocks last, anywhere on the stall, ladies.

TRICIA It's lies and deceit I fear. Yours and mine. *(she approaches him)* Listen to me.

CARNEY Get your silk flowers. Everlasting roses two for 50p.

TRICIA That's what you need, isn't it, love? An everlasting rose. But would she still want you in ten years?

CARNEY   Your garden gnomes!

TRICIA   An everlasting rose would be the one to prick your fingers. She'd be the one to throw you over for a younger model. Perhaps you wouldn't be the first . . .

CARNEY   Anywhere on the stall.

TRICIA   Maybe you'd be husband number one, or two or three or four. One day you'll meet and marry everlasting Rose, it's bound to happen, it's only a matter of *time*.
(Silence) Love are you okay? Carney.
(He remains looking in the mirror) Look what I've got. *(she holds up a 50p piece so that he can see it in the mirror)* What've you got for 50p? *(she stands so he can kiss her. He doesn't move)* Anything on the stall? What bargains can I tempt you with this morning, sir? *(she unbuttons her top)* Everything 50p, anywhere you like. *(she takes her top off)* Take your pick, feast your eyes on these, feel the quality. *(she starts to unfasten her bra)*

Carney exits.

TRICIA *(she refastens her bra, approaches 'Rhonda')* You've seen it all, haven't you? Your life acted out again and again and again. *(pause)* I like your dress. May I? *(she slips the 60's style dress off over 'Rhonda's' head. She puts it on, over her jeans and tries to imitate as best she can 'Rhonda's' hairstyle and posture)*

Enter Nym, wrapped in a towel. He is shocked to see Tricia in his mother's dress. He cannot look at her, nor the naked 'Rhonda'.

NYM   Dad said to ask if you're okay.

TRICIA   Is he okay?

NYM   Yeah.

TRICIA *(goes to Nym)* I'm sorry, I'm sorry about this, but it was what you said about lies and deceit, about making Carney face up to the truth.

NYM   You look nice. *(he smiles shyly)*

TRICIA   Your mother's dress! Oh Nym, what must you think of me? *(she moves to take the dress off)*

NYM   Don't, Patricia.

TRICIA   I'm almost decent underneath. Or leave me a moment, if you'd rather.

NYM   I'd rather you wear it than the effigy.

TRICIA   Do I remind you of her?
(Nym shakes his head) I'm not pretty, like her . . .

NYM   You're beautiful. *(overcome)* I've got to get a clean shirt.

Exit Nym. Tricia removes the dress and puts it back on the dummy. She puts her top back on and sits down by the window. Enter Nym wearing jeans, buttoning up a shirt.

TRICIA   Is he sulking? *(she indicates to Nym that she would like him to sit down beside her. He does so, leaving a distance between them and not looking at her)* Is he talking to himself?

NYM   No.

TRICIA   Is he upset?

NYM   He's in the bathroom.

TRICIA   I better go to him.

NYM   He's alright.

TRICIA   I ought to apologise.

NYM   He threw me out the bath. He wants to wash his hair.

TRICIA   Oh. There's still your blood on the tide.

NYM   *My* blood?

TRICIA   No I didn't mean . . . I meant because you showed me it.

NYM   It's beautiful when the sun shines on the algae. I think it looks like roses growing underwater. Have you ever been down on the shingle bank, right at the water's edge?

TRICIA   I haven't . . .

NYM   You ought to.

TRICIA   You can come with me, you can go out today now you've got all your clothes clean to wear. We'll go for a walk later, shall we?

NYM   I'd like that. We can go every day . . .

TRICIA   I lied to Carney earlier.

NYM   We don't look like brothers.

TRICIA   You do, you could honestly . . .

(Nym stands up)
Sorry, I keep saying the wrong thing today. Don't let me upset you as well. Sit down. *(he sits)* I was too hard on him. I wasn't hard enough on myself. Instead of telling him the things he likes me to say, I said the things he hates to hear.

NYM   Like I do.

TRICIA   We shouldn't do that.

NYM   We shouldn't lie to him.

TRICIA   You're very honest aren't you?

(Nym shrugs) You're honest with me, I like that.
(He looks at her shyly and smiles. She takes his hand) But you're not truthful to yourself. You think something awful will happen if you don't set up routines and keep to them. If you did something different, if you stopped bathing for a month, if you lived in filthy, dirty clothes, lived like a pig, Nym – would anything terrible and frightening happen? Would it?
(Sheepishly he shakes his head) Of course not. You believe that now don't you?
(He nods) Trust me. I trust you. I trust you to help me. Will you?

NYM   Yes.

TRICIA   I don't love your dad . . .

(Nym wrings his hands. Tricia stops him, holding his hands)
I don't think I was ever 'in love' with him. I didn't feel the way you're supposed to – all light and tummy fluttery . . . I've never felt like that, had that tingling 'in love' feeling, well apart from with rock singers and actors on the telly.

NYM   Yes.

TRICIA   Have you felt like that about anyone?

(Nym gets up and moves to the dummies, his back to Tricia)
I'm sorry I didn't mean to be nosy.

NYM   I'll see if he's out of the bathroom.

Exit Nym. He re-enters moments later.

NYM   He's still in there.

TRICIA   Do you think he's okay? Can you call out to him for me?

NYM   He's singing and splashing about.

TRICIA   Oh.

NYM *(goes over to the dummies again. He looks at 'Maureen' and then at Tricia)* I was in love with Maureen. Don't tell Dad!

TRICIA   How long ago was that?

NYM   I was eight.

TRICIA *(laughs)* That wasn't really love though was it? More of a schoolboy crush. *(she walks over to 'Maureen')*

NYM   I thought she was the most beautiful woman in the world . . .

TRICIA   And was she still beautiful when he ditched her?

NYM   She was so beautiful . . . *(he strokes 'Maureen's' hair and clothes)*

TRICIA   Do you ever see her now?

NYM   Never saw her again.

TRICIA   I bet you were upset when she went.

NYM *(shakes his head)* I was out of love with her by then.

TRICIA   Because she was getting older . . .

NYM   She hated me. I loved her and she hated me. It was terrible. She had a nickname for me.

CARNEY *(offstage)* The towel's sopping wet! Nym! Is there a dry one anywhere?

NYM   She used to call me 'filth'.

Exit Nym. Tricia twists 'Maureen's' head round to an unnatural angle, becoming bolder. She starts to re-position the dummy's arms. An arm comes off. Tricia starts to dismember 'Maureen'. She is sitting on the floor pulling the legs off, when Nym re-enters.

NYM   No! Don't!

Carney wrapped in a towel stands in the doorway. He is amused, but concerned about Tricia. Tricia jumps up guiltily. Nym starts trying to reassemble the pieces.

TRICIA *(breathlessly)* What was she like?

CARNEY   My second wife, who you've just dismembered? Like I'd made her look, there. Pretty. But you're pretty too. There's no need to be jealous of an effigy. I doubt if she's very pretty now . . .

TRICIA   It *was* a long time ago.

CARNEY *(takes hold of Tricia)* What's with you this morning? If this is the effect of sleeping on that hard sofa, we'd better make sure we've the duvet back tonight, if nutty as a fruit-cake's finished with it.

NYM   That's what she used to call me.

TRICIA   Maureen?

NYM *(shakes his head)* Carol.

TRICIA   What was Maureen like, her personality, I mean?

CARNEY   Spirited, quite sparkly, like you this morning.

TRICIA *(quietly to Carney)* What was she like with Nym?

CARNEY   Nym, was Maureen a good step-mother to you? *(Nym has fixed 'Maureen's' legs. He stands her torso up)* She tried to be, but that wasn't quite how he saw her. He used to crouch down beside the wall outside and watch her when she was in the bath or undressing.

TRICIA   Did she see him?

CARNEY   She suspected what was going on, but she was too embarrassed to say anything until she actually caught him. Which she did eventually of course. But by then it had been going on for a couple of years . . . He'd become so confident, that he'd creep into the corner of the bedroom, you know between the old chest and the wall, and he'd stop there for hours. He was what, nine years old then. He's too tall to fit in that space now, so you needn't worry. Anyway, Maureen was obsessed by the way she looked . . .

TRICIA   *She* was?

CARNEY   Women often are. I'm glad you're not though. So she'd only go to bed with me in the dark. Didn't want me to be able to look at her. I maintain to this day that Nym's seen more of her than I have . . .

NYM   Carney . . .

CARNEY   Why didn't you take pictures? I should've just brought you a camera and left you to it.

Exit Nym. The sound of running water.

CARNEY   He's going to clean the bath after me.

TRICIA   You've upset him.

CARNEY   You don't understand him.

TRICIA   Did you catch him spying on Maureen, or did she?

CARNEY   We both did. Maureen carried on alarming. She thought he was some dreadful degenerate, 'ought to be put away'. He was a nine year old kid, with a healthy curiosity, that's all. Where's the harm in it?

TRICIA   So you weren't angry with him?

CARNEY   I'd have done exactly the same, so how could I be? But Maureen, she never forgave him. She called him 'filth' for the rest of her time here. Never called him by his name again. 'Filth do this, filth do that.' Poor kid.

TRICIA   Is that when it started? The washing?

CARNEY   Yeah, but he's a lot worse now than he was then, and that's mainly due to Carol . . .
(Tricia walks over to the dummy 'Carol'. 'Maureen' is still only half-repaired. She grips the dummy's arms and lifts off its feet. With some satisfaction she throws it on the floor and stands over it. She stoops to start taking it apart. Carney stops her)
Who're you angry with, them or me? Is it me you want to rip limb from limb? I'd better be careful, especially while there's a blood

tide. It's when murders happen, according to Nym. Did he tell you that?

TRICIA It was a woman who was murdered.

CARNEY Did he tell you where it happened?

TRICIA Was it very near here?

CARNEY *(grinning)* It was in America. You take Nym seriously. You're the first one of my ladies to do that since his mum. *(he puts his hand on Tricia's head)* You're hot.

TRICIA What's my skin feel like?

CARNEY Sticky, you might be running a temperature.

TRICIA Is it soft?

CARNEY *(stroking her face)* Mmmm.

TRICIA What about the lines, the shadows under my eyes, Carney?

CARNEY *(looks at them together in the mirror)* You're a little hot that's all. *(he releases her to comb his hair straight)*

TRICIA Wilting like a flower.

CARNEY *(picks up his cap and then puts it down again)* A little fresh air would do you the world of good. Why don't we go for a walk, down by the river? I can convince you once and for all that it's just a red algae on the water, nothing sinister.

TRICIA I rather like Nym's description of it, though.

CARNEY We could kneel down on the shingle bank and hold hands under the water. Just to see them looking red, like we were seeing our hearts entwined.

TRICIA Red hands? What are you on about?

CARNEY *(smiling)* Don't ask me.

TRICIA You're completely crazy.

CARNEY I'll get some clothes on and then we can go.

Enter Nym, wearing his own coat.

CARNEY Have you cleaned the bath?
(Nym nods. He sees 'Carol' lying on the floor. He looks at Tricia)
Another job for you, I'm afraid.

Exit Carney. Nym stands 'Carol' back on her feet. He carefully brushes her off.

TRICIA   I did that, I'm sorry.

NYM   She can wear something of mine while her dress is in the wash. I've got lots of clean clothes now. Don't have to wear a duvet. *(he smiles at Tricia)*

TRICIA   Her dress looks clean enough to me.

NYM   It's been on the floor.

TRICIA *(sighing)* And you can't see germs can you?

NYM   You can't see them but they're there.

TRICIA   You've forgotten what I said to you earlier.
(Nym shakes his head)
I said that if you stopped washing everything, if you lived in dirt like a pig, nothing terrible would happen. And I asked you to believe me, Nym. Can you? Will you?

NYM   Okay.

TRICIA *(goes to Nym who is continuing to repair 'Carol')* Promise.

NYM   Yes.
(Tricia hugs him)
Do you . . . I thought you might like to go for a walk.

TRICIA   Yes, Carney thought I needed to get out in the air.

NYM   I'll clean my shoes . . .

TRICIA   Nym, what will happen if you don't?

NYM   If I don't clean them? *(shrugs)* Nothing.

TRICIA   So don't do it!

NYM *(delighted)* Yeah! *(he puts his dirty shoes on, proud of the achievement)*

TRICIA   Supposing you never cleaned them again. What would happen?

NYM   Nothing!

TRICIA   You've got it, love. *(she gives him a peck on the cheek. He is startled but pleased)* No more baths today.

NYM   Definitely not.

Enter Carney, fully dressed, wearing his coat.

CARNEY   Ready then?
      (Tricia picks up her coat, Nym is bewildered)
      We're just going for a walk.
TRICIA   He knows. He's coming.
CARNEY   It's very muddy out.
NYM   I don't mind.
CARNEY   It might well rain again.
NYM   Well, I'm not wearing a duvet today.
      *(Tricia takes Carney's arm and then Nym's. At the door, he
      hesitates)* I left the bath taps running.

Exit Nym.

CARNEY   Come on.
TRICIA   Wait, Carney.
CARNEY   He can catch us up.
TRICIA   He won't be a minute.
CARNEY *(goes back to the mirror)* My hair's going to blow about.
      (he sprays it liberally) Better. Are my teeth alright? I brushed
      them after breakfast . . .
TRICIA   They're fine, love.
CARNEY *(ties his neck-scarf around his neck)* Is that straight? He's
      taking his time, isn't he?

*Exit Carney. Tricia looks at her watch, she takes a flower from a
vase and sniffs it. Enter Carney.*

CARNEY   He's having another bath.
TRICIA *(annoyed and disappointed)* Oh no.
CARNEY   Nutty as a fruit-cake.

*Carney opens the front door. Carney and Tricia exit; Tricia with a
glance behind.*

Enter Nym. He is still wearing his coat and shoes. He runs to the window and looks out. He can see Carney and Tricia on the river bank. He stands rubbing and wringing his hands, lost. Then he takes down a pot plant. Emptying out the plant, he rubs the soil on his hands and then his face and clothes.

Blackout.

ACT THREE

Several weeks later. Carney's mobile home. Carney and Nym are discovered on. Carney, wearing dark glasses to cover the bruises around his eyes, is shaving in front of the mirror. Nym, unwashed and dirty, carries a washing-up bowl of mud into the centre of the room. He sits stirring it with a spoon.

CARNEY   She was there this time. I finally got to her and not her mother.
(Nym smears himself with mud)
And she's coming back. Does my face look okay? *(lifts his glasses, momentarily)*Should I get rid of the effigies? Do you think they're what upset her? I really was beginning to think I'd lost her this time. *(combs his hair)* To think she might *be* everlasting Rose. *(walks over to the flowers in the vases, which are dead)* I'd better pick some more. Hadn't you noticed the flowers had died?
(Nym takes the dead blooms, shreds them and rubs them in his hair)
God you stink, Nym, like an old tramp. I never thought I'd hear myself suggesting it, but why don't you have a bath?
(Nym shakes his head)
What will Trish think if she sees you like this, eh? Before she left she was convinced you were getting better. *(picks up the bowl of mud)* If you must play mud pies, you can do it outside. I'm sick of clearing up after you. We're still getting through as much soap and water a week, only now it's me that's doing all the bloody cleaning.

NYM   She's not coming back.

CARNEY   I phoned her and she is.
    (Nym shakes his head)
    You're a fruit-cake.

*Exit Carney with the bowl of mud and the dead flowers. He re-enters
with some fresh flowers which he arranges in the vases. He pauses
in front of the mirror where Nym joins him.*

NYM   We could almost be brothers.

CARNEY *(tries to comb some of the mess from Nym's hair)* What's
    this? A potato peeling? I don't want that blocking the plug hole.

NYM   I'm not having a bath.

*Carney tries to wipe some of the mud from Nym's face, then exits.
Nym puts Carney's cap on.*

NYM   50p, anywhere you like, ladies.

Enter Carney with a bowl of water, flannel and soap.

NYM   All your bargains today.

CARNEY   My cap! *(snatches the cap from Nym's head and
    brushes it off. Nym wanders to the window)* Yeah, best keep an
    eye out for her. She'll come across the bridge. *(sits down besides
    Nym and gives him the flannel. Nym grips it but does not wash.
    Carney offers him the bowl of water. Nym looks out of the
    window)* Here, clean yourself up. *(he takes the flannel back and
    wipes Nym's face, cleaning him up)* Like when you were a little
    kid and I used to buy you an ice-cream and you'd spread it all
    around your face. Remember that?

NYM   Years ago.

CARNEY   And when you were in your high chair and you'd
    have a tantrum and put your soup bowl on your head . . .

NYM   Ages and ages ago.

CARNEY   It doesn't seem like that to me. So much water under
    the bridge.

NYM   Blood on the tide.

CARNEY   Not today there isn't. I suppose it gets washed out to sea. Or does it just die and disappear?

NYM   You and Tricia went down to the shingle bank . . .

CARNEY   You watched us?

NYM   You both held your hands under the water to see the blood on your palms.

CARNEY   We splashed the water on our faces, caught water droplets on our tongues to taste the salt . . . *(studies Nym critically)* A little better.

NYM   Is my face smooth?
(Carney feels Nym's face)
Smoother than yours?

CARNEY   Come into the light. *(drags Nym in front of the mirror again. He holds Nym's head and shaves him)* There. Look, the glass hasn't cracked. A miracle. Smile, can you? Or would it kill you? The coroner attributed the death of Mr. Nym Carney to an excess of smiling and recorded a verdict of misadventure.
(There is a knock at the door)
Get in that bath! Now. Get out of here! *(he opens the door to Tricia)*

TRICIA   I haven't come back.

CARNEY   Angel, we've missed you. *(ushers her into the room)*

TRICIA   What's the matter with your face? Have you and Nym been fighting?

CARNEY   I've a bottle of wine in the fridge. We haven't started it either. Want some?

TRICIA   How's Nym?

CARNEY   In the bath.

NYM *(in the doorway)* Hello Patricia.
(Tricia embraces him. He is shy)

CARNEY   Patricia – she hates being called that, don't you, babe?

TRICIA   Not as much as I hate being called babe and angel. Anyway I've changed my name. *(pulls away from Nym)* Ugh, what've you been doing? For once you really do need that bath.

CARNEY   He's been gardening. What've you changed your name to? Not back to your maiden one . . .

TRICIA   I'm not Tricia anymore. I'm Rose.

NYM   That's a beautiful name. Suits you.

TRICIA   Thank you, Nym. What do you think, love?

CARNEY   I don't like being called 'love'.

Exit Carney.

TRICIA   Darling? Something I said?

NYM   I'm glad you came back.

TRICIA   So the routine repeats, over and over. Nothing bad can happen because Tricia goes and Tricia comes back. Then Tricia's replacement will go and come back. Isn't life safe and predictable?

NYM   I'm glad you came back because I've missed you. I don't care whether it's a routine or something new. I'm not frightened by changes anymore.

TRICIA   That's good, Nym. that's really good.

NYM   I want to make changes, to make the best of my time. I might go back to the college. I might do something which even surprises me.

TRICIA   That's great.

NYM   Patricia . . . Rose, I . . .

TRICIA   Still Trish to you, Nym. Everlasting Rose to Carney.

NYM   Trish I . . . I ought to show you something . . .

Enter Carney with the wine and three glasses. He pours the wine.

CARNEY   To Trish's very happy return.

TRICIA   Rose.

CARNEY   Your return. *(they toast Tricia and drink)*

TRICIA	I haven't returned.
CARNEY	We can talk about that.

Exit Nym.

TRICIA	I'm leaving you.
CARNEY	You've come back to tell me?

TRICIA   I need to prove to myself that I can walk in here, say goodbye and walk away forever. I'm everlasting Rose, I'm the one who's dumping *you*.

CARNEY *(snatches up his cap)* You wouldn't leave me . . .

Enter Nym with another shop dummy dressed as Tricia. Carney remains oblivious to its entrance for a moment.

CARNEY   I love you.
       (Tricia sees the dummy and gasps. Carney notices it for the first time. He is shocked)
       Shit! What the?. . .

TRICIA   That's it then. That's the end of me.

CARNEY   Nym! *(catches hold of Nym and shakes him)*

TRICIA   You *had* already decided then. Time to find wife number five . . .
       (Carney drops Nym on the floor and goes to Tricia)
       Or is she already waiting in the wings? Like I was, when you were divorcing Carol?

CARNEY   I divorced Carol because it was the honest thing to do. I'd met you and we were in love.

TRICIA   You were in love.

CARNEY   I'm not responsible for that thing. It's not my doing. It's *his*. It's his idea of a joke.

Exit Nym.

TRICIA   It doesn't matter.

CARNEY   I didn't make that effigy, please believe me, Trish.

TRICIA   Rose.

CARNEY   Please angel.

TRICIA   Alright, alright, the fault's mine, I know. I was in the wrong from the start.

Carney pours Tricia another glass of wine. Enter Nym with a bunch of flowers which he gives to Tricia.

TRICIA   Why Nym?

NYM   They looked pretty and so do you.

CARNEY   Why did you make an effigy of Tricia?

NYM   I missed her being here.

TRICIA   Why did *you* make effigies of the others?

CARNEY   With Rhonda, because she'd left some of her clothes here, and I was used to having her about the place . . .

NYM   You couldn't break the routine. You thought something awful would happen if she just went out of your life completely?

CARNEY   Something awful? Like what? I just wanted to be reminded of her prettiness, the eyes I could dance all night in. And it seemed right and fair to commemorate the others in the same way. They accepted it, Maureen lived with Rhonda's effigy and Carol lived with two of them. Maureen and Carol were able to accept it. Why can't you?

TRICIA   Perhaps they didn't understand you or try to. Maybe they loved you.

NYM   Tricia doesn't love you.

TRICIA   I'm sorry, Carney.

CARNEY *(sharply)* When did it happen? When did I change?

TRICIA   You haven't changed love . . .

CARNEY   Is it the bruises? They're starting to fade already and no more bags or lines under my eyes . . .

TRICIA   My God, you didn't!

CARNEY   But what about the other changes? Does my skin feel coarser, drier, can you not bear to touch it?
(Nym picks up Carney's cap before he can take it)
Did these things occur overnight? Did you wake one morning to find I had more thread veins around my nose? Liver spots on my hands?

NYM *(quietly)* Anywhere on the stall.

CARNEY   Was it when you came back last time? Didn't you say I'd changed then? Did you mean the lines on my forehead were deeper? I might try collagen when I can afford it.

NYM   All your bargains, ladies, 50p.

CARNEY   And for the wrinkles at the corners of my mouth.

NYM   Strictly while stocks last.

CARNEY   My hair's greying at the sides and thinning on top.

NYM   Last chance for a bargain.

CARNEY   My profile's softening too I know, and my cheeks are becoming hollow.

NYM   An offer not to be repeated.

CARNEY   This is what you've done to me, Trish.

TRICIA   I . . .

CARNEY   There won't be a number five. *(picks up the dummy 'Tricia' and carries it to the end of the line)* This is where the line stops.

NYM   The routine ends.

CARNEY   Everything ends.

TRICIA   No, Carney . . .

CARNEY   Time's caught up.

TRICIA   I shouldn't have married you. But it was you – or staying with my mother . . .

CARNEY   It had to eventually.

TRICIA   I did fancy you, and you flattered me, but that's not enough is it? The gentle art of subterfuge.

CARNEY   Yeah.

TRICIA   Lies and deceit. Nym opened my eyes to it. It was a routine – leave, return, leave, return. Stay here for a while, go home to Mum. And meantime time passed . . .

CARNEY   It was catching up.

TRICIA   On us both. I've been wasting my life, when I could be living for real, feeling new sensations, seeing new places and faces, instead of being caught in a circle, a loop of tape, the hands of a clock. You're caught too, Carney. You've been caught for far longer than I have. Since you were my age, since Rhonda, through Maureen and Carol . . . and Tricia. Through every Saturday at the market, putting up the poles and taking them down, unfolding the canvas and folding it up again, setting out your wares and packing them away.
(Carney strokes the face of the 'Tricia' dummy)
Now's your chance to make a change, to break out of your routine . . .

NYM   I've done it, Dad. You can do it.

TRICIA   It's never too late. You'll come to see it was for the best.

CARNEY *(quietly)* I love you.

Exit Carney.

TRICIA   I've made a mess of it. I didn't want to upset him, well I did because he annoys and irritates me so much. Because if I'd lived this life of lies for another year or two, given him another couple of years of my life, what would he have done at the end of it?. . .
(looks at the flowers. The sound of water running, off)
Look the petals are beginning to curl already.
(looks in the mirror, drops the flowers on the floor) Are mine?
(Nym takes Tricia's hands) What've you been doing to yourself?

NYM   I haven't been bathing. I've stopped cleaning and washing.

TRICIA   Are you happy?

NYM   Yes.

TRICIA   You've given me my freedom and I hope I've given you yours. I don't think I can go to him, to say goodbye. Would you just check he's okay for me?

Exit Nym. He re-enters a moment later.

TRICIA   Is Carney alright?

NYM   He's having a bath.

TRICIA   He's not too upset?

NYM   He's singing.

TRICIA   He didn't love me. I was an animated mannequin, warmer than plastic in bed, but otherwise he won't notice the difference. He'll still have my effigy. I was just an ego-trip, an aid to his vanity. *(pause)* He was my escape from my mother.

NYM   I'll come to see you, at your Mum's, or we could meet at weekends sometimes, just to talk. We don't need to get into a routine – see each other when we want to.

TRICIA   I'm leaving this town, I'm not going back to Mum's. I've booked myself a holiday. Then I might travel on around Europe, different jobs, different rooms, different scenes and different languages. No routines, plenty of changes!

NYM   Will you write to me? I'll write back and perhaps we can meet up again somewhere, in different circumstances . . .

TRICIA   I write you, you write to me, I write to you. It would be a routine, Nym. You go back to your university, make new friends, learn new things. *(she opens the front door)* Look after Carney. Don't let him work too hard, eh? See if you can't find him wife number five . . .

NYM   There won't be a number five. You're everlasting Rose. You're leaving him. And me. There won't be anyone else, ever.

TRICIA   Don't be stupid. You know Carney and his eye for the girls. There'll be five, six, seven and eight quite likely . . .

NYM   No-one's ever left him before.

TRICIA   Nym don't! Goodbye.

Exit Tricia. Nym goes to the window to watch her depart. He half lifts his hand to wave, but does not do so. He sobs. A red sunset has been gathering outside the window.

NYM   Like underwater roses . . .

He gets up, goes to the dummy of 'Tricia'. He wipes his tears on her hair. He wrings his hands. Picks up the dropped flowers. Starts to take off his dirty clothes. He washes again with the water Carney brought, then wanders out. Exit Nym.

NYM *(screams off)* Carney!

Enter Nym, supporting Carney who is bleeding heavily from cut wrists. Carney sinks down on the floor. Nym has Carney's blood on his hands. He stares at them.

CARNEY   See what they look like red, *(he grips Nym's hand)*
     . . . hearts entwined.
     (Nym fetches the duvet. He wraps it around Carney)
     (weakly) It'll need washing.

Blackout

The end.

Judy Upton

An award-winning playwright whose stage plays include **Everlasting Rose** (London New Play Festival, Old Red Lion) 1992, **Ashes and Sand** – winner of the 1994 George Devine Award, (Theatre Upstairs, The Royal Court), **Temple** (The Room, Richmond Orange Tree) 1995, **The Shorewatchers' House** (The Red Room, Kentish Town), **Bruises** – winner of the 1994 Verity Bargate Award, (Theatre Upstairs, Royal Court), 1995; **Stealing Souls** (The Red Room), 1996; **Sunspots** (The Red Room) 1996, transferred to BAC; **People on the River** (The Red Room at the Finborough) 1997, **To Blusher with Love** – winner of the 1997 Open Stages competition, (The Man in the Moon) 1997, **Pig in the Middle** – Y Touring, (National Schools tour) 1998, **The Girlz** (The Room, Richmond Orange Tree) 1998.

Judy has had two radio plays produced by BBC Radio 4 –**Tissue Memory,** 1997, **Long Time Man**, 1997.

Ashes and Sand, Bruises and **The Shorewatchers' House** are published by Methuen. Judy Upton is writer-in-residence with the Red Room Theatre Company.

Strindberg Knew My Father

by Mark Jenkins

Strindberg Knew My Father

It all began rather spookily in a deserted Welsh manor house. During the filming of my first teleplay, I found a book lying in the middle of the floor of a vast empty library – **Confessions of a Madman** by August Strindberg. I was immediately struck by the honesty with which this great writer gave voice to his neuroses and struggled to make sense of his deranged vision. Not long after, I learned of the bizarre circumstances under which Strindberg laboured to produce his masterpiece, **Miss Julie** and I began to wonder how he could possibly have fashioned a tragedy out of the series of hilariously comic events on which his story is based. So I set about **Strindberg Knew My Father**, in which an alchemist turns the base metals of infidelity, prejudice and misogyny into theatrical gold. I reduced **Miss Julie** back into its original farcical elements. A hard-drinking literary critic then informed me that I had *deconstructed* the great Swede. This was news to me.

I was greatly encouraged when the finished script was rejected in vitriolic tones by a dozen or more theatre companies whose repertoires I despised for their servile political correctness. Three years later, I got a phone call from a young director, Areta Breeze, who said she wanted to direct it and that a producer, Phil Setren, would put it on at the London New Play Festival. She assembled the finest bunch of actors I have ever worked with – Sean Patterson, Annette Eden, Yvonne O'Grady, Charlotte Bronte-Elmes and Ben Cole. From the Old Red Lion Theatre we took it to the Sherman in Cardiff. With a minimal set and a tight budget this amazing team resurrected the gothic atmosphere of the Danish castle in 1888, handling the hairy moments of levitation, mesmerism and alchemy like true magicians.

Strindberg, by the way, did not know my father, and my father had never even heard of him.

This play is dedicated to the memory of my father William John Jenkins born Caerfarchell, Solva, West Wales 24:11:1911 died Oxford, England 3:11:90

Notes:

After the publication of **A Madman's Defence**, August Strindberg spent the period from April to September 1888 with his family on an extended holiday in a run-down castle in Skvolyst-at-Lyngby in Denmark. Here his marriage to the long suffering Siri von Essen finally broke up whilst he wrote his masterpiece **Miss Julie**. The castle was owned by the eccentric Countess Frankenau (Anna). Dogs, cats, peacocks, ducks and rabbits wandered at will through its corridors. The castle's slovenly bailiff was Ludwig Hansen, half-gypsy, semialcoholic dabbler in levitation and mesmerism. He is in fact the Countess's half-brother and illegitimate son of the late Count and a local gypsy woman, though this fact is kept secret from the world to protect the family's reputation, and Strindberg did not know the truth. Ludwig's sister, (Martha), was a housemaid in this zany establishment, beautifully understated in the wry chapter, *Miss Julie* in Michael Meyer's wonderful biography of the Master.

I see this as a 'gothic' piece, in which all the characters appear grotesquely larger than life, as they might have seemed to Strindberg in his delicate mental state. He was, even then, showing signs of the paranoid schizophrenia which later afflicted him. Being chased from the castle by a pack of Great Danes, with Ludwig firing buckshot after him, probably did not assist. Yet, out of all this madness came **Miss Julie**, based partly on Strindberg's imagined affair between Anna (Miss Julie) and Ludwig (Jean) and partly on his own tortured relationship with Siri. In my play, Strindberg deals with everyone as if they were his own fictional creations over whom he is slowly losing control.

In this play all of the incidents, except the most trivial, are true.

Mark Jenkins

. . . the ménage Strindberg, make ideal material for a surrealist biodrama that Ken Russell would have slavered over . . . The Guardian

Strindberg Knew My Father

or
Making Miss Julie
by Mark Jenkins

First performed at the Old Red Lion Theatre, Islington in 1992 as
part of London New Play Festival, transferring to the Sherman
Theatre, Cardiff.

Directed by Areta Breeze

Designed by Michelle Dado

Countess Anna Frankenau   Yvonne O'Grady

Ludwig Hansen, her bailiff, a gypsy,   Ben Cole
and secret half-brother.

Martha Hansen, his sister   Charlotte Bronte-Elmes

August Strindberg   Sean Patterson

Siri (Von Essen) Strindberg, his wife,   Annette Eden
an actress.

ACT ONE
SCENE 1

*Spring 1888, in Skvolyst, Denmark, daytime. The scene is a large
airy living room of an old castle, but naturalistic scenery is not
called for. Long grey drapes should give an impression of spacious-
ness. Strong, clear morning light floods in between the drapes, right,
indicating generous windows. The furniture should suggest faded,
shabby, one-time glory. There is a writing desk, right, with a retract-
able working surface, which can be locked. In front of it, a chair. In
the back right corner there is the main exit and entrance 'door'
which leads out to a hall and the rest of the house. Centre right rear
is a chaise longue and above it, a mirror. Centre left is another exit
to the Countess' private rooms. The script suggests that this is a
lockable door, but these intricacies can be avoided if the door is*

*imagined to be offstage in the wings. In the back left corner there is
a large potted plant, dying for lack of water. At the front of the
stage, centre could be a low coffee table which we imagine to be set
in front of a fireplace. Either side are two low stools. There should
be one 'gaslight' rear and one near the front of stage so the
audience can accept that at times frontstage or backstage can be lit
up or plunged into darkness. There are thus three or four areas
where the actions may be concentrated within this space.*

*Ludwig, in his mid-thirties, might have a suggestion of gypsy-like
features. Realism might suggest he wore a bailiff's uniform, leather
gaiters and generally black clothing with a white shirt and black tie,
but this is not essential. Strindberg, from time to time, steps back
from the other characters, scrutinising them as an artist does his
canvas, perhaps even making notes about them as the models for the
play he is working on. He is, after all, making **Miss Julie**. Ludwig
and the Countess never touch physically, except at the very end of
the play. This heightens the 'electricity' between them. Ludwig
should have an air of quiet menace. He tries to appear super-
confident.*

Enter Anna, left, looking for a cat.

ANNA *(calling)* Ibsen! . . . Ibsen! . . . puss, puss, puss, puss . . .
*(she gets down on her hands and knees to look under the chaise
and feels underneath it with her hand)*
Oh dear !
*(Anna wipes her hand on a handkerchief then stands and looks at
the shabby state of the chaise, vainly flicking the dust off it with
the handkerchief. She sighs at the futility of it. She walks back to
the entrance left and calls again as she looks up the chimney)*
Ibsen!
*(The sound of half a dozen large Great Danes barking at various
pitches. She holds up her finger and shouts firmly)*
Stay! . . . Stay!

*The dogs stop immediately and she turns her back on the door. She
hears Ludwig approaching at the rear right entrance. As he enters*

*we see a half-full bottle of claret in his jacket pocket, but he is well
in control of his faculties. He is a man capable of wild recklessness
in pursuit of what he thinks the world owes him. Despite Anna's
laid-back but zany aristocratic style there is a hint of tension and
even attraction between them. She finds his earthy, gypsy side
engaging but is irritated at his pathetic yearning for status. He looks
at her, strolls to the writing-desk, sits, takes a swig and sits back,
stretching his legs.*

ANNA   Ibsen's gone missing. Have you seen him?

LUDWIG   Him, Countess? She would be more appropriate . . .
or rather it.

ANNA *(puzzled)* Ibsen's a tomcat?

LUDWIG   Was a tomcat, Countess. Was!

ANNA   Poor Ibsen! You'd no right to take his masculinity.

LUDWIG   I am responsible for all livestock, you said. *(he
drinks)*

ANNA *(moves around the room quickly to stem her irritation. She
indicates the wine)* You're slowly emptying the cellars. I hope
that's not a *Chateau Val Fleury*, sixty-eight?
*(Ludwig checks label, slips bottle back into pocket. Anna is still
busy)*
Can't we have a rule – no wine before lunchtime?
(she plumps the cushions on the chaise. Dust flies out)

LUDWIG   Don't talk down to your bailiff, Countess!

ANNA   Ludwig! Our Swedish guests arrive before lunch . . .
Great Dane hairs all over the cushions and piles of dogshit behind
the chaise . . . Guests notice these things!

LUDWIG   So . . . offer them a reduction.
(Anna glares at him)
Alright . . . I'll get Martha to see to it.

ANNA *(examining the chaise)* Oh God! Othello's been chewing the
upholstery again . . .

LUDWIG   What do you expect if you serve him breakfast on it?

ANNA   . . . the dogs must eat . . .

LUDWIG   From porcelain dishes? On silver trays?

ANNA   The wine's playing tricks with your eyes!

LUDWIG   Why is it the aristocracy treat dogs better than
servants?

ANNA   They're obedient . . . and they don't ask for
wages . . .

LUDWIG   Ah, yes, wages . . . I remember them well . . . How
long is it now – three months? *(shouts)* Christ! Why do I put up
with it!

*(The dogs start barking. Anna advances towards the door left and
shouts at the dogs, but Ludwig has his back to her)*

ANNA   Silence!

(The dogs cease immediately, as Ludwig swings round)
Don't start them off like that . . .

LUDWIG   These days – crap on the carpet and you shoot up the
social scale . . . from skivvy to animal . . . Ludwig Handson,
bogcleaner!

ANNA *(smiles)* You've never cleaned a toilet in your life! Heaven
knows . . . all I ask is a modicum of deference . . . for appearance
sake.

LUDWIG   I am a living example of premature ejaculation! One
day! . . . One day I'll blow the whole story.

ANNA *(firming up)* Still you'd have no rights in law . . . My 'trusted
servant'! Act the part!

LUDWIG   Damn the injustice of it!

ANNA   Twenty years supply of vintage wine – seems like a
good deal to me . . . Have another bottle.

LUDWIG   Perpetual piss-artist? What about my children ?

ANNA   You haven't got any.

LUDWIG *(whispering with lustful menace)* Neither have you.

ANNA *(in a sexually provocative manner)* Don't be disgusting.
That's incest!

LUDWIG   Half incest . . . who's to know? *(he nibbles her ear)*

ANNA *(in a sexy whisper)* It's a sin isn't it?

LUDWIG   Half a sin . . .

ANNA   Animal! See a vet.

LUDWIG *(sensing her interest, whispers excitedly)* Don't trust yourself with me, do you? Admit it! Not getting any younger . . . Going to waste on that bed every night, Great Danes draped across your quilt. Tomcats. Peacocks.

ANNA   Jealous! *(walks away from him haughtily, nervously)*

LUDWIG *(pursues her and whispers menacingly in her ear)* No heirs . . . The estate will go to your poncey cousin. Life's passing you by like a wind round a corpse in a tomb. No passion . . . *(he runs his hands through his hair anticipating her submission)*

ANNA *(nervously changing the subject. Makes herself busy)* I promised the Strindbergs I'd change the curtains. Is there clean linen on the beds? The floor's not been swept. We should open the windows. Let some air in. Are the bedrooms prepared?

LUDWIG *(angrily)* How should I know!

ANNA   Tell Martha it must be done . . . They're paying good money . . . It'll be nice to have some intellectual company. She's an actress and everybody's talking about his new book.

LUDWIG   Book?

ANNA   'Getting Married.' Word had it she was livid when she read it . . . on the point of leaving . . .

LUDWIG   Brilliant! He can write the sequel, 'Getting Divorced.' P'raps that'll bring 'em together again.

ANNA   He was tried for blasphemy . . . They say Queen Sophia was the instigator . . . but he won the case . . .

LUDWIG   So, entertaining heretics and blasphemers now, are we? Wait till that gets round the village.

ANNA *(laughs)* From propositions of incest to propriety . . . and you didn't even stop for breath . . .

LUDWIG   What d'you expect from a gypsy bastard?
(he breaks into an old Russian folk song 'Kalinka'. She smiles. The song gets faster and faster as they swirl around, never touching)

Kalinka, Kalinka, Kalinka Maya

Kalinka, Kalinka, Kalinka Maya Oy!

Kalinka, Kalinka, Kalinka Maya etc. etc.

(They stop and look at each other, breathless, suddenly the dogs start barking at a commotion outside. A carriage has arrived)

ANNA *(breaking off and running to windows right)* The guests! They're here! *(she adjusts her headscarf)* Ring for Martha!

Anna dashes out as Ludwig casually pulls a bell-rope and wanders to the window. Voices of greeting can be heard outside. He pulls back a drape to observe more closely. Enter Martha rear right. She is a chambermaid and Ludwig's sister by his gypsy mother. Ludwig is still preoccupied at the drapes and talks over his shoulder as Martha checks her hair in the mirror and admires her profile.

MARTHA   Yeah . . . What do you want?

LUDWIG *(correcting her with quiet menace)* 'You rang, Master Ludwig!'

MARTHA *(still primping)* You're Ludwig. I'm Martha. Get it right! *(Ludwig swivels round, advances and armlocks her)* Ow! Stop it!

LUDWIG *(menacing whisper)* 'You rang' . . .

MARTHA   You rang, Master Ludwig . . . You rang Master Ludwig!

LUDWIG   Have you put fresh linen on the beds, swept the floor, changed the curtains?

MARTHA   No.

LUDWIG *(twists her arm)* Do it!
(She breaks free) The playwright's in the tower room . . . His wife – next door.

MARTHA *(sensing a problem)* Oo-er!

LUDWIG   Exactly! *(steers her towards the windows)* Shoo the chickens out of the wardrobes . . . Clear the rabbits from the top hall. Understand? . . . And those peacocks nesting in the grand piano – it's wicked what they do to Chopin's nocturnes!

MARTHA   I'll close the lid on 'em, Master Ludwig. *(she blows on her fingernails, polishes them on dress. They go to window)*

LUDWIG   Now. Take a gander . . . That's our quarry little sister.

MARTHA *(admiring)* Hmmm! Looks like the devil himself . . .

LUDWIG   . . . and partial to witches . . . Pucker those lips . . . *(she does)* Suck in those cheeks . . . *(she does)* Smile . . . *(she does)* and flutter those eyelashes . . . *(she does)* and remember he's a poet . . . They're suckers for still waters, hidden depths.

MARTHA *(walks away)* The mystery of the unspoken promise; the sigh of the oppressed creature longing for the touch of wisdom . . .

LUDWIG   You're a bloody witch! Chop! Chop! *(he claps his hands and she scampers off at great speed. He stops her at the doorway)* Martha!
(She halts) The grey buck rabbit . . . He's hyper-active. Skin him. We'll have him for dinner . . .

MARTHA   I'll save the blood for gravy. *(she licks her lips and dashes away. He takes a last look through the window)*

SCENE 2

Afternoon the same day. Strindberg doesn't smile much. His humour is black with fantasies which oppress him. Siri is walking on egg-shells. She tries to keep calm and composed, knowing that to sympathise is to feed his paranoia. Strindberg is writing as Siri enters.

It is important that Siri wears trousers/slacks.

SIRI   Writing?

STRINDBERG *(preoccupied)* Mmmh?

SIRI   I see you're writing.

STRINDBERG All these years I've tried to keep it from you but there! The secret's out! I do this for a living you know.

SIRI   Don't start, please . . . How's your bedroom?

STRINDBERG My bedroom doesn't like me.

SIRI *(sighs, undaunted)* Hans' room is lovely . . . Karin and Greta are sharing . . . beautiful views overlooking the orchard

STRINDBERG There's a duck in the bath-house . . . It's nesting in the hand basin!

SIRI   It's the country . . . We're on holiday . . .

STRINDBERG It's like a prison here . . . I'm in the tower.

SIRI   You loved it when we came to view. The whole
Danish landscape spread out before you . . . I'm right next door.

STRINDBERG Oh . . . if I'm too close I could move . . . to the
stables perhaps . . .

SIRI   Look if you're not happy . . .

STRINDBERG No improper suggestions, please . . . Conjugal
rights. That sort of thing . . . People might talk.

SIRI   I meant we could swap rooms, that's all . . .

STRINDBERG So . . . a masturbation holiday! Home from home!
Think I'll chuck my condom . . . Its only taking up space . . .

SIRI   Don't be selfish. Don't my feelings matter to you?

STRINDBERG Feelings? . . . you?

SIRI   I just cannot bear the idea of sex the way things
are . . .

STRINDBERG Sex? sex? No . . . Sorry . . . Doesn't ring a bell . . .

SIRI   After all the public humiliation . . . the things you
said about me . . . in print! Your own wife!

STRINDBERG I suppose I could try buggery. There must be some
good-looking men around . . .

SIRI   Do do! Have a man, if you must. A woman . . .
anything!

STRINDBERG Right then. That's settled. Infidelity it is. You can
watch if you like . . . Might spark off some hidden passion . . .
You still have memories?

*(Siri stares at him with a wry smile. Her mood changes. She
starts stroking his forehead, running her fingers through his hair)*

SIRI   Do you remember how it was . . . in the beginning?

STRINDBERG Wait. Wait. It's coming back to me. Yes . . . You
were rather fed up with your husband who was . . . screwing his
pretty young cousin, as I recall . . .

SIRI *(moved by the memory, she is in a trance of fond reminiscence,
not listening to his cynical remarks)* My God . . . I was so
unhappy. . .

STRINDBERG The noble baron had also lost a fortune on the stock exchange . . .

SIRI *(upset. She is elsewhere)* We never went short. Let's be fair . . .

STRINDBERG . . . you were in urgent need of a provider for your daughter . . .
(Siri draws away sadly) Enter . . . our hero *(indicating himself)* Wide-eyed, innocent to the perfidy of woman . . . I believed your story . . . imprisoned by the wicked baron, prevented from pursuing your 'great talents' as an actress.

SIRI *(sadly, dramatically)* You've never forgiven me, have you? Your worst play, a feeble melodrama . . . But my reviews! They loved me! 'Never again!' you said. Then I became your prisoner.

STRINDBERG Oh this portrayal of oppressed woman! Brilliant! Christ! If you could act like that on the stage! We could clear our debts . . .
(Siri beneath her anguish still tries to salvage some fond memories and understand her past)

SIRI When we met I thought, I felt you loved me enough to let me be what I wanted to be . . . You gave me such encouragement, and I believed in you . . .

STRINDBERG *(claps slowly three times in irony)* Bravo! The show's over Baroness. As the wife, you're miscast . . . Great love story becomes farce. Ta ra! . . . Mud pie in face of Romeo. Exit Juliet with dildo in search of lesbians!

SIRI *(disgusted)* You must live in a nightmare or a jungle.

STRINDBERG Well, man and woman are descended from the apes. But! – different species of apes. Man – the higher primate; woman – the little spider monkey!

SIRI You never saw me as I was! I was some apparition to you. A virgin mother, stage Madonna – like Pygmalion of ancient Athens, waiting to be fashioned into a Strindberg saga. The moment I tried to be myself your saintly ideal of me was shattered. I became your 'oppressor'! . . . Sometimes . . . I don't think you ever loved me, Not love. Not me. No. You didn't.

STRINDBERG *(plays melodramatic violin music on an imaginary violin, mocking.)* Cross my heart and hope to die. I was infatuated with you . . . and you know it . . .

(Siri takes a cigar from his top pocket. Lights it. Walks to drinks cabinet, pours a drink)

SIRI   Why did you try to drown me, then?

STRINDBERG That was later . . . Anyway, you asked for it.

(Siri knocks back the Schnapps)

SIRI *(with irony)* Oh yes! I 'changed my sex'!

STRINDBERG Well – You wear men's clothes, smoke cigars, drown yourself in Schnapps. You chase young girls! Intercept my mail . . . Try to get me certified insane! . . .

SIRI   You're paranoid!

STRINDBERG There! You're at it again! Just because I'm paranoid doesn't mean you're not a lesbian! No. Drowning's too good for you. I'll think of something else . . .

SIRI   Women friends, August! Not sex! My God! Without them I couldn't have survived this marriage . . . Even now I'd still try to make a go of it . . . Even if my career suffered for it.

STRINDBERG You malignant little nun! All unremitting sacrifice and self-denial. How do you suppose that makes me feel?

SIRI *(exhausted)* Rotten, I imagine. Oh . . . I know . . . your great gifts . . . I didn't mean to . . .

STRINDBERG Please! Not another performance . . .

SIRI   It's not a performance!

STRINDBERG Believe me – I hate myself for wanting you physically because spiritually, I feel only a deep loathing.

SIRI *(turns her back on him, lights one of his cigars and blows smoke at him over her shoulder)* You can't hurt me!

STRINDBERG *(wearily)* All women have a virulent reforming streak. They see a man and think: 'Underneath that self-assurance, is a pathetic little masturbator trying to get out' . . . They work at it till the man's reduced to a pleading infant, begging to be let back into the womb. Well . . . I'm not going to beg any more.*(he sits)*

SIRI *(trying to keep her temper)* Please, please . . . This is a holiday . . . For the children's sake . . . Can't we have a truce? *(she approaches him from behind as he sits, placing her hands gently on his shoulders. He stiffens warily)*

STRINDBERG The end is near . . . Our final battle, my little
 serpent!

SIRI *(nods knowingly)* Please! . . .

*There is the sound of a concertina offstage. The Countess is playing
'Kalinka' again. Strindberg's head turns fearfully at the approach of
yet another woman. The Countess enters playing the concertina from
stage left, as dogs bark.*

ANNA *(to the dogs)* Stay! *(to the Strindbergs)* So how are we
 enjoying our second honeymoon?

STRINDBERG *(risen from his seat and backing off right at the
 sound of the dogs)* Forgive me, Countess, but I have an aversion
 to dogs . . . and they know!

ANNA 'Countess?' I haven't been called that in years . . .
 You must be a socialist. They're the only people who take class
 seriously.

STRINDBERG They can't escape, I hope?

ANNA I find socialists frightfully bourgeois . . . It's the
 aristocracy who are the real egalitarians. Don't you think?

STRINDBERG *(trying to get through to her)* Permit me. Just what
 is in there . . . apart from kennels? . . .

ANNA Please call me Anna . . . That's . . . my bedroom!

SIRI *(smiling politely)* Dogs? In your . . . bedroom? How many?

ANNA Eight Great Danes . . . I sleep with them.
 (Strindberg's face has to be seen to be believed)
 . . . on my bed . . .

STRINDBERG Does the door . . . lock?

SIRI It's nothing personal . . . Anna, you understand . . .
 Eight you say?

ANNA Let me see . . . There's Hamlet, Caesar, Brutus . . .
 he's a sweetie . . . Falstaff . . . a heavy drinker . . . Macbeth and
 Othello . . . He's black, you know . . . Then Titus and Cassius . . .
 never turn your back on him . . . All my favourite characters. But
 do keep the door locked if you'd prefer . . . Now come on . . .
 tell me all about the theatre *(she rings the servant's bell)* . . . I'll

get Martha to bring us some coffee . . . Oh . . . I'm not intruding am I?

(Siri and Strindberg exchange humorous glances)

SIRI *(trying to make polite conversation)* Is it a . . . large estate?

ANNA   I haven't the slightest idea . . . Ludwig handles all my business affairs.

MARTHA *(enters as if in a trance)* You rang, Countess?

ANNA *(puzzled)* Are you alright Martha?

MARTHA   Last night the sunset over Lyngby Heath set the woods aflame and figures in the fields were lit with gold, like angels . . .

ANNA   Quite so! Bring us some coffee will you . . . Mr Strindberg . . . some schnapps?

STRINDBERG *(intrigued by Martha and becoming more sociable)* Mmmmh? Thank you yes!

ANNA   Run along then Martha and . . . Martha . . . The peacocks are roosting on the grand piano . . . not a good idea, darling . . . and ask Ludwig to join us will you?

MARTHA *(curtsies and exits with slow elegance)* Yes Ma'am.

ANNA   Gypsies! Does sunset inspire you that way Mrs Strindberg?

SIRI *(being polite)* Some say our whole being is governed by heavenly bodies . . . Personally I . . .

STRINDBERG That girl . . . she's in a trance . . .

ANNA   Ludwig's sister . . . Romanies . . . I treat them as part of the family . . . as long as the whole tribe don't camp on the lawn . . . There is a limit . . .

SIRI   Are they reliable?

ANNA   Beneath the deference there is a kind of well . . . nihilism, I suppose . . . A desire to demolish civilised life . . . Hardly the right credentials for a servant, really, but . . .

STRINDBERG I know the feeling . . . I am the son of a kitchen maid.

ANNA   There, there! Never mind! . . . Yes, Ludwig would surprise you – Such talents!

STRINDBERG He was talking to the horses this morning . . . and they were nodding in agreement . . . whispering in his ear.

SIRI   Oh really!

ANNA   Quite a conversationalist – the stallion, that is . . . What are you writing at the moment, Mister Strindberg?

STRINDBERG Oh! . . . I've given up writing – haven't I, Siri? *(Siri has heard this all before, she sighs)* All audiences want these days are morality plays about 'social justice', 'identity', and oppressed womankind destroyed by men. Feminist fairy tales. That's why old bluestocking is so popular . . .

ANNA   I'm sorry? . . .

SIRI   Mister Ibsen . . . August thinks he's a lesbian.

ANNA   We've got a cat called Ibsen. It's just been castrated.

STRINDBERG How very apt! Now . . . get the cat to write feminist plays . . . He'll make a fortune . . . No . . . I'm going into banking. It's well-paid and it deals in fiction, paper shadows that wield power . . . At least women haven't taken over the City . . . yet!

ANNA   I do believe you're pulling my leg . . .

SIRI   Oh! . . . He means it.

Voices are heard, off.

LUDWIG *(voice off)* Now Martha . . . I'm going to leave you here . . . You will not enter until the word 'peacock' is spoken by a woman's voice . . . Remember 'peacock'.

ANNA *(moving towards rear right door)* Oh . . . It's Ludwig into his black arts again.

SIRI *(getting anxious, she stands)* I'd . . . better see to the children.

ANNA   There's nothing to fear . . . Don't you find hypnotism enthralling?

STRINDBERG *(rising)* There's a time and a place . . . *(he puts his arm around Siri, anxious for the children)*

Ludwig enters, a bottle of wine in one hand, and a folded white sheet over his other arm.

LUDWIG   Now . . . if you'll take your seats . . . a short demonstration . . . Come.
(They all take seats downstage except for Siri)
SIRI *(dashing out, rear right)* Excuse me, I'll just check the children are asleep . . .
LUDWIG *(as if he knows exactly what is going to happen next)* Perfect, perfect! Now wait.

We hear Siri running offstage and a door slamming. Siri shrieks. A peacock calls.

SIRI   Ah! There's a peacock on the banisters!

The moment the word 'peacock' is uttered, Martha enters, trance-like from rear right with a tray of coffee and schnapps and walks to the coffee table.

LUDWIG *(softly, to Martha)* Stop! . . . Now . . . listen carefully . . . The very moment Siri enters the door . . . not before . . . I want you to place the tray on the coffee table . . .

Martha has her back to the rear right entrance and therefore cannot see as Siri quietly appears and waits before crossing the threshold. The minute her foot crosses the threshold Martha places the tray down on the coffee table. Siri takes her seat downstage not under-standing why the other three are clapping. Martha remains trancelike.

LUDWIG *(raising his finger to his mouth for silence, speaks in quiet measured tones)* Countess . . . ready with the lamp?
(to Siri and Strindberg) We need complete darkness for this experiment . . . *(then, in a clear voice to Martha)* Turn around,

Martha . . . Now . . . You will walk to the chaise and lie down on it.

Slowly Martha does so, and Ludwig opens the white sheet, walking towards the chaise.

LUDWIG *(to Anna)* Lights! *(to Martha)* Now, Martha . . . You are reclining . . . You are comfortable . . .

As she does so the lights, rear, are turned down, plunging backstage into darkness. Simultaneously frontstage, where all the other four characters are situated is strongly lit to hide the backstage trickery. Anna also walks up and down frontstage, playing the balalaika to distract attention from backstage goings-on. Since Martha is dressed totally in black, including black gloves, and a veil which she can pull across her face the moment the lights go down, she can easily move rear of the chaise and place a body profile, unseen, onto the chaise itself and exit in the darkness. Ludwig moves towards the chaise and places the white sheet over the body profile, and then moves front of stage again.

LUDWIG Martha . . . You are weightless . . . Free of the earth's pull . . . There is no sun . . . no gravity . . . You can feel the heavens drawing you . . . up . . . up . . . *(he gestures with his arms)* . . . You are free as air, Martha.

The body profile with the sheet covering it, is lifted by Martha, who cannot be seen by the audience.

LUDWIG Martha . . . I want you to float . . . out of the room . . .

The sheet moves slowly right of the chaise and vanishes through the door, carried by Martha.

LUDWIG Lights!

Anna turns up the rear lamp and the downstage lights come up simultaneously.

SIRI   Amazing!

STRINDBERG Fantastic!

(Everybody starts to applaud)

ANNA   Ludwig . . . Do go after her . . . We don't want her floating all over the house *(to Siri)* . . . It frightens the dogs, you know . . .

SIRI   How's it done? Is it a trick?

STRINDBERG Hypnosis . . . Auto-suggestion . . . I've read of it.

ANNA   Martha is particularly receptive . . . Some only manage two or three seconds suspension. I've seen him suspend an eighteen stone cow-hand . . .

SIRI   And did the man know . . . afterwards?

ANNA   . . . Laughed . . . Didn't believe us . . . Until he realised he was on top of the wardrobe.

STRINDBERG And then what?

ANNA   He gave in his notice . . . Became a Marxist or something. His last words to me were . . . 'We have nothing to lose but our chains!'

STRINDBERG *(looking around)* That makes a lot of sense to me.

Lights out.

SCENE 3

(From here on Strindberg always locks up his script when not working on it.)

One month later. Late in the evening. Strindberg sits at the writing desk, thoughtful, writing feverishly in spurts. He stands, walks around and rushes back to the writing desk as a new idea hits him. We can hear Ludwig approaching, singing softly, an old gypsy song. He stands at the door full of bonhomie and slaps his belly. Strindberg is mildly irritated but since it is very late, decides to welcome the interruption.

STRINDBERG By all means! . . .

Ludwig enters, one half- empty wine bottle in his pocket and another full one in his hand. He also has a wine glass in the other pocket, ready to produce it at the right moment.

LUDWIG   One in the morning . . . Still at it . . .

STRINDBERG You too, I see. Living in this castle for a month . . . the imagination struggles . . . I find my wildest fictions dull, prosaic.

LUDWIG   How d'ye mean?

STRINDBERG Oh . . . peacocks flying past you on the stairs . . . Rabbits eating the carpet. Bodies floating through space. Drunken dogs!

LUDWIG   All part of the service! Hasn't stopped you writing has it? *(indicates desk full of paper)*

STRINDBERG A little idea of mine . . . it's beginning to take me.

LUDWIG   Are all writers crazy?

STRINDBERG It's life that's crazy . . . Sometimes after reading the newspapers I can barely find my way to the kitchen . . . It's impossible to write plays in this day and age . . . We're all rushing towards some mighty undiscovered waterfall that drops into nothingness . . . Fill me up . . .

LUDWIG   Take the bottle . . . I'll start on this one.

STRINDBERG *(drinks a long draught from the bottle)* Tell me . . . Do you read?

LUDWIG   Can do . . . But don't . . . Dulls the senses . . . I'm a man of action . . . When I get round to it.

STRINDBERG You're right . . . The world's grown effete with intellectualising . . . Like the Roman empire before the Huns came thundering across the plains . . . *(he drinks again)* Ah! All Europe is ponsified . . . I want to tear down the whole rotten structure to the last stone.

LUDWIG   What . . . with a pen and scraps o' paper!

STRINDBERG It's inescapable . . . We'll wake up one morning and civilised Europe will be gone. *(he grows ominously pensive)* . . .

Vanished in a pall of smoke. *(pause)* . . . I can see it in the way a complete stranger simply . . . looks out of a window or a woman brushes her hair in the mirror . . .

LUDWIG   No disrespect, Mister Strindberg . . . but if you think that . . . you're barmy . . .

STRINDBERG Very soon I shall be able to turn base metals into gold . . .

LUDWIG *(engrossed. In harsh whispers)* How's it done? Swear to God, I won't breathe a word . . . Just me and you against the world.

STRINDBERG Three characters in a room . . . three ordinary people . . . a table, chairs and no sunrise . . . They struggle, dream and die . . . All existence in a few terse lines . . . and people pay to see the blood . . . in gold.

LUDWIG *(drinking)* No . . . no! . . . I mean the real thing . . . Lead into gold, no messing . . . Slap, bang wallop . . . the goods!

STRINDBERG What do you want out of life, Ludwig?

LUDWIG   Na . . . nothing really . . . I'm a contented man.

STRINDBERG Rubbish . . . Why do you drink? . . . What are you looking for . . . running away from? . . . What do you hate?

LUDWIG   I don't 'hate' . . . hate, indeed!

STRINDBERG *(almost as if he is hypnotising Ludwig, and drawing out his responses)* What a dull existence! No enemies? You might as well be dead, a priest or something! . . . Come on! Who do you hate?

LUDWIG *(instantly)* The aristocracy!

STRINDBERG You're in good company . . . Go on.

LUDWIG   Centuries of incest, and they call it pedigree . . . Result? A race of dickless anaemics with atrophy of the brain . . .

STRINDBERG . . . That's more like it!

LUDWIG   Preoccupied with horses, dogs and bloodstock. Why? Because racially, they're dodos . . . But still you can't beat the bastards . . . I'd love to fuck a blueblood, wouldn't you?

STRINDBERG Nothing to it . . . my wife is a Baroness.

LUDWIG   Ah! . . . to lay a Countess! . . . strip off the privileged knickers and get down to basics . . . A few good plebeian thrusts . . . and then the blissful groans of submission . . .

STRINDBERG Not . . . bad!

LUDWIG   Helpless, lost! The princess trampled by her sweaty cow-hand . . . Then, stand up, button your flies and tell her to sling her hook . . .

STRINDBERG Not so fast . . . She's got you, now . . .

LUDWIG   Naa! . . . The minute you come inside her . . . she's the servant . . .

STRINDBERG You really believe that?

LUDWIG   Too right! . . . This *(pointing to his crutch)* . . . determines the fate of women . . . It's the one thing they can't get from their own sex.

STRINDBERG But now, revenge! Ever seen a she-cat turn on her mate? Wives leave tigers in the shade for savagery.

LUDWIG   What's the problem?

STRINDBERG Woman is the enemy of magic. Without magic there is no art, no science. If women had their way we'd still be living in the stone age.

LUDWIG   Subjugate woman in the name of progress . . . I like it!

STRINDBERG There never was a female Mozart, nor a Michaelangelo. Its not an accident . . .

LUDWIG   By God you're right! They can't make it to the top unless they're born to it. Do I know that! One good fuck and she'd be done for. *(he nods towards the Countess' door)* It's magic!

STRINDBERG Knock and enter. Don't mind me.

LUDWIG   But the dogs. They'd eat me alive!

STRINDBERG Feint heart, never one fair Countess.

LUDWIG   The balcony windows! If I can reach them first . . . there are steps down to the garden . . .

STRINDBERG Midnight walkies. Dogs love 'em.

LUDWIG   What if she says 'no' . . .

STRINDBERG The most unlikely citadels fall easily. Perhaps the Countess wants her bailiff more than he wants her . . .

LUDWIG   There's something you don't know about her . . .

STRINDBERG My God! She's not one of . . . *them* . . . ?

LUDWIG   *Them?*

STRINDBERG *(whispers)* 'Lesbians!' *(conspiratorially)*. Siri once confessed her passion for her husband's cousin . . . even though the Baron himself was having an affair with her . . .

LUDWIG   So it's true what they say about Sweden! *(holds his head)* What ever happened to morality! . . .

STRINDBERG . . . A year after our marriage I surprised her with our maid . . . In Germany we barely escaped punishment when she accosted schoolgirls . . . She even . . . made advances to the town Mayor's daughter in the middle of a Schubert song cycle . . .

LUDWIG   You poor man . . . How you've suffered . . .

STRINDBERG Yes . . . She probably is attracted to the Countess . . . and *(conspiratorially)* Watch out for your sister, Martha . . . Nothing that wears a skirt is safe . . .

LUDWIG   I'm just a simple farm hand. But I know where my duty lies . . . We must stand up for normality whatever the cost . . . Fancy Martha, do yer?

STRINDBERG You seem to exercise remarkable power over her.

LUDWIG   Oh . . . she'd do anything for me, Mr Strindberg . . . anything you could wish . . .

STRINDBERG No! . . . Female distractions in the middle of my new play! I'd have to talk to her. Tell her how pretty she is . . . I don't have the time . . .

LUDWIG   She's a girl of few words . . .

STRINDBERG *(his mind elsewhere)* I'm going for a walk . . . *(locks up the writing desk)* Back in an hour . . . I don't yet know the ending . . . *(he moves towards the door)* Ludwig . . . *(nods towards Countess' door)* Good luck . . .

LUDWIG   Its an honour to have such deep discussions with a man of your intellectual stature, Sir.
(he stands, shakes Strindberg's reluctant hand)

Strindberg exits.Ludwig takes a long swig from the bottle, places it down, adjusts his belt, waistcoat and jacket, smoothes his hair, breathes in, puffing out his chest, strides towards the Countess' door, unbolts it and charges in. Wagner's 'Ride of the Valkyries' is heard. Frantic sounds of dogs barking.

Lights down.

SCENE 4

One week later. Early morning. A few balls of paper and empty wine bottles are strewn around. Siri enters rear right in dressing-gown. She pulls back the grey drapes right and takes in the beauty of the morning as she stretches. Enter Martha

MARTHA   And how is the Baroness this morning?

SIRI   Wonderful, Martha, wonderful!

MARTHA   All this paper . . . reams of it . . . *(starts collecting up Strindberg's rejected bits)* I'll take it down to the bin.

SIRI *(immediately anxious)* No . . . No . . . Never throw anything out. August says he's struck a rich seam . . . Up all night.

MARTHA   Aye . . . drinking . . . with my brother *(she picks up the empty bottles and takes them to the door and places them down)* Ludwig's asleep in the stables . . . Falstaff draped across him.

SIRI   Writing keeps August sober . . . he was still at it when I looked in at six . . .

MARTHA   Probably just drunken ramblings.

SIRI *(points finger firmly but nicely)* You and I could write after a few glasses and be ashamed of it next morning . . . but not my husband . . .

MARTHA *(head down)* I'm sorry, Ma'am, I've spoken out of turn.

SIRI *(collecting up remaining scraps)* I'll lock these up for safe-keeping . . .

MARTHA   Aren't you going to read it?

SIRI   It's too painful. Where we see love, he sees a kind of war between men and women – a war that never ends . . .
(she shuffles the papers, sits, and Martha squats at her feet)

MARTHA   How can love be war?

SIRI   It doesn't start as war, Martha. Its wonderful – a kind of joyous madness . . . which you both surrender to.

MARTHA   But it is quite violent . . . isn't it? You know . . . when they 'do it' to you.

SIRI *(musing)* In pagan times, each spring, the tribe would sacrifice a young virgin . . . cut her open . . . to ensure fertility.

MARTHA   Eergh! Then I'd have had a lad away at Christmas time – to be on the safe side!

SIRI *(smiles)* Enjoy it while you may, Martha! For marriage sometimes . . . Oh, never mind . . .

MARTHA   Ma'am . . . why did they sacrifice a girl and not a boy?

SIRI *(wiping a tear away)* Because the elders of the tribe were men.

MARTHA *(pouting)* I don' understand none o' this!

SIRI *(a little upset)* Neither do I, Martha . . . neither do I . . .

Strindberg's head appears around the door, manic, staring.

MARTHA *(raising her face to Siri)* Oh Ma'am . . . Are you alright? . . . I'd do anything to help . . . anything . . . just say!

SIRI *(cupping Martha's face in her hands)* I know . . . I know. *(she kisses Martha on both cheeks)*

Strindberg's horrified face disappears, comically. His worst fears now 'confirmed'.

SIRI *(brightly)* And what are the children up to today?

MARTHA   This morning . . . milking cows with Larsen . . . feeding chickens . . . The yard at noon to see the piglets suckling. Then the men are going to brand the calves . . .

SIRI   Oh no . . . I really think . . .

MARTHA   It hurts no more than a kiss, and afterwards we give them names . . .

SIRI   Well if you're sure . . . *(lies back)* . . . It's so good for children to see farm life.

MARTHA   Karin is such a little Mistress, explaining all to Greta and Hans . . . as if she were a farmer's wife . . .

SIRI   Poor Karin. The eldest always assumes the role of parent. She's so responsible. *(stands)* Go out into the yard . . . see that they are happy

MARTHA   Yes, ma'am.

Martha exits and Siri takes a seat at the window, looking out. The sound of children's laughter is heard. Enter Anna from left.

ANNA *(dishevelled, yawning)* Oh . . . I need coffee . . . What time is it? What day? Is this Denmark?

SIRI *(turns smiling)* Had a bad night?

ANNA   The dogs were dreaming of a hunt. Falstaff was howling with a hangover. The men were carousing till late and then Ludwig . . . strange . . . strange . . . Dammit look at that . . . the hem of my dress is trailing.

SIRI   Sit down . . . There's needle and thread on the writing desk . . . Here we are.

(The Countess sits and Siri squats at her feet, inserting her left hand inside the dress to sew with the right. As she does so Strindberg again appears, unseen)

ANNA   A little higher, sweetheart, yes, yes . . . That's lovely . . . beautiful. *(she lets out a tired sigh as she leans back. Strindberg construes this as passion, clutches his head and disappears. Anna thinks she catches sight of him)* Was that your husband?

SIRI   I didn't see anything.

ANNA   Are we keeping him from his desk?

SIRI   He uses the bedroom table most mornings.

ANNA   Ludwig and he seem to have struck up quite a friendship.

SIRI   Male company is good for August. He gets insanely jealous of my female friends.

ANNA   Let him, my dear. Men think they're indispensable. Ludwig's the same *(defensively)* about his job, I mean.

SIRI   I have this one particular friend, Marie. He can't abide her. He's published such hideous calumnies against her, she was obliged to sue to protect her reputation . . . and mine, by implication.

ANNA   Implicating you . . . Oh really . . . That! Well, if she's a nice girl, my dear, give it a whirl. Some find it quite refreshing.

SIRI   You misunderstand me . . .

ANNA   Have you never taken a lover?

SIRI   Well, not a woman . . .

ANNA   I have two friends of that persuasion positively swear by it. Suffragettes, you know. English of course . . . The men are 'good chums', too.

SIRI   Its not my inclination. Marie helps . . . helps keep us together as a family. The children just adore her. And this brings on such violent feelings in him . . .

ANNA   You must stop defining yourself in terms of your husband . . . I trust he never lays a hand on you?
(Siri takes the needle and thread back to the desk)
Does he?

Martha enters at this point.

MARTHA *(brightly)* I've just taught the children to say 'boo!' to a goose. Good morning, Ma'am. Shall I get the hairbrush?

ANNA   Do . . . and let the dogs out through the French window. It stinks in there . . . Bring a mirror!
(As Martha departs, to Siri) Sit down on the floor here. I've been dying to plait your hair.

SIRI *(does so)* I remember doing the same to my cousin when I was a child. When times are trying, change your hairstyle!

MARTHA *(returning)* I passed your husband on the way up . . .
Stared at me as if I were a ghost.

ANNA   You are probably a character in his latest play who
just died in the last scene.

SIRI *(laughs)*   He gets like that.

MARTHA   I felt like a criminal.

SIRI   Did he say nothing at all?

MARTHA   'Et tu Brute!'

(They all snigger)

ANNA   He's Caesar. You're a conspirator. Its obvious.

(They laugh)

SIRI   Oh. Poor August . . . He should be pleased. He's just
had some excellent news from his publishers . . .

ANNA   Really . . . then . . . *(whispers)* . . . we should plan a
little surprise celebration . . .

*Anna gathers them round, conspiratorially. They whisper their
plans, sniggering. Strindberg appears at the door unseen, again.
Martha stoops low over Anna's shoulder with her arms round Anna
and Siri. Siri's arms are folded on Anna's lap. The whispers get
quieter and Strindberg strains to hear.*

ANNA   Oh Yes!

SIRI   Mmmmmh!

MARTHA   That's woooonderful!

*Strindberg believes he has witnessed an 'example' of 'three way
lesbianism'. Strindberg holds his face. He strides away.*

STRINDBERG Aargh!

The three women break apart and look towards the door, puzzled.

Lights down quickly.

SCENE 5

A fortnight later. Morning. Strindberg at the writing desk. He writes feverishly, making corrections, searching back through the script, reshuffling the page order. Enter Siri.

SIRI   Still writing then?

STRINDBERG You make it sound like something young boys do to themselves in bed.

SIRI *(trying not to antagonise)* Comedy? Tragedy?

STRINDBERG *(still pre-occupied)* . . . the greatest piece of modern drama ever to flow from a pen . . .

(Siri genuinely tickled by the remark, laughs)

STRINDBERG *(deadly serious)* Why are you laughing?

SIRI   Well *(defensively)* Where's your modesty? . . . I thought it was a joke.

STRINDBERG I inform you of my greatest achievement to date and general hilarity breaks out . . . *(dismissing her)* Find something to occupy your mind!

SIRI   Don't try to make me feel small.

STRINDBERG You are small, ma petite . . .

SIRI *(after a pause, treading carefully)* Am I in it ?

STRINDBERG In the beginning God created heaven and earth and Eve said *(mocking)* 'Am I in it'. No, little one, this is a play for large people . . . people with normal sexual desires. *(he sharpens a quill feverishly)*

SIRI *(snapping)* I just need to know whether you plan to rip my heart out again in public.

STRINDBERG Not *your* heart . . . *the* female heart . . . if indeed I manage to locate one . . .

SIRI   I read a little of it . . .

STRINDBERG A little . . . well, you would, wouldn't you?

SIRI   This heroine . . . Miss Julie . . . I hope you're not planning to libel the Countess on stage . . . sleeping with her servant . . . really! Do you want another court case . . . damages?

She'd clean us out . . . Needs the money. The estate is virtually
bankrupt . . .

STRINDBERG So. You've got it all worked out. Miss Julie is the
Countess . . . and Jean . . .

SIRI   . . . is Ludwig. It's pretty obvious . . . To suggest
on stage they're having an affair! It's courting disaster. If she
doesn't sue, he will. I strongly suspect they're actually brother
and sister . . . Haven't you noticed the likeness round the eyes.

STRINDBERG So, it's incest. What do I care!

SIRI   That's a horrendous suggestion to make on a public
stage.

STRINDBERG What then? A private stage? For God's sake Siri . . .
I'm not a gutter journalist grubbing around for scandals.

SIRI   No. You devise your own, and drag me with you
through the slime. Miss Julie . . . the tragic tale of a noblewoman
led to self-destruction by a member of the servant class with
hang-ups about status . . . sounds like you and me!

STRINDBERG Miss Julie's none of us. All of us. It's called
'universality'. *(he makes a squeaking noise with his mouth)*

SIRI   You insufferable, arrogant –

STRINDBERG *(loudly)* People agonise about the divorce rate.
What baffles me is the marriage rate. A woman needs that special
person on whom to vent her own inadequacies. The husband . . .
becomes the focus of all the fears and failings in the wife, till he,
poor swine, loses the will to live. Adultery's more honest.

SIRI   See how that stands up in court . . .

STRINDBERG The only courts I care about are drama and
posterity.

SIRI   But it's a lie!

STRINDBERG Love's a lie. Marriage is a damned lie . . .

SIRI   You can't go round telling lies. It's simple human
decency.

STRINDBERG Decency! I do believe you're besotted with the
Countess!

SIRI   What?

STRINDBERG Even Martha! . . . a sixteen year old . . . or is it fifteen?

SIRI   Don't palm your fantasies about her, off on me. Oh. I've seen you looking at her. You can barely keep your hands off her!

STRINDBERG There's nothing abnormal about that . . . under the circumstances . . . What do you expect of a normal healthy male? Masturbation? . . . It's true. It does affect your eyes . . . I see . . . I think I see . . . monstrous things . . . the three of you!

SIRI   What are you talking about?

STRINDBERG *(softening)* I'm isolated . . . exiled. *(he puts his hands on her shoulders)*

SIRI   You hate me.

STRINDBERG What does that matter? Men and women have hated each other for centuries. They still do it.

SIRI   If only we could get to know each other as people.

STRINDBERG As *people*! As dogs perhaps, but never people!

SIRI   This is sick . . .

STRINDBERG In sickness and in health . . . for better for worse.

SIRI   Don't quote that vow at me. You don't believe in it. God, anything! What is it you call marriage? . . . Legalised prostitution? Well, it's true!

STRINDBERG What am I to do?

SIRI   Try Martha.

STRINDBERG And then I suppose you'd cite her in divorce proceedings.

SIRI   If I cared, I would . . . *(Strindberg looks crestfallen)* Ah, at last . . . message received! You dominate every aspect of my life. Every day I have to fight for my existence. If I can't build a life for myself, I'm done for. I may as well be dead . . . and I'm not getting any younger.

STRINDBERG Let me get this right . . . You're telling me to find another partner?

SIRI   Stop leaning on me!

Siri exits.

STRINDBERG *(stands confused, slightly deflated. He sighs and slumps onto the chaise longue. After a pause, he starts talking to himself)* Martha . . . or total blindness? Martha it is! Would she find me too old? *(feels face, smoothes hair)* No, of course not. *(snaps fingers)* Hypnosis! She wouldn't even know. *(he picks up a pillow pretending it's Martha and starts to 'hypnotise' it)* You will have three orgasms in quick succession . . . My God that'd be a novel experience! . . . But was it all a trick? Does it matter? Even if she was faking three orgasms ?

He kisses the pillow, lays it down on the chaise and starts to push his loins into it, chewing his tongue, as if in a fit. Enter Anna, quietly, with fresh flowers in a vase. She glances at Strindberg's antics and isn't the slightest bit put out. Strindberg is startled and embarrassed and moves from the sexual position imperceptibly to a reclining pose. He picks his teeth, nervously.

ANNA   In the throes of creativity are we? I thought fresh flowers might inspire. *(she begins a stream of chatter at quite a fast pace, stunning Strindberg into horrified silence)* Please do continue . . . Don't mind me . . . the dogs do it all the time you know . . . armchairs, kneeling servants, each other sometimes . . . The vicar's knees are highly favoured. But he doesn't object. So polite. *(she fusses over the flower arrangement and pulls curtains, etc.)* There. Aren't they pretty? Your wife, Mister Strindberg, is such a fine woman. I'd say you need to talk to her about . . . your problem. Men do neglect their wives, I find . . . but you can always rely on a dog. *(Strindberg's mouth drops open)* Dogs are so loyal . . . Have you ever stroked a Great Dane? The warm muscles of his chest, rippling under the smooth coat . . . *(Strindberg stares into space)* I hope they don't interfere with your work. I've given them a good talking to. I said: 'Mister Strindberg is a brilliant man . . . and he's writing something absolutely spellbinding.' And, do you know? I think they understood. Oh, and I hope you don't mind, I borrowed your volume of Nietszche, that awfully strange German fellow . . .

Can't say it's my cup of tea exactly. What I always say is – we Nordic folk are a cut above . . . The Vikings were absolutely right to rape and pillage . . . improved the stock . . . ask any dog-breeder. No. It's this Superman nonsense I object to. What Herr Nietschze needs is a damned good night in bed with a Danish peasant girl. That'd soon stop his headaches. Yes, a good fuck with a serving wench. Oh, I haven't fed the dogs. Do excuse me. *(moves to the door)* If you meet Herr Nietschze, do tell him what I've said. *(smiles)* Superman indeed! I only hope the Germans don't take it literally. Happy writing . . . Now, Hamlet, Brutus, Othello . . . Where are they?

She breezes off.

Light on Strindberg's horror-stricken face.

Lights down.

ACT TWO
SCENE 1

Siri is surreptitiously reading the draft of 'Miss Julie.' She glances nervously over her shoulder once or twice. Her face betrays both admiration and deep concern. Enter Ludwig with a bottle and glasses.

LUDWIG   Oh . . . er . . . I'm sorry Ma'am . . . Thought it was your husband.

SIRI *(after initial nervousness about being caught reading the play she has the measure of Ludwig)* He's gone into town . . . to buy some paper.

LUDWIG   Aye . . . Reckon he must get through quite a lot . . . being a writer and that . . . I thought . . . he might like a drink . . . Best be off . . .

SIRI   I'll have a drink with you. *(she's having a game)*

LUDWIG   I beg your pardon Ma'am . . . but, well . . . it's not 'right' is it . . . I mean . . .

SIRI   Nonsense . . . here's a glass. Fill me up!

LUDWIG   It's dirty . . . I'll . . .

SIRI   Sometimes dirt excites me . . .

LUDWIG   You'd best not start drinking wi' me. Drinkin' man, I am. I'm known for it!

SIRI *(takes the bottle, fills her glass, drains it, hands the bottle back and offers her glass)* Now. Fill me up again.

LUDWIG *(does so and fills one for himself)* Well . . . if you say so . . . Vintage stuff this . . . No rubbish here . . . The dogs love it.

SIRI   Why did you come up here?

LUDWIG   Like I said, I . . .

SIRI   You knew perfectly well August's in town. You drove him there yourself. *(she knocks back the second glass)*

LUDWIG   Hadn't you better . . . slow down?

SIRI   Why?

LUDWIG   Well . . . it looks bad . . . a lady, and that . . . drinking with a servant . . . What if your husband came back, sudden.

SIRI *(holds out glass and Ludwig hesitates)* Serve me! You are a servant, aren't you?

LUDWIG *(pours, begins to think he might 'have a chance' with her)* I warn you. This is potent stuff. Bouquet like a mule's hind leg!

SIRI   I could drink you under the table any day of the week. *(she puts one of Strindberg's cigars in her mouth)*

LUDWIG   How's about Monday?

SIRI   How's about . . . now. Martha's taken the children out and your mistress is out with the dogs for the afternoon. She is your mistress isn't she? Light me!

LUDWIG *(lighting her cigar)* I'd best be going.

SIRI   You haven't answered my question . . . Why did you come into this room?

LUDWIG   Well, to be honest, I thought you'd been looking unhappy recently . . . I thought, as you'd been left all on your own again, you might fancy . . . well, some company.

SIRI   You're a very sensitive man, aren't you Ludwig?

LUDWIG   Well I do 'ave an understanding of women, ma'am. So I'm told . . . I can tell when they've something on their minds . . . I'm a very good judge of character.

SIRI   Sit down . . . Now tell me, Ludwig . . . What do you make of me?

LUDWIG   You're . . . very beautiful . . . and a lady . . . not afraid to break the rules, mind. I think you mostly get what . . . and who you want. I, I . . . I must say this . . . I don't understand how he can treat you the way he does, and you so desirable . . . Scribbling away all day on bits of paper when he's got a real, beautiful creature right under his nose. Is that why you did it? Turned to drink . . . and acting, like?
(Siri laughs)
I mean . . . acting. Surely a woman of your status could have found something . . . well . . . respectable.

SIRI   So. Its alright for you to drink and play the parts . . . but not me?

LUDWIG   What! I've no interest in plays. That's for city folks and lunatics. All the men are nancy boys and the women wear trousers . . . And the audiences aren't much better . . . Present company excluded!

SIRI   You are very perceptive, aren't you?

LUDWIG   It's not book-learning mind you. Its the university of 'Life'.

SIRI   Ah 'Life'. That's the big one, isn't it, Ludwig?

LUDWIG   You know what it is makes people tick?

SIRI   I'm just an actress and my husband's a playwright.

LUDWIG   Exactly. But I'm a man of the world. *(confidentially)* It's . . . money! With money you can climb the social scale . . . and sex is dirt cheap. Not that I've ever sunk to that mind you. Never had too.

SIRI   No. You're a fascinating man. It's not just physical. This hypnotism and levitation . . . You're really deeply into it, aren't you?

LUDWIG   I'll let you into a secret . . . That time I hypnotised Martha . . . remember . . . It were all a trick . . . an illusion . . . Quickness of hand deceiving eye!

SIRI   You mean theatre stuff . . . for city folk and lunatics? *(mimics his accent)*

LUDWIG *(smiling uneasily)* Here . . . You're taking the rise out of me, aren't yer?

SIRI *(filling glasses)* We're all in the same business, Ludwig . . . the actress, the Countess, the playwright, the serving wench and the plain blunt bailiff . . . All of us acting out the roles we hope will bring us one step closer to our dreams. My husband does it so much better.

LUDWIG   You're playing games wi' me!
(he rises. Siri pushes him back into his seat)

SIRI *(raises her glass)* Skol!

LUDWIG   'Skol!' That's lager talk! This is *Chateau Val Fleury* . . . a votre santé!

SIRI *(bows, clicks heels,clinks glasses)* Now. Let's take your premise. That it's money makes people tick . . . It isn't true for my husband . . . and it certainly isn't true for me. But let us say that for a certain person . . . it holds true. Let us suppose this person lacks . . . *(a)* money and *(b)* social position, and wants desperately to obtain both.

LUDWIG   Here! Wait a minute!

SIRI   What strategy would he employ? What resources could he muster? Why sex of course! He might imagine he could seduce a Countess or a Baroness . . .

LUDWIG   I'll have you know I came here in good faith, out of the kindness of my own heart . . .

SIRI   And we haven't mentioned blackmail yet, have we? Sex and blackmail can often be found in the same bed. And if illegal methods fail him, our scoundrel would think nothing of recourse to law itself!

LUDWIG   I don't have to listen to this . . . *(rises to leave)*

SIRI   You came here for this? *(holds up the script)* Didn't you? . . . to obtain evidence for a possible court case!

LUDWIG   I'm not interested in your husband's bloody fantasies . . .

SIRI   My husband is a deeply troubled man. I love him. Do you understand? This play is frightening and I hate the vision which inspires it. It is about you, if you must know. It's about all of us . . . If you do anything to hurt him, you'll have me to contend with, and your mistress too . . .

LUDWIG   He won't thank you for defending him. Not from what I know of him. By my book his heroine is about to make a shabby exit. There's no part in it for you . . . But how the plot will end . . . That I'm working on. I never give away the ending . . . spoils the story.

He strides to the door and turns then he leaves. Siri pours a drink and slams the glass down angrily.

Lights down.

SCENE 2

Evening. Some nights later. A dark stage with Strindberg in a pool of eery light. He wears a white apron and stares manically at some test tubes and flasks he has on top of the writing desk. He adds liquids from one to the other and shakes them. They foam.

Siri enters. She is very slightly drunk.

SIRI   What's that? Your laundry?

STRINDBERG Experimenting with liquids, like you, it seems.

SIRI   Is Gus having lots of fun with his chemistry set? Huh! Alchemy . . . I prefer alcohol . . . Don't burn your little panties with that nasty acid.

STRINDBERG *(tries to restore his dignity)* An amalgam of iron and copper. A chemical wedding. A union of natures . . . Mars . . . Venus . . . their fusion is a love affair . . .

SIRI   And I thought I was pissed!

STRINDBERG Not physical, you understand . . . celestial natures. A union of opposites! Science! . . . will be the death of God!

SIRI   Poor old God! He's got no chance against you, has he? He must be quaking in his boots . . . You'll never make gold! Sell 'Miss Julie' . . . now there's gelt for you!

STRINDBERG Good plays never get done. Except by back street abortionists with knitting needles. *(holds his belly)* 'I'm three months gone with this play.' 'Alright . . . inside! There we are! All better!' Great writers are despised. Jews run the theatre.

SIRI *(mocking)* Lesbians everywhere! Jews everywhere!

STRINDBERG *(serious)* You've noticed?

SIRI   You've got a persecution complex.

STRINDBERG Its not complex. I am persecuted. Every Stockholm publisher turned down 'The Father'. The world is run by socialists who detest the strong and the intelligent. The feeble and feminists . . .

SIRI   So. You've given up socialism too . . .

STRINDBERG Socialism – it's caused by breastfeeding. Before I had my teeth . . . Can you imagine . . . turned down 'The Father'! If I'd called it 'The Mother' I'd have been drowned in adulation and showered with money. *(he rises and perambulates)* First I want to wash my spirit clean. Then a cool draught of cyanide . . . That's after I've got rid of you, my little gorgon-princess!

SIRI   I am the mother of your children!

STRINDBERG . . . in writing please! *(holds up a pen)*

SIRI   Sometimes I think you need to fail . . . as husband, father and as writer . . . to prove the world's against you.

STRINDBERG Oh I'll succeed despite the lot of you . . . but not if it means crawling to wet-behind-the ears directors, promoting the latest line in 'radical fashions', 'worthy causes' and *(spits it out)* 'social problems'! They get a living out of human refuse. Why don't they piss off out of the theatre and join the rest of the pious rabble in parliament? Pass a bill and lo! Woman becomes man's equal.

SIRI   You're just jealous of Mister Ibsen's success! Women rather like him.

STRINDBERG A Christian beggar, rattling his cup for charity! I blame the publishers!

The next section consists of interwoven excerpts of a dialogue of total non-communication. Each is, in effect, talking to themselves and the audience, but not to each other. Strindberg stands arms outstretched à la crucifixion.

SIRI   The nails driven into the hands with hammer blows . . . bang, bang, bang . . . There! Comfortable?

STRINDBERG No! They don't want plays that disturb the complacent reformist conscience. Just dare suggest such a thing as an insoluble problem and you're finished . . . 'Arthritis . . . the socialist solution.' Bravo! Encore!

SIRI   . . . and now the feet! Would you mind crossing them please . . . It saves on nails . . . There . . . That's better *(pulls an imaginary nail from her teeth and hammers it into the air)* Enjoy the pain!

STRINDBERG I blame the theatre directors! Next time . . . the next time one of those shits sends me a rejection slip, do you know what I am going to do? I'm going to reject it! Yes! 'Dear Publisher . . . Your rejection slip I found unconvincing . . . The opening was weak, apologetic . . . It sagged badly in the middle and the ending was sheer crap . . . But do keep trying. I am sure you have a good rejection slip in you but this is not yet it. Yours etc. . . . Strindberg . . .'

SIRI   'Likewise also the chief priests mocking him with scribes and elders said . . . 'He saved others. Himself he cannot save'

STRINDBERG Women who can succeed, do. Those who can't . . . become feminists.

SIRI   Trample me! Revile my name for I am the light of the world . . . Er . . . Pass the crown of thorns . . . Thank you.

STRINDBERG *(holding his head as if in pain)* Oh Christ! Is it me? Or has the world gone mad? Nietzsche's right. God's dead. Did you know I am pregnant by Nietszche? I have conceived by correspondence.

SIRI *(screams)* I can't take any more of this!

STRINDBERG *(mood changes to one of calm)* Everything alright, dearest? Can I get you something? . . . some water to drown in? I must tell you about my latest play . . . It's about a servant who destroys a noblewoman. Know how he does it? Guess. Guess! *(he produces a razor from his inside pocket)* He gives her a razor to shave with. *(laughs)* Nice touch that. A razor . . . Here . . . take it. *(offers her the razor. Siri rises and backs off)* Strange world isn't it? A man gets pregnant and a woman cuts herself shaving.

Siri leaves.

STRINDBERG Inverted . . . like the image in a camera. *(shouts after her)* You're trying to kill me. You're trying to drive me mad!

He walks front of stage, raises the razor to his throat, lifting his head to get a good stroke in. He appears very distressed. Enter Ludwig with a bottle and glasses to destroy tension.

LUDWIG   Five o'clock shadow? I'm the same. Twice a day man, me . . . Fancy a drink?

STRINDBERG *(coming out of his brainstorm. Still spaced out)* Well . . . alright then. One for the road. *(puts razor away)*

LUDWIG   She, er . . . alright . . . your wife? Strange, women . . . yes . . . creatures of passion . . .Time of the month, no doubt. Still . . . where would we be without 'em? . . . the fond embrace, the idle chatter . . .

STRINDBERG My wife, Ludwig is . . . mentally . . . She has brainstorms . . . She thinks I'm trying to kill her . . .

LUDWIG *(laughs)* Complaints, complaints. That's all you get from 'em. Never satisfied. Still . . . Knock this back *(pours the drinks)* No. You're not the murderin' type, you . . . How's the . . . er . . . *(nods towards the desk)* . . . play . . . going alright, is it?

STRINDBERG *(locks the desk)* It's turning out different to the way I'd planned . . .

LUDWIG   What? You plan it all out first? That's brilliant, that!

STRINDBERG But then it develops a life of its own . . . The characters begin to take over. They tell me what to write. They talk to me . . .

LUDWIG Really? *(knocks it back and pours another)* Good year, this. Bags of alcohol, 1852. Enough to float a battleship . . . Oh women are unfathomable. No logic in 'em. Take my Martha. She was only saying to me today, she said: 'That Mister Strindberg, for a middle-aged man, he's really rather dishy.' You know how they get these crushes. Amusing really . . . I suppose you get a lot of that.

STRINDBERG *(coming out of his 'spaced out' mood)* I don't have the time to indulge it. The play comes first.

LUDWIG   Well of course, but this one's . . . nearly finished, would you say? Oh, I'd love to see a real manuscript . . . in the raw . . . in the process of creation, so to speak . . . like watchin' someone having it away.

STRINDBERG I never divulge my current projects. It's a personal thing.

LUDWIG   Is it a . . . topical subject, or personal?

STRINDBERG It's both.

LUDWIG   Very wise. Fusing the general with the particular, to use agricultural parlance.

STRINDBERG I'm feeling rather tired tonight . . . not good company, I'm afraid.

LUDWIG   Oh never say that Mister Strindberg. I mean a man of your intellect is bound to come up with something profound even when he's knackered . . . *(Strindberg smiles)* I'll bet you find us country folk a bit o' light amusement eh? No. We take life as it comes here . . . rhythm o' nature, all that guff . . .

STRINDBERG *(butting in quickly)* Could you hypnotise your sister for me?

LUDWIG *(fast response)* Done! She's like a fart in a trance at the best o' times.

STRINDBERG Young, pretty, vital!

LUDWIG   Absolutely vital, sir. And yet behind the childlike innocence . . . mysterious depths . . .

STRINDBERG *(impatiently)* Yes, yes, yes, yes. When?

LUDWIG   Tonight. Where you sleepin'? On the chaise? *(Strindberg nods)* Right, an early breakfast then. Say, five? . . . Then . . . I'll be leavin' you now, sir. *(he glances at the writing desk)* Going out tonight, sir, are we?

STRINDBERG A long stroll, I think . . . A tavern and some company.

LUDWIG   Not too far, I hope. Save your energy, sir . . . if you get my meaning.

Lights down.

SCENE 3

Later that night. Martha is tidying up. She polishes the writingdesk which is locked. Enter Ludwig. He approaches the desk and pulls her roughly to one side.

MARTHA   Hey, watch it!

LUDWIG *(grasping her wrist, roughly)* I'm sorry, Master Ludwig!

MARTHA *(breaking free)* Bully!

LUDWIG *(rattling the desk-top)* It's locked. *(snaps his fingers)* The key! The key!

MARTHA *(carries on polishing)* I ain't got no key . . . He took it with him.

LUDWIG *(pulling jack-knife from pocket and trying to prise the lock)* Get out the way! I must know the ending!

MARTHA   It ain't right, stealing his scenarios . . .

LUDWIG   Call yourself a gypsy! You're a disgrace to the profession!

MARTHA   That's the Countess' writing desk!

LUDWIG *(mimicking and mocking her propriety)* Countess' writing desk . . . If your mother could hear you now! She'd puke all over her crystal ball! . . .

MARTHA   Burgling a play! It's not been done before. You've no right! . . .

LUDWIG   I've every right. I'm bloody in it. That's why! You too, I reckon . . .

MARTHA *(indignant)* Sod me! You can't call your life your own!

LUDWIG   Once the secret's out . . . reputation's ruined!

MARTHA   What you on about . . . secret? . . .

LUDWIG *(stops momentarily)* You're too young to know. Shadows from the past! Human failings! . . .

MARTHA   I'm as good a human failing as you are!

LUDWIG *(resumes lock-picking)* Sins of the flesh . . .

MARTHA   You . . . and the Countess . . . That's the secret, isn't it?

LUDWIG *(grabs her by the arm)* Never . . . say that again! The secret, my little nymph, you'd never guess in a million years . . .

MARTHA   Ow! Leave go . . . You're hurting!

LUDWIG   Cos it's a damned lie. And if he's put it in this drama, I'll have him for every penny he's got . . . and he's worth a few bob! *(pushes her aside roughly)*

MARTHA   Why're you so horrible to your own . . . sister . . . unless . . . I'm not your sister . . . leastways not entirely . . . *(Ludwig pursues her round the furniture, but she dodges)* Aha! . . . It's true, then . . .

LUDWIG   Shut your trap. I'll have your tongue out! You're enough my flesh and blood for me to want advancement for yer. Think big! Think money! . . . Look at yourself! Famous man . . . comes to the house, loaded wi' brass . . . wife as frigid as a bent penguin . . . Poor bugger hasn't had a good shag in months and still you haven't had him away! Call yourself a Jezebel!

MARTHA   He thinks I'm a dyke!

LUDWIG   Then stick a tit in his eye!

MARTHA   He's always working . . .

LUDWIG   You've been had by every farm hand for ten mile . . .
How do you stop them working?

MARTHA   I takes their dinner out in the fields. Hot rolls wi'
butter meltin' in 'em . . . wrapped in cool-white linen. I lays the
linen down. and . . .

LUDWIG   Gets really hungry do they? . . . Right! Hot rolls it is
for Mister Strindberg . . . The butter melts at dawn!

MARTHA   What shall I wear?

LUDWIG   A necklace!

MARTHA   What if someone comes?

LUDWIG   It'll be him . . . Two minutes flat! I'll put money on
it! And while you're at it . . . ask him for the key to the desk!
Well . . . after! Maintenance payments and the laws of libel . . .
screwed both ways . . . What'll you call the baby?

MARTHA   What baby?

LUDWIG   Never . . . take up fortune-telling!

(Children's voices are heard from outside)

VOICES   Martha! Martha! Can we lock the chickens up?

*Martha runs to the window and gesticulates that she is coming
down. She exits as Ludwig finally prises open the desk and starts to
read the play avidly.*

LUDWIG *(reading aloud from it)* What! That I should have an
amour with a servant . . . You, great, strong lout . . . What
muscles you . . . have! . . . The dirty bastard! He'll pay for this!

Lights down.

SCENE 4

Very early next morning. Barely light. Strindberg is tossing and turning on the chaise. He has a blanket over him and his trousers and shoes are on the floor. Enter Martha carrying a silver tray with rolls and coffee. She is pretending to be in a hypnotic trance. She places the tray down on a chair nearby, then lets slip her dressing-gown.

STRINDBERG *(suddenly wakes, eyes popping)* Good God! He's done it!

MARTHA   A new day, sir, full of promise, and a new season. I love the springtime and its ritual.

STRINDBERG *(slowly waves his hand in front of her face to test if she is in a trance. To himself)* A trance or the perfect imitation of a trance? *(to Martha)* Which is it, Martha?

MARTHA   I only know what I must do.

STRINDBERG Yes. Silly question really. If you weren't in a trance, you wouldn't say and if you were, you wouldn't know.

MARTHA   You make things awful complicated, sir.

STRINDBERG Do you come to me of your own free will?

MARTHA   When you want someone bad enough, you're not in control of yourself. That's how things are. Love is a trance. No logic in it. Nor should you look for none for fear you'd break the spell. Surely . . . you'd know that.

STRINDBERG So. I'll never know what's really going on here.

MARTHA   It's awful cold, sir.

STRINDBERG *(to himself)* Hoist on my own petard. I set this up and now she could be setting me up. I'm a victim of my own plot . . .

MARTHA   The proof of the puddin' is in the eatin', sir. Taste it, and see if it's real. *(to audience)* I should never have got involved with an intellectual!

STRINDBERG You realise I'm old enough to be . . .

MARTHA   . . . my father, sir. Yes, sir. More's the better *(she jumps into bed with him)* I shan't breathe a word to no-one. Cross my heart *(goes to cross her bare breast. He covers her up)*

STRINDBERG Yes I know where your heart is.

MARTHA *(kissing his neck)* Oh. My brother's told me all about how famous you are. I always wanted to be an actress . . .

STRINDBERG Well. You seem to have learnt the first lesson. Now let's just run through this little scene together. *(he lays her on her back underneath the blanket)* I'll see if I can offer you the part . . .

MARTHA   Oh Mister Wolf . . . what big eyes you have.

STRINDBERG *(getting playful)* GGrrrrrrrr!

They toss about under the blanket coming up for air and breathing frantically. The lights go out and we hear the parodied sighs of orgasm, followed by yawning and finally snoring. The stage stays in darkness for thirty seconds. When the lights gradually go up again Martha is asleep under the blanket and Strindberg is smoking and editing his script at the writing-desk in a half-dressed state. Suddenly he realises the time. It is getting light. He dashes to the chaise and wakes Martha.

STRINDBERG Quick . . .The children are up . . . Get your clothes on. *(he holds the dressing-gown for her)*

MARTHA *(kissing his neck)* I think I loves you Mister . . . what's your first name?

STRINDBERG August . . . Come on, will you? Take the tray!

MARTHA   What about tonight?

STRINDBERG Yes. Where?

MARTHA   In the stables.

STRINDBERG I can't abide the smell of horses . . . What about the hayloft?. . .

MARTHA   Alright. Eleven o'clock.

STRINDBERG And Martha . . . Have a bath, first . . .

There is a knock on the door connecting with the Countess' room. Martha exits quickly. Strindberg tidies himself hurriedly and adjusts the chaise.

STRINDBERG Come in!

ANNA *(voice off)* Undo the bolt!

*Anna enters. Her mood is quite different to the end of the last scene.
She is thoughtful and introspective, though not without humour.*

ANNA   Forgive me intruding. I'd like a word before
everyone's up and about . . . You had a restless night. So did I.
Dreams, you know. And Othello is not well. He may have to be
put down . . . Poor Othello!

STRINDBERG A tragedy!

ANNA   He's always been so devoted to me . . . and jealous
of the other dogs. Hence the name . . . Mister Strindberg, there is
a matter on which I would welcome your opinion. I would not
burden you with it, but since you deal in matters of the soul . . .

STRINDBERG I'm listening . . .

ANNA   Ludwig is . . . my bailiff, as you know. He and I
are, however, on closer terms than mistress and servant . . . I
can't elaborate . . .

STRINDBERG I've no wish to delve into your private life . . .

ANNA   . . . and you a writer. Investigation is your brief,
surely . . .

STRINDBERG Life invents us all . . . none of it's of any substance.

ANNA   I'm very fond of Ludwig. Our families have been
obligated to each other for centuries . . . It's a trust, you see, a
bond. I feel myself responsible for his welfare . . .

STRINDBERG Noblesse oblige! How quaint!

ANNA   But his actions and their consequences reflect upon
this household . . . *(pauses, sighs)* Mister Strindberg – Ludwig's
hardly spent a night here for three months now . . . Where he
goes, I have no idea . . . I have been unable to pay his salary
during that same time. . . And yet, he's never short . . . He's even
. . . lent me cash. Let me be blunt. In Skvolyst there have been
numerous unsolved burglaries . . . friends of my mine. Local
dignitaries are becoming restive . . . Were the police to ask me to

vouch for his movements, I could not in all honesty provide an alibi . . . What am I to do?

STRINDBERG You mean . . . you need the money?

ANNA It is a help . . . How did I get into such a bizarre reversal of roles?

STRINDBERG Confront him. Demand an explanation. If he is innocent he has nothing to fear. The law is just. I myself was cleared of blasphemy, though God knows why!

ANNA Poor Ludwig. He believes that life has dealt him a poor hand . . . eaten up with resentment at his lowly origins . . . He will do damage to himself, to Martha, to me . . . and anyone he comes into contact with . . . Be careful.

STRINDBERG He is the perfect rationalist. All his schemes backfire on him. He's born to lose . . . and keep us all amused in the process . . .

ANNA Not a humane judgement, Mister Strindberg . . . Unworthy of you . . . Think at least of Martha . . . an innocent child . . . She believes that everything he counsels will bring happiness . . . Oh, if only people could be satisfied with what their station in life –

STRINDBERG All very well for you to say . . . But what of the Countess, with her aristocratic concern for all and sundry . . . is she satisfied?

ANNA Aspiration for me seems pointless . . . Had I been poor, I might have achieved much.

STRINDBERG Had you been poor you would have been denied the right to achieve anything! Take it from one who's been there!

ANNA But I would have had the choice!

STRINDBERG Ah yes, the *choice*. To be free to choose. What a wonderful endowment. Have you any idea how hard it is for those with infinite choice and absolutely no means whereby to avail themselves of it . . .

ANNA There. You are a socialist. I knew it . . .

STRINDBERG Socialism is just another means of self-advancement for those ashamed of their talent . . . Let me tell you, as the son of a servant . . . You need extraordinary gifts, heroic perseverance or incredible luck to make choice work in your favour . . . and as for happiness – forget it. It's one long struggle against the pygmies, the stupid and the indolent . . . who, by and large, run the show.

ANNA   But you're a man!

STRINDBERG Oh no! Please. Spare me the sexual pleading! You. A woman of standing!

ANNA   Yes. And intend to remain so. Do you imagine I have not wanted to marry? Why! I'd lose it all. Instantly a wife and a subordinate. Men know this. I've been sought not for what I am but for the status I endow men with. This crumbling edifice is what they're after. I have no choice but to remain single and to grow eccentric. You see . . . I cannot marry . . .

STRINDBERG Will not.

ANNA   Choose not, then.

STRINDBERG *(wistful)* Each choice is a denial. And all the spurned alternatives become a chain of regrets that weight us down . . .

ANNA   You regret your marriage?

STRINDBERG No more than you regret not marrying. My problem is that life with a woman is hell, and life without one, purgatory.

ANNA   You're looking for a mother, not a wife . . . I do hope you and Siri can resolve your present difficulties, before the holiday is over. Will you stay another month?

STRINDBERG *(considerately)* Ah, yes . . . the September rent. Fifty Kroner, wasn't it? *(he goes to pay her)*

ANNA   No, no, please . . . Give it to Ludwig.

STRINDBERG *(returns the money to his pocket)* Siri will probably return to Taarbaek in a fortnight, but I shall certainly stay on . . . I can't desert my characters. They're going through a difficult time. They need me . . .

ANNA   Talk to Siri . . . It would be a tragedy for the children
if –
(She shakes her head but Strindberg is already engrossed in his manuscript)

Lights down.

SCENE 5

Martha is seated, sniffing into a handkerchief, her other hand on her belly. Ludwig is holding a shotgun, pointing ceilingwards and striding up and down as he speaks. They await Strindberg's arrival to confront him. Ludwig practices aiming out of the open window. The writingdesk is open with the script on it. Ludwig is having a bit of fun, here. At times clearly 'acting'. It is deliberately farcical.

LUDWIG   Rape! That's what it is, rape . . .

MARTHA   No-one heard me shout or scream . . .

LUDWIG   You weren't yet sixteen. Technically that's rape! Christ! At this rate he'll be suing you! . . . Right. Final rehearsal!

MARTHA *(trying not to make a mistake)* I came into his bedroom with the breakfast tray . . .

LUDWIG   Not the bedroom, God save us!

MARTHA   The study . . . the study!

LUDWIG   Then what happened?

MARTHA   Well. He raped me of course . . .

LUDWIG   What? Breakfast tray in hand? Without spilling the coffee? Think, girl, think . . . tell the Court what was on the breakfast tray . . .

MARTHA   Coffee, hot rolls and butter . . .

LUDWIG *(as if to a court)* Coffee . . . hot-t r-rolls and-d . . . but-butter. Hardly a provocative breakfast, gentlemen of the jury. *(to Martha, again, as if still in court)* Tell the Court, had you served similar breakfasts to previous male guests?

MARTHA   I had, sir . . .

LUDWIG   And did instant erection and uncontrollable lust result on those occasions?

MARTHA   They did not, sir.

LUDWIG *(to Martha)* Good! Keep your eyes downcast. Speak in whispers. Remember, the court's a theatre! You play the victim. He's the villain. *(to 'the court')* Did you say anything at all to the accused?

MARTHA   I said: 'It's awful cold, sir' . . .

LUDWIG   And what occasioned this . . . innocent observation on the state of the weather?

MARTHA *(whispering loudly at Ludwig)* I din' 'ave no clothes on.

LUDWIG   Inadmissible evidence, dear child . . . a naked woman cannot testify against herself. It's ultra vires! So let me change my line of questioning . . . How did the accused inveigle you into the removal of your maid's uniform? . . . What did he say?

MARTHA   He just told me to strip off.

LUDWIG *(holding his temples and addressing Martha)* Think for a moment, think! Here we have one of Europe's leading word-smiths – a man skilled in the art of the subtle phrase, the delicate juxtapositioning of noun and adjective . . . now again I ask . . . what did he say?

MARTHA   Kindly remove your undergarments . . .

LUDWIG   . . . and why did you feel so disposed to comply with this unbreakfastlike request?

MARTHA   He promised to give me . . . a part . . . in one of his plays.

LUDWIG   What guile, gentlemen of the jury! What cunning! And tell me, Miss Hansen, is this *(holds up the script)* the said dramascourge? 'Miss Julie'?

MARTHA   It is, sir.

LUDWIG   A play, m'lud, in which a local bailiff of this county is portrayed as having an affair with his employer, a Countess! *(to Martha)* At this point, gasps from the courtroom *(to 'the court')* And what part did he have in mind for you in this scurrilous piece?

MARTHA   I was to be a maid. He said I was made for it. He said he wanted to see if I could do it.

LUDWIG   He wanted to see . . . if she could . . . 'do' . . . 'it'.

MARTHA   He said an actress had to be uninhibited, specially in love scenes . . .

LUDWIG   And so, this virgin child was taken in by the accused's seductive prose, his propositions of fame and fortune to the point where she gave away her bodily integrity, and now finds herself at the tender age of fifteen years . . . with child.

The imagined court room drama is now over.

MARTHA   If they swallow that, there ain't no justice.

LUDWIG   *(a)* he slept with you *(b)* you're under-age. Open and shut case. If he's got any sense, he'll settle out of court. We could go for a lump sum maintenance payment, one-off . . . or the royalties from that damned play . . . or both!

MARTHA   I feel sorry for his wife. He said she doesn't understand him . . .

LUDWIG   No bugger understands him. That's how he makes his money.

MARTHA   I'm very fond of his children . . .

LUDWIG   Just as well . . . You'll have one all to yourself soon! Now stop the sob stuff. This is business. You know the gentleman we spoke to yesterday – the journalist from Taarbaek. He knows a good story . . . This could make his name.

MARTHA   It's not in the papers is it? I can see the headlines now – 'Prominent playwright impregnates pretty parlourmaid!'

LUDWIG   'Swedish scribbler sued by screwed servant!' . . . 'In a dramatic move today the Bailiff of Skvolyst-at-Lyngby lodged a libel suit against August Strindberg, alleging defamation. The scandal-prone dramatist simultaneously faces a charge of rape of a minor, whom he violently rogered across the breakfast table'. Oh yes, the public will love it!

MARTHA   Does the Countess know about this?

LUDWIG   By the time she's back from her shopping safari, the whole world will know . . .

A door slams off.

LUDWIG   That's him now! Quick . . . in with the dogs . . . The door's not bolted.

MARTHA   Are you sure 'bout this? You said he was mad.

LUDWIG *(holds up the pistol)* If you hear this, release the dogs!

Martha slips into the Countess' room. Ludwig puts the pistol under his belt, hidden, and walks over to the writing desk, picking up the top sheet of the play. Strindberg arrives, standing in the doorway, composed.

STRINDBERG So. Your thirst for literature finally overcame discretion.

LUDWIG   Beg pardon, sir?

STRINDBERG You've broken into my desk, you scoundrel *(snatches sheet from Ludwig and replaces it)* And . . . you're reading my private papers! What would the Countess make of that?

LUDWIG   I was just thinking the same thing myself, sir . . .

STRINDBERG Cut out the 'sir'. Only servants use it, and you've probably just lost your job.

LUDWIG   Oh I hardly think so . . .

STRINDBERG Deceit, theft, invasion of privacy, not to mention insolence? She'd take a dim view of that.

LUDWIG   Oh very dim. She's an extremely moral woman. If someone, shall we say, deceived her, stole her reputation, invaded her privacy, that someone might expect to find themselves doing handstands in a cesspit, or more likely, considering her breeding . . . the subject of litigation.

STRINDBERG She's my Countess and she can sleep with who she bloody well likes . . . though what she sees in that obnoxious little creep of a bailiff, I can't imagine. Still there's no accounting for the behaviour of woman.

LUDWIG I'll have you know I've never laid a finger on her . . .

STRINDBERG Well that's your pathetic inadequacy as a man . . . You've certainly wanted to . . . and for the basest of motives. Don't throw away the best part you've ever had. In life you're a miserable failure but in this, your wildest fantasies, imprisoned by your total lack of will, are realised.

LUDWIG A dreamer who can't satisfy his own wife . . . Oh I know! . . . Havin' it away with pillows! Don't try to put me down. *(mocking)* I want to tear down civilisation to the last stone! Oh, you vicious beast, you!

(Strindberg sits on the chaise, hands behind head, laughing and enjoying every minute of it)

LUDWIG You think you can go round distorting the world, putting words into people's mouths and forcing them to unspeakable acts of murder!

STRINDBERG Come! Come! Has murder never crossed your mind? I tried it once, but compassion got the better of me. Besides . . . it's stupid . . . right up your street I'd have thought.

LUDWIG Oh no. This character's written his own plot. I've got an ending all worked out . . . a courtroom drama . . . and a second sub-plot . . . How does it feel to be outwitted by one of your own creations?

STRINDBERG A sub-plot! My word, we are inventive. Don't tell me . . . Pregnant child raped by smooth-talking bard. I take it she is with child?

LUDWIG Fifteen years old and up the stick.

STRINDBERG Her pregnant state has been certified of course? By a qualified doctor? Or did you do the examination yourself, you know, with a torch, shouting up the orifice: 'Anybody there'?

LUDWIG *(furious)* You evil bastard!

STRINDBERG Come on Ludwig. You'd love to have your hand up your sister's vagina. Admit it.

LUDWIG *(pulls out the pistol, breathing heavily with anger)* I'll kill you. I'll kill you!

STRINDBERG *(still laughing)* Oh. You're changing the plot then? What about due process of law . . . By the way . . . speaking of law, there are two gentlemen waiting to see you downstairs *(shouts to them)* You can come up now!

LUDWIG   That'll be my lawyer and the journalist . . .

STRINDBERG I hardly think so . . . They're wearing uniforms . . . *(he rises slowly and walks to the desk, picks up his play, shuffles the papers, tucks them under his arm and walks towards the door, delivering the following lines as he does so)* They have, I believe, a warrant for your arrest . . . some burglaries in Taarbaek . . . the Countess told me all about them . . . your unexplained night absences . . . Pretty convincing case it seems to me . . . *(stands at the door)* In my next play, 'Tschandara' an evil gypsy who tries to trick a noble professor is eaten by his own dogs . . . Lovely touch that . . .

LUDWIG *(shaking with anger he points the shotgun at the doorway as Strindberg turns to leave and the lights go out just as he fires).* Release the dogs!

Blackout on stage. Pandemonium. Two more shots. The baying of dogs.

STRINDBERG *(voice off)* There's your burglar!

POLICEMAN *(voice off).* Grab the gun! Now come along quietly sir . . .

Dogs are heard baying in the distance.

SCENE 6

Postscript. Morning. Some days later. Siri, dressed for travel, with cape and bag, enters, looks around and knocks on Anna's door.

ANNA *(enters)* All packed and ready to go?

SIRI   Any more news of the dogs?

ANNA   Hamlet's back. Falstaff's drunk, of course. Titus and Cassius were exhausted by the chase. Macbeth and Caesar . . . are still on your husband's scent . . . I do hope they'll be alright . . . Othello's been spotted in Taarbaek . . . And where's our genius?

SIRI   August left a message at the station. He's gone to Berlin with a friend.

ANNA   Dear, dear! . . . Writers are so odd. How do you live with it?

SIRI   Thank God I shan't have to any more . . .

ANNA   Oh, that business with Martha . . . a foolish flirtation . . . give him another chance . . .

SIRI   I think I'll give myself a chance for once. The children need stability . . . I'm sorry he's caused so much trouble.

ANNA   Nonsense. It's done me the world of good . . . Martha has admitted she's not pregnant . . . Ludwig's being released this morning . . . I haven't had so much excitement in years . . . Is it all over then?

SIRI   I can't compete with Nietszche . . . his latest passion . . . First I'll go to Taarbaek. Then home to Sweden. I'm not exiled. Only he.

ANNA   He's a gorgeous lunatic. How does he get through each day?

SIRI   He'll stalk around the battlefield at dusk, collecting up the chunks of flesh and bone, sinews, torn out hair and eye-balls dancing on their coils . . . stitch them all together then fill the skull with fear and make it stammer incoherently. Have you read 'Miss Julie'?

ANNA   I must admit. I did sneak a peek. Eccentric I may be, but I've never slept with my bailiff . . . not yet at any rate . . . Well goodbye, and if you ever need a quiet holiday again . . .

Siri kisses her and walks to door with bag.

ANNA   How is it that he writes so profoundly about us when he totally misconstrues our characters? He's like a babe in arms. He doesn't understand a thing.

SIRI *(shrugs)* Goodbye Countess.

ANNA   Goodbye Baroness.

(she walks slowly to the desk where a single piece of paper lies alongside a razor. This is the last page of 'Miss Julie'. She picks up paper and razor in either hand. Reading from Strindberg's script)

'Miss Julie', final page. Jean puts the razor in her hands. Miss Julie *(rousing herself)* Thank you I'm going to have peace at last . . . What is all this?. . . Ah! She puts the razor to her throat. *(she does so dramatically and then recites the lines melo-dramatically)* Jean: 'It's horrible but there is no other way out!' With a firm step Miss Julie goes out through the door . . .

She heads for the door of her bedroom, holding razor in front of her. She stops. Ludwig appears in back doorway leaning on door-post.

LUDWIG   Burglaries in Taarbaek!

ANNA *(turns. She is suddenly flustered and excited)* Oh! And how did you enjoy prison?

LUDWIG   It was you, wasn't it, spun him that yarn?
(Anna shakes her head)
Why did you do it?

ANNA   That Taarbaek woman, your paramour . . . She dresses like a streetwalker! No breeding! You're . . . too good for her.

LUDWIG   It's my life!

ANNA   She can't have you. You're my Bailiff.

LUDWIG *(kissing her hand)* My Countess!

ANNA   Brother!

LUDWIG   Sister!

Each puts right arm round front of other's waist and begins to circle in 'Kalinka' dance. The dance speeds up to very fast.

BOTH   Kalinka, Kalinka, Kalinka, Maya!
Kalinka, Kalinka, Kalinka, Maya.

They stop suddenly.

ANNA   'Jean!'
LUDWIG   'Miss Julie!'

They laugh. Continue to dance slowly, then faster.

Blackout.

The end.

Mark Jenkins

Born and brought up in Islington, London, he now lives, as a writer in Cardiff. His first film **The Scarlet Tunic** was released at Cannes in 1997 and he is currently commissioned by the Arts Council of Wales to write a film of the life of Welsh boxer, Jim Driscoll.

His one-man show **Playing Burton** was a sell-out at the Edinburgh fringe in 1997 and is on a two year world tour, sponsored by the British Council. His first play, **Birthmarks**, won first prize awarded by the Drama Association of Wales in 1987. **Downtown Paradise**, his most recent play, is currently seeking an American producer.

Maison Splendide

by Laura Bridgeman

Maison Splendide

Maison Splendide started life as a 20 minute commission to be shown alongside two others in a trilogy entitled *Gay Marriage in Suburbia* in The London New Play Festival 1996. It was always my feeling that the heart of the play would be in the location and not the event. In the little time allocated I wanted to concentrate on the world and the tone and create a distinctive vernacular that would run to the names of all the characters and the title. Two women (Honey and Moon) are house-sitting in Buckhurst Hill for a supposed small time gangster and his wife (Tiny and Delores) who we never see. The women steal their culture and appropriate it through a sequence of discoveries and dressing-up culminating in a private wedding ritual. The mood is celebratory and not issue-led. A single sex marriage currently in this country cannot be officially blessed and gives you no legal benefit. I wanted to show characters driven by their own financial and emotional needs and sense of play as opposed to a desire to change the world with a sexual politic. This could be filled in by the audience.

It ran in the 6:30pm slot to full houses, was critically well received and short-listed for Best Play in the Festival, that year. Fuelled by the encouragement of its success I wrote more. The tone began to change and the serious underworld became more about make-believe. The house took on a living identity for a specific purpose. The doorbell, the phone, the metal case, all controlling the action to one room. In this way it now spoofs the gangster genre but retains a real notion of it, where darkness and violence constantly pervade. The characters escape their own registers of pain and disappointment through the release and comfort of fantasy and dreams. The relationship of the women sometimes echoing and eventually reaffirming that of the older heterosexuals. All are complicit (even after the dénouement) in their desire to keep the bubble intact. *Maison Splendide* with its drinks trolley and karaoke machine provides their perfect pleasure parlour from which to flee the abrasive outside world.

Laura Bridgeman

Maison Splendide

by Laura Bridgeman

First produced as part of the London New Play Festival's *'Gay Marriage in Suburbia'* Trilogy in 1996 at the Young Vic Studio.
Directed by Sarah Frankcom
Designed by John Howes

MOON	Ursula Lea
HONEY	Michelle Butterly

ACT ONE

The time is present. A hot August evening. Delores and Tiny's front room. Honey and Moon are discovered sitting on a chaise longue. There is a drinks trolley and a Karaoke machine behind them. Two cardboard boxes are underneath the chaise longue. Three flying ducks are mounted on the back wall. The front door is at the back wall with a letter box. A metal case is on the floor against the back wall.

Honey is holding a take-away rice dish in a tinfoil container and Moon is holding a paper in her hands. Neither eat nor read but stare into space beyond. The décor is bright. They are monochrome. Moon wears a vest and trousers. Honey wears a white dress with poppers down the front similar to a nurse's uniform. Both have stockinged feet. Their shoes are near the door, arranged in a row.
Silence. Honey begins to place her take-away on the floor.

MOON	I said no.
HONEY	Don't want anymore.
MOON	It'll stain the carpet.
HONEY	Can't finish it.
MOON	Chuck it in the rubbish.

HONEY   You told me not to move!

MOON   Don't.

HONEY   How can I *find* the rubbish?

MOON   Give it here.

HONEY *(passing her the takeaway. Moon juggles the paper in one hand and the container in the other. Eventually she places them both on the floor, the container and the paper)* Smart.

MOON   That's it.

HONEY   I wanna explore!

MOON   We're housesitting not on *Star Trek*.

HONEY   You're here regular – I wanna look!

MOON   Sit still – you'll break something.

HONEY   I got to move sometime!

MOON   I'll get you everything.

HONEY   Everything?

MOON   Yeah.

HONEY   What about the toilet?

MOON   Cross your legs, think of something else.

HONEY   What we supposed to do?

MOON   Guard the house. Make sure no-one breaks in or asks questions about Tiny and Delores's whereabouts.

HONEY   Who wants to know?

MOON   Plenty.

HONEY   Why?

MOON   'Cos of his business.

HONEY   What's that?

MOON   Helping people. Finance. He gives out money.

HONEY   Sounds like Santa Claus.

MOON   Yo ho ho.

HONEY   He works at night, like Santa Claus.

MOON   When repayment's overdue he's got to give people a little reminder.

HONEY   Why don't he phone?

MOON	More effective in the flesh.
HONEY	What d'you and Delores do?
MOON	I wait in the car, she stays in and organises the paper- work.
HONEY	I seen her at the club – gets a massage once a week.
MOON	Takes care of herself.
HONEY	Nice figure. Strong features. That deep scar down her cheek –
MOON	Yeah, that scar –
HONEY	Covers it with Max Factor. Good with her make-up – skilful.
MOON	Used to be a chorus girl on the cruises. They wanna start a chain of casinos next and do the whole Las Vegas bit.
HONEY	A *casino* in Buckhurst Hill?
MOON	That's why they're over there. Pick up some pointers.
HONEY	A *casino* in Buckhurst Hill?
MOON	Be good for us – I do the bouncing, you work the floor.
HONEY	I work the health club not the sleaze pits!
MOON	Could double your money. We need to think big. Now we got two weeks to keep this place spangly. When they get back we're fixed for future employment. One good favour deserves another. We shake and vac – he'll send some of that freshness back our way. *(making a money sign)*
HONEY	She don't even smile when she come in for her massage.
MOON	She don't have to. She's Tiny's wife.
HONEY	So?
MOON	Don't you get it?
HONEY	What?
MOON	They're important.
HONEY	So are we.
MOON	They got no kids. They're sifting a generation. They wanna pass things on to the suitable. We're talking inheritance.
HONEY	I'm talking convenience. I'm not gonna stay still for two weeks.
MOON	For now. Stay still for now. Till we're settled.

HONEY   I am settled. *(pause)*

MOON   We take care of things here for a couple of weeks and our future is as sweet as the Kipling pies deep in the freezer, safe as the maisonettes lining the cul de sac, neat as the gnomes fishing in the Japanese water garden –

HONEY   We're cheap labour, money for old rope –

MOON   He hasn't asked *anyone* – he's asked us!

HONEY   The others have more sense.

MOON   Think of it as a working vacance.

HONEY   Working full stop. A vacance means sitting in the sun, hitting the happy juice and sex anytime, anyplace, anywhere – apart from the hotel bedroom.

MOON   Naughty.

HONEY   We'll be lucky to snatch a glimpse of the flaming orbit. Let alone the rest of it!

MOON   You *can* sit outside.

HONEY   Are you sure?

MOON   'Course.

HONEY   Better look it up. Don't want to be soaking up rays when it's against the gospel! Get out the chapter according to Saint Tine. Read me the written. Lay down the law. Refresh my fading memory. *(pause)* What you waiting for? Give it to me one more time – The contract all signed and sealed – The list of 'dos and don'ts.'

(Moon produces a list from her pocket)

HONEY   Begin at the beginning.

MOON   Contract of employment and list of 'dos and don'ts' whilst looking after *Maison Splendide* for the period of thirteen nights and fourteen days – as established between Tiny Lavender's Chauffeur – Moon (hereafter known as the house-sittee) and Tiny Lavender Esquire (hereafter known as the boss) and witnessed by Mrs Delores Lavender (hereafter known as the witness). Any failure to comply with the contract and the list will result in a dismissal from current employment as the boss's Chauffeur and could result in receiving specific methods of enforcement frequently used by the boss and known by the housesittee. Anything that happens to the house throughout the duration of this time will be the direct responsibility of the housesittee. Anything that happens to the garden, furniture, crockery, etc., will be the direct responsibility of the housesittee. Anything that is heard or seen should be forgotten. Anything that is discovered should be ignored. Anything that is unusual should be taken note of and not ignored. On completion of this contract this document will be burnt and never discussed by any of the three parties again. Signed and dated . . .

HONEY   I'm surprised it has to be burnt. I'm surprised it doesn't simply self-destruct on our departure.

MOON   What?

HONEY   Mission impossible. *(starts singing the theme tune)* Da da da da da da da.

MOON   D'you wanna hear the list?

HONEY   'Course, Da da da.

MOON   What do you wanna know?

HONEY   Um. Dos and don'ts. Soaking up the rays.

MOON   Sunbathing. Do. Told you – you can sit outside.

HONEY   Kind. What about the happy juice?

MOON   Alcohol. Do. Drink what we like – no replacement.

HONEY   Generous. What about sex?

MOON   Sex. Sex. Sex isn't here. Not even mentioned.

HONEY   And me?

MOON   You? – not even mentioned.

HONEY   He knows we're a team?

MOON   He knows.

HONEY   But me and sex is not even mentioned?

MOON   No.

HONEY *(whispering)* I'm not supposed to be here?

MOON *(whispering)* No.

HONEY   Me and sex is not mentioned. Da da.

MOON   Stop it –

HONEY   The names have been changed to protect the
innocent.

MOON   Now –
(Honey falls silent)
You and sex is not even mentioned.

HONEY   I suppose that could mean either our team is *not*
allowed sex *or* we can have it anytime, anyplace, anywhere apart
from their hotel bedroom. *(taking the list out of Moon's hands
and making it into a paper plane)*

MOON   What are you doing?

HONEY   I'm not here. I'm not doing anything.

MOON   With that list –

HONEY   Talking to yourself – bit of a worry.

MOON   What are you doing with that list?

HONEY   How does our team start a vacance?

MOON   Pack our bags.

HONEY   Then what?

MOON   Turn the heating off at the time switch. Put on the
ansaphone. Leave the hall light on and the curtains drawn. Set the
video for the pick of the week and then head for the bus stop.

HONEY   Good. Then what?

MOON   Stay on the bus till we get to the tube.

HONEY   Then what?

MOON   Stay on the tube till we get to the airport.

HONEY   Then what?

MOON   Pick up mags, comics, bubblegum, coke and see if
Boots has got those waxy earpluggy things for you.

HONEY   Good. Then what?

MOON   Passport check. Bag check. The bleeper check up
and down the body.

HONEY   We like that.

MOON   What?

HONEY   The bleeper check. Then she does the hand check.

MOON   Yeah.

HONEY We like that.

MOON Yeah . . .

HONEY She's in a uniform, dominant, running her hands in between our legs, all over our bonanzas –

MOON Cheap thrill.

HONEY We like that. A lot. Then what?

MOON Duty free. Down to the gate. Ready to board. Ready to board.

HONEY On the plane and take off. *(grabs Moon's hand then sends it flying into the air)* We've landed. Off the plane and onto the hospitality bus which takes us to our hotel –

MOON How do we know the hotel?

HONEY I booked it.

MOON Who did that?

HONEY Me.

MOON When?

HONEY Two weeks beforehand.

MOON Last minute bargain?

HONEY Last bookings left.

MOON Nice one.

HONEY Thanks. We check in. Get our key. Go up to the room. And before we even unpack – before we even think about going down to the heated pool and having our first dip of the season, what do we do to kick off the vacance?

MOON Get something to eat?

HONEY We fuck.

MOON Right.

HONEY Right. I suggest we make a start. We've landed. We've booked into the hotel. The sun has already departed. The happy juice is quite content clinking on the trolley 'til we're ready. That leaves only the fuck. Now the fuck is always a good way to get the girlie in the mood for a two week break. What d'you say?

MOON Hello girlie –

HONEY Hello. Help us unwind –

MOON   Yeah.

HONEY   Stop us squawking like a couple of old crows.

MOON   Yeah.

HONEY   If we're imprisoned here, might as well be happy captives and happiness is not always a cigar called Hamlet. More often a fuck on someone else's sofa. A shag on someone else's shag pile. A delve into deep recesses of pink flesh on someone else's borrowed time. Ooooh, I want to. Don't you?

MOON   Yeah.

HONEY *(unbuttons her dress)* Getting hot just thinking about it.

MOON *(undoes her trousers)* Me too.

HONEY   I love to play away from home.

MOON   I *love* playing in our team.

HONEY   What position are you?

MOON   I'm always changing.

HONEY   Yeah?

MOON   Sometimes I'm mid-field. *(kisses her stomach)*

HONEY   I remember –

MOON   Sometimes I'm wing. *(kisses her armpit)*

HONEY   That's right.

MOON   But most frequently I'm in goal. *(kisses her lap)*

HONEY   I love to see you in goal. You're better in goal than anywhere else.

MOON   What about you?

HONEY   My position? That changes too. Tonight – being the first time playing away on this pitch. Gonna indulge myself. Gonna choose the best position of all.

MOON   What's that?

HONEY   Referee.

MOON *(lifting her head)* Oh!

HONEY   Don't worry. *(shoves her head down)* Play on.

    (More frantic undressing and groans. Suddenly the doorbell rings – a cacophony of sound – it has a tune attached to it. Both their

heads spin round. Moon tries to get up but Honey then takes her head down again to carry on.)

HONEY *(clamps her with her legs)* I'm the referee. Haven't blown the whistle.

MOON   There's someone at the door!

HONEY   Just a spectator! They'll go away at the end of the match.

MOON   Want them to go away now!

HONEY   Carry on. You're in goal.

(The doorbell goes a second time. Moon yelps, leaps up and starts to get dressed at manic speed. Honey slowly rearranges herself)

MOON   Who can it be?

HONEY   Don't know but it's the end of the game.

MOON   Put your clothes on.

HONEY   Just as we were warming up.

MOON   D'you think they've been watching? Spectator like? D'you think they have?

HONEY   How should I know?

MOON   It might be a neighbour!

HONEY   It might be a pizza!

MOON   We didn't order a pizza!

HONEY   Joke.

MOON   Nah. Some anorak head – I bet you – Frotting off in the bushes! Those French windows are big – you know. He could have been out there, past the patio getting his rocks off by the Japanese water garden!

HONEY   Go and see who it is.

MOON   *Dirty, dirty* man –

HONEY   Sooner you go – quicker we found out.

MOON   Why don't you go?

HONEY   Not supposed to be here, am I? How can I get the door if I'm not here?

MOON   Good point.

HONEY   You go.

MOON   Can't.

HONEY   Why?

MOON   On the list of 'don'ts.'

HONEY   You sure?

MOON *(picks up list)* Don't answer the telephone – don't get door. Knew I'd seen it!

HONEY *(lights cigarette)* Well, that's sorted.

(The doorbell rings a third time)

HONEY   Let it ring.

MOON   Wait a minute. *(gets paper out again)* Oh, yeah – Do. You can smoke.

HONEY   Thank you.

MOON   What should I *do*?

HONEY   *Bang!*

MOON *(jumps)* Freaked me!

HONEY   You're a walking coronary.

MOON   Shut it! Now I'm going to squint through the letter slat, see if I can see something.

HONEY   If you must.

MOON   That's the only way we find out.

HONEY   Good idea.

MOON   I'm going to open the slat and squint through.

HONEY   O.K.

(Moon approaches the letter box. Honey stands up)

MOON *(spins 'round)* What you doing?

HONEY   Ashtray.

MOON   Sit down while I do this!

HONEY   Why?

MOON   In case something happens!

HONEY   If it's a pervert – he'll run off. If it's one of the boys – you can talk. If it's a pizza – it's the wrong number.

MOON   Could be a client.

HONEY   What?

MOON   Someone we do business with.

HONEY   Why would it be one of them?

MOON   Some of them get upset. With the specific methods
of enforcement.

HONEY   What does that entail ?

MOON   He snips people.

HONEY   Where?

MOON   Pinkie. Smallest digit. Cut-throat razor. Takes him
seconds.

HONEY   Charming!

MOON   Guns are for the gangsters. Snips, slices and cuts.
Swift and inexpensive. His wrist. Very skillful. Dances through
the air.

HONEY   You've seen him cut people?

MOON   Seen him practice. Takes it serious. Keeps all his kit
in a metal suitcase.

(Both their heads turn to the case on the floor)

HONEY   Either open the door, squint through the letter slat or
pretend it never happened and pour us both a drink!

MOON   One, two, Scooby Dooby Doo; three, four, who's at
the door? *(prizes open the letter-box and peers through)* That was
close. Very close.

HONEY   Get me a drink.

MOON   What you having?

HONEY   Snowball.

*(Moon starts preparing Honey a Snowball and herself a large
neat whisky)*

MOON   I was picturing magnums. Letter bombs. Threats.
Never know with the clientele. One time had one follow me
round in the car for days on the Vespa. Scooter boy I titled him.
Young lad. All kinds of trouble. He was six months overdue.
Tiny didn't take to him at all. His reminder went on for hours.
Serious specific method enforcement! See . . . he starts on the
pinkie but if things are bad he works up to the top half of the

body. In extremis, he slices the face. This boy must have been
that, 'cos he was on the Vespa following me in a rubber mask. In
extremis, incognito, on wheels behind me for days! Every time I
looked in the rear mirror, there he was. Dressed in black. Like the
angel of death. A faceless fucking omen on a Vespa! Makes me
come over parched and trembly just thinking about it. Still think I
see him now. Behind me on the road. My mind playing tricks.
Never knew what he wanted. But I stopped once in the car. And
told him: 'Tiny warns once. The slice on the face gets fatal next
time round'. Tiny laughed. In Extremis Deo. He said it was a
warning too. Life is full of them. Pay them heed he said, there'll
be more. *(hands Honey her Snowball)* Get that down you girlie.
Clean your pipes. Cheers.

(Honey drinks) The job's not always that. Sometimes smooth as
silk. Civilised. Only a question of getting there. Up to the
doorstep. Ring the bell. Wait. Ask for the client, if it's not them
that answers. Speak: 'Good evening. I work for Tiny Lavender.
You have forgotten to return the favour we did for you. That's
alright we all forget, but I'm your reminder in the flesh. Now I
can wait on your doorstep while you fetch the favour to return. Or
I can ask Mr Lavender to step this way into your front room.'

MOON	No work now. Just you and me.
HONEY	Shut it.
MOON	What?
HONEY	Squawking Polly.
MOON	Polly?
HONEY	Pretty Polly Parrot – you.

MOON *(parrot's voice)* Hello.

HONEY *(making a gun out of her fingers)* Meets – Honey the
Hunter – Click, click, boom, boom, shriek, shriek, flap flap, flap,
feather, beak, claw, hit and stick to the ceiling, the sofa, the shag
pile.

MOON	Someone has to talk 'round here!
HONEY	Honey the Hunter will talk.
MOON	Alright.
HONEY	You never mentioned snips or scooter boy.

MOON   Must have forgot.

HONEY   Yeah.

MOON   Don't want you fretting.

HONEY   Touching.

MOON   *I'm* safe.

HONEY   *You* don't get snipped. Not yet.

MOON   I'm smart.

HONEY *(rising)* So am I.

MOON   Yeah.

HONEY   Why d'you do it?

MOON   What?

HONEY   Work for a twisted. *(drags the suitcase downstage)*

MOON   He looks after me!

HONEY   He's a twisted! *(pulls out a pair of handcuffs)*

MOON   Got to enforce pressure.

HONEY   Like Delores?

MOON   What?

HONEY   She felt pressure enforced.

MOON   She's part of the team?

HONEY   Yeah?

MOON   He needs her. She does the accounts. Got a Xerox
head.

HONEY   What if she stopped respecting?

MOON   Wouldn't happen.

HONEY   One day, maybe . . .

MOON   Nah!

HONEY   Never say never.

MOON   They're solid –

HONEY   Teams change.

MOON   Been together twenty odd years –

HONEY *(shouts)* What would he do?

MOON   Dunno –

HONEY   Specific method enforcement?

MOON   Not Delores.

HONEY *(with handcuffs)* When he practices, does he use these?

MOON   Has them with him.

HONEY   Style.

MOON   Where d'you find them?

HONEY   In the box of tricks.

MOON   Put them back.

HONEY   The case was open.

MOON   Put them back.

HONEY   No. We are going to finish what we started.

MOON   What's that?

HONEY   The fuck . . .

MOON   Not with his gear.

HONEY   I want to play on. I want to get what you get when you reach the hotel bedroom. I want my vacance to start with some frottage on the three-piece suite.

MOON   Please –

HONEY   Turn over.

MOON   Get rid of his gear.

HONEY   Turn over.

MOON   Put the snappies back in the box!

HONEY *(rolls Moon over onto her stomach)* No I'm still referee. I still call the shots. The game was suspended by uninvited interruption. Bad weather stopped play. Now the clouds have passed and the players are back on the pitch. We continue where we left off. But before that happens we're going to check a few things over. You and me.

MOON   What you gonna do? Check my arse?

HONEY   No.

MOON   Sluice my tubing?

HONEY   Calm, calm.

MOON   I don't want a liquid internal!

HONEY *(pushes her down and sits astride her)* I'm not giving you one!

MOON   My arse is fine, just fine.

HONEY   No dispute.

MOON   Why've you rolled me?

HONEY   Convenience. *(attaches the cuffs behind her and sits her on the settee)* Comfy?

MOON   Perfect.

HONEY   Good. Because you don't seem to be picking up here.

MOON   What?

HONEY   Hot night. Still. Even those gnomes look thirsty. They don't wanna fish. They wanna dive right in and guzzle up the whole of the Japanese water garden. *(gets a drink)* Ooh that's good. Sweet stuff. Remember getting hooked on these, Snow-balled 'til I was avocadoed out. Friday night. Hotfoot out of make-up class. Key in the latch. Drop my bags. Run Radox and hot H_2O up to my earlobes. Madonna on the turntable . . .
(sings) 'Some boys kiss me, some boys hug me and I think they're O.K . . . '
'If they don't give me copper pennies I just walk awa-ay.'
Transform my form into something nightlife. . . mascara, lacquer, lipstick.
(sings) 'We are living in a material world and I am a material girl'
Hit the high street. Follow that neon sign till I reach The Blue Monsoon. Slot myself on my wicker chair at the end of the bar. Watch you mixing drinks. Shaking, stirring, sloshing them out. With the olives and the cherries and the ice and the lemon. All glitzy, greeny, reddy, yellowy. All crunch and cut and elegance. Keep those Snowballs coming right up to me till you knock off. Midnight. Rip off your elasticated dickie-bow crackly with too much starch. Walk me back home through the Essex streets. Not enough between us for the take-out and my twenty Silk Cut. So we pool your tips. Share savaloy and chips on our fifteen minute walk. Your eyes starry bright. My teeth sweet with Snowball. Steal kisses on the doorstep of our two rooms above the pet shop. *(pause)* But we could be anywhere. Anyone. Because we weren't part of the Essex night, you and me. Not like the chip-shop

queuers. We were different. Elevated to where the stars come out all furry with prosterity and the sun never sets! I'm not doing make-up classes at college. I am a pop star with dyed blonde hair and a passion for rum truffles. Slipping my way through fans like a hot knife through Vienetta. Bringing you back home in the limousine we sit by the pool all twinkly with stardust. Skinny dip till our bodies hold close. You and me. Steal kisses on the doorstep of our two rooms above the pet shop. Tongues like Kenwood mixers. Mashing up the moments while the canines in the cages howl. *(pause)* Now I get the steady readies in cosmetics and the weak spot for happy juice. You get in debt up to your eyeballs.

MOON   I'm not in debt.

HONEY   Shut up talking.

MOON   Thought you wanted to fuck.

HONEY   Wanna get your head on first! You were always alright! Straight down the line. Reliable. Like fucking Timex! Now it's all rubber masked omens, cuts, snips and slices and ghosts at the doorbell. What the hell happened?

MOON   Changed jobs.

HONEY   Changed personality. Now you signed a bit of paper keeping us here two weeks. You're in debt and I'm right in there fucking with you.

MOON   It's a working vacance.

HONEY   This is no vacance, this is shit deep enough to drown in –

(The telephone starts to ring. Both their heads turn to look at it)
Hells Bloody Bells!

MOON   Who is it?

HONEY   My mum. Joke.

MOON   Well who is it?

HONEY   It might be a client.

MOON   Clients don't ring.

HONEY   Well someone is – *(shoves Moon towards the phone)*

MOON   I can't.

HONEY   Why not?

MOON	It's on the list of 'don'ts'.
HONEY	Don't care.

(The telephone rings off)

MOON	Wrong number.
HONEY	Must be.
MOON	Maybe those tele-research people. They ring at night. Catch people in.
HONEY	Really.
MOON	You know – surveys and that.
HONEY	I know.
MOON	Or it could be Tiny. Maybe he's reached Las Vegas!
HONEY	Their flight was at six p.m.
MOON	Yes.
HONEY	It takes more than three hours to get from Stansted to Las Vegas!
MOON	Maybe they had strong winds.
HONEY	I haven't finished with you. *(goes to the suitcase and pulls out a rubber mask)* What's this – your scooter boy?
MOON	Looks like his.
HONEY	What is he now? Deceased? Departed and Tiny took his trophy?
MOON	Maybe –
HONEY	Maybe there's no scooter boy. Maybe the masked omen was Tiny himself trying to fuck you up or send you off the trail.
MOON	I saw the boy – young he was – no more than nineteen . . .
HONEY	Never saw him in extremis? Never saw him change into the masked omen angel of death and follow you down Chingford High Street?
MOON	No.
HONEY	How d'you know he had a Vespa?
MOON	Tiny told me.
HONEY	How d'you know his face was sliced?

MOON   Tiny told me.

HONEY   Ever see scooter boy when Tiny was in the car?

MOON   No.

HONEY   Who's Batman?

MOON   Bruce Wayne.

HONEY   How d'you know?

MOON   'Cos he's never there when Batman is.

HONEY   One and the same. Batman and Bruce Wayne.
Scooter boy and Tiny Lavender. Two men. Two disguises. Both
made of rubber. *(places it over Moon's head)* Now you can be
scooter boy too and go freaking people out.

MOON   Don't understand.

HONEY *(pulls out the cut-throat razor)* I'll help. This is what he
uses when he practices?

MOON   Yeah.

HONEY   Shows you how he cuts, slices, wrist dancing
through the air. Whoosh whoosh whoosh –

MOON   You can't use it! –

HONEY   Nor can you – your hands are tied!

MOON   Put it down –

HONEY   What a buzz! Buzz buzz buzz.

MOON   You'll hurt me.

HONEY   Now you know how *she* felt.

MOON   Who?

HONEY   Delores.

MOON   When?

HONEY   When he sliced her.

MOON   He's never touched her.

HONEY   She has the mark to prove it! Got that cleft down her
cheek. Tiny's mark. The mark of a professional. *His* for life. Now
I've a good mind to slice you myself. *My* way. Not the face but on
your fucking arse! Now turn over.

MOON   Don't –

HONEY   Mine for life.

MOON	I'm trembly –
HONEY	I'm trembly too *(pause)* Where d'you go?
MOON	Nowhere.
HONEY	You have.
MOON	Take off the latex.
HONEY	Not yet.
MOON	Please.
HONEY	Come back.
MOON	I will.

(Honey goes towards Moon. The telephone rings a second time)

HONEY	And again!
MOON	Take off the latex!
HONEY	Get the phone!
MOON	On the list of 'don'ts'.
HONEY	Get the fucking phone.
MOON	It'll ring off.
HONEY	I get the receiver and you talk.
MOON	What do I say?
HONEY	He-llo.
MOON	Right.
HONEY	Think you can manage?
MOON	Think so.
HONEY	Good. One, two, three . . .

(goes towards receiver. The phone rings off)

HONEY	And again!
MOON	Next time we ignore it.
HONEY	Next time we get it regardless.
MOON	Take off the gear.
HONEY *(takes off the mask)* Voila!
MOON	Now the snappies.
HONEY	No. *(pause)* What do you call me?
MOON	Honey.
HONEY	Why?

MOON   'Cos your tooth is sweet and you like it on your
    toast.

HONEY   What do I call you?

MOON   Moon.

HONEY   Why?

MOON   'Cos I work nights and my eyes look like stars.

HONEY   Put them together and what have you got.

MOON   Gold and silver.

HONEY   And the best vacance ever created.

MOON   Yes.

HONEY   Say it.

MOON   *Honeymoon.*

HONEY *(takes off the handcuffs)* Don't swallow this.

MOON   Alright for you. You got something. Upstairs.
    Something worth keeping. What have I got? The only thing
    school gave me was you. The only thing I left with. Sixteen
    Certified unqualified. You get the make-up course. I get the
    sandwich bars. The restaurants. Turn eighteen and turn my hand
    to public houses. The cocktail bar. All the way learning one
    lesson only. Keep my motor on the run. Talk my way out of
    anything. Talk my way into a whole new world. Enter Tiny
    Lavender. The only man to treat me like I had something to give.
    Employs me. Buys me clothes. Hands me money and the keys to
    his tip-top Cadillac. Feel like I've come home. Don't talk about
    old times. I washed more floors and served more dickheads on
    two pounds fifty an hour than you've had fucking facials. Now I
    don't know why he's doing a Bruce Wayne and following me
    'round on Vespas. I don't know how Delores got that scar. But up
    till now he's treated me good and if there's more to come I'm
    staying in.

HONEY   He cuts his wife's face.

MOON   You don't know that.

HONEY   Damn sure.

MOON   What d'you want me to do?

HONEY   You can't respect *him.*

MOON   Oh I'm alright. I've got my nice little job with my nice little perks. Free saunas. Free facials and free fucking sushi at dinner time.

(The telephone rings a third time. Both look at it)

HONEY   Never know Tiny might have just got off Concorde with that wind hurtling behind its wings.

MOON   Never know.

HONEY   One way to find out.

MOON   No.

HONEY   Pick up. Pick up. Pick up.

MOON   Alright.

(picks up the receiver. The lights start to flicker bright and dim. Honey looks around) Hello . . . Tiny Lavender's residence, Moon speaking – the chauffeur and housesittee.

HONEY   Never mind who's there – who the fuck's here ?

MOON   Hello . . . Hello.

HONEY   Look at the electrics!

MOON *(tapping the receiver button)* Hello . . . Hello.

(The lights are flicking and there is a rush of a wind)

HONEY   Woooah! What's that?

MOON   The line's dead.

HONEY   There's a fucking poltergeist, I know. A gooly!

MOON *(still tapping the phone)* Hello . . . hello.

(Another rush of wind)

HONEY   Woooah!

MOON   Is . . . anybody . . . there?

HONEY *(going over and slamming down the phone)* Put your shoes on, we're going –

MOON   Why?

HONEY   Because I said so.

MOON   I signed a contract.

HONEY   I don't care. I want to live and if I have a choice I want to live with you. In order to do that both our hearts have to be beating. So put on your fucking shoes.

MOON   Why?

HONEY   Because doorbells are singing when there's no- one outside and telephones are ringing, when the line is dead. Lights are flicking. Winds are howling like under the wings of Concorde and I am about to piss myself! –

MOON   Go to the toilet!

HONEY   Remember twenty-five Cromwell Street! Bodies under the patio. If you think I'm leaving here to sprinkle the daisies in the uncertainty of what is out there . . .

MOON   What happened to – 'We can be anywhere. Anyone we want. Because we're not part of the Essex night, you and me. Not like everyone else.' What happened to *'Material Girl'*?

HONEY   She got the heebeejeebies.

MOON   There is a fault on the circuit.

HONEY   What?

MOON   The electrics. Setting off the door. The phone. The lights.

HONEY   We just had a gale force wind blow through here as well! Hurricane *Maison Splendide* ripping through the front room.

MOON   Only the noise. There was no wind as such. No movement.

HONEY   This house is alive. Spirits or something . . .

MOON   Spirits?

HONEY   Watching us. Sounding us out. Getting angry. Trying to scare. Trying to control.

MOON   The only spirits here are these. Get them down you.
(hands her a drink and swigs some whisky herself)

HONEY   Ooh.

MOON   Better?

HONEY   Ooh. I love freeloading this liquor.

MOON   Yeah. Anyway. Thought you wanted to fuck.

HONEY   Not now.

MOON   I do. *(smiling)* All that rowing.

HONEY   Forget it.

MOON   Please.

HONEY   No.

MOON   Fuck me.

HONEY   Fuck yourself. Go on. In the corner.

MOON   Honey I want to –

HONEY   You sound like a cheap record.

MOON   We haven't finished the game.

HONEY   I'm not playing.

MOON   The referee can't pull out.

HONEY   She can. It's her prerogative.

MOON   What grounds?

HONEY   Injury.

MOON   What kind?

HONEY   Personal.

MOON   That's internal damage.

HONEY   Yes.

MOON   Smoking makes it worse.

HONEY   Really?

MOON   Only touching heals.

HONEY   Yeah?

MOON   Feel . . . *(they start to touch)*

HONEY   Oooh.

MOON   Don't wanna shout.

HONEY   Nor me.

MOON   Wanna keep you . . .

HONEY   Wanna keep you . . . *(unbuttons her uniform)* getting
hot again.

MOON *(takes off her trousers)* Me too.

HONEY   Start of the *vacance*.

MOON   Begin as we mean to go on.

HONEY   Anytime.

MOON   Anyplace.

HONEY   Anywhere.

(Their touching becomes more frantic. Kissing and groans. The doorbell rings one time. Both lift up their heads and turn around. Then a cough from outside)

MOON   That's it!

HONEY   Leave it!

MOON   There's someone at the door!

HONEY   Leave it!

MOON   Every time we start!

HONEY   Forget!

MOON   It's a chain reaction –

HONEY   Ignore!

MOON   We snog and Peeping Tom pokes the bell!

HONEY   Lose yourself –

MOON   Can't believe it! –

HONEY   Lose yourself in me –

MOON   He's on a flaming trigger switch!

HONEY *(dropping at Moon's feet)* Forget the world!

MOON   Go back to the leather.

HONEY   Anything!

MOON   Gonna try an experiment.

HONEY   Oooh yes Doctor.

MOON   Call me over.

HONEY   Help me Doctor Moon I've got a problem. Well, I've got two actually *(pointing at her breasts)* One here and one here. Come to me now. I can't stand this professional distance between us. Don't be so cold Doctor Moon. Help a woman in pain. A patient in need. So much shag pile between us! I don't need a Snowball, clogging my pipes. Speed yourself here . . .

MOON   I'm speeding. I'm speeding.

HONEY   Too too too too too too long!

(The doorbell rings a second time followed by a cough)

MOON   Yes.

HONEY   Yes.

MOON   National.

HONEY	Lottery.
HONEY / MOON	Jackpot.
MOON	Every time we snog –
HONEY	The doorbell goes –
HONEY	Good.
MOON	Bad.
HONEY	Leave the door!
MOON	Getting the heebeejeebies!
HONEY	It's the electrics.
MOON	It's the house.
HONEY	You haven't come.
MOON	It's getting stranger.
HONEY	It's sexual tension.
MOON	The doorbell.
HONEY	You need to unwind.
MOON	The cough.
HONEY	We'll beat it, baby.
MOON	Where's the razor?
HONEY	What are you going to do?
MOON	Where's the snippy?
HONEY	With the snappies. In the box of tricks.

MOON *(going over and getting it out)* Right.

HONEY	Don't act soft!
MOON	I'm gonna do an experiment.
HONEY	Again?
MOON	Get on the leather and roll like we're active.
HONEY	What?
MOON	Just do it!

HONEY *(begins to toss and turn as Moon creeps up to the door)*
Ooh Transportion. Ooh professional distance. Ooh shag pile.

(The doorbell rings a third time followed by a cough)

MOON *(opening the letter box and ramming the knife through)* Die,
die, die on a hot night in August, dirty Peeping Tom from Essex,

frotting yourself off on the doorstep whilst we discover delights
so delicious!

HONEY   Did you get him?

MOON   No.

HONEY   Try again.

MOON *(rams the knife and pulls out)* Not a trace.

HONEY   My turn *(she takes knife and shoves it through the
flap)* Nothing. Must be already deceased, already a phantom. A
see-through spectacle on the doorstep. Maybe he was another of
the clients. Tiny's slicing went too far. Slit his guts and down he
dropped. Coming back now. For visitations.

MOON   There are electrics everywhere. Cable all over the
place. Running underneath the carpet. There's bugs in the phone.
Cameras in the garden. Trigger switches on every surface. Tiny's
rigged up the house to keep us both in check. And that sofa has a
current connected from the leather to the doorbell that starts
heating up when the frotting gets active!

HONEY *(goes over to the sofa and starts chucking the cushions on
the floor)* Oh!

MOON   What is it?

HONEY   A scar. *(reaching down picks up a fake rubber scar
from the inside the sofa and holds it out)*

MOON   What?

HONEY   A fake rubber scar.

MOON   Eh?

HONEY   Delores. Her scar. From her face.

MOON   She must have left it.

HONEY   Yes.

MOON   Must have forgot to stick it on.

HONEY   Or Tiny forgot to stick it to her.

MOON   I don't understand.

HONEY *(putting it to her face)* Hiya I've got a three p.m. massage
with Cherise, my name is Lavender, Delores Lavender. Very
good with my make-up, skilful.

MOON   Don't understand.

HONEY	Tiny doesn't slice. Never sliced anyone.
MOON	I've seen him practice. Specific method enforce-ment.
HONEY	You've never seen him do it!
MOON	Must do.
HONEY	Expect he never gives out money.
MOON	Must do.
HONEY	Ever seen the wads?
MOON	No.
HONEY	Ever seen a client?
MOON	'Course.
HONEY	How many?
MOON	One.
HONEY	One?
MOON	Scooter boy.
HONEY	Scooter boy doesn't exist!
MOON	We should go home.

HONEY   No. There's stuff you better say. Because I'm way out of the picture here and when people are out the picture they either do something stupid or they push to get themselves in. Now I'd prefer the latter. Otherwise I might just not forget to put out my cigarette on this settee. Or piss all over the shag pile. Or snip at the wallpaper. So I suggest *you* finish the fable. Then *I* say what we do.

MOON	Can't.
HONEY	Why's that?
MOON	I promised him.

HONEY   Promised him shit. What did he promise you, wads of crispies? Clients? Casinos?

MOON	Yeah.
HONEY	Swallowed it?
MOON	Wanted to.
HONEY	You played right into his hands.
MOON	He needs me.

HONEY   He's a twisted. He's not Bruce Wayne. He's not
even Batman. He's joker and he's laughing all over Las Vegas.
Sitting in Caesar's Palace with his jaw on the floor. Splitting his
fucking sides. Tiny Lavender. Small time gangster. Big time wind
up.

MOON   You're wrong.

HONEY   Why?

MOON   He's not in Las Vegas.

HONEY   Where is he?

MOON   Walthamstow.

HONEY   You've got to give him credit! We come here on a
two week house sit. He gets a holiday in Walthamstow! This is
good. Very good.

MOON   We go out driving five nights a week because –

*(A spotlight comes up on one of the flying ducks and it quacks
loudly. Honey and Moon turn their heads around to look)*

MOON   What was that?

HONEY   Don't know.

MOON   It came from back there – sounded like an animal –
something farmyard.

HONEY   You and Tiny in the car five nights a week.

MOON   Not a pig.

HONEY   Sometimes drive to the coast.

MOON   Not a cow.

HONEY *(slapping Moon)* Get on with it.

MOON   We get to the coast. Canvey Island. Southsea. It's up
to him. When I started we'd get as far as Leytonstone. Sit in the
Tandoori. Just parley really. This and that. Chicken Vindaloo.
Bombay potatoes. Tiger beer. Only out till midnight. Drive him
back home. Delores would be waiting. In her dressing-gown.
Watch them embrace as she closes the door. Remote control in
her hand. Then we did the job. Scooter boy. Went round his flat.
Buzzed the bell. Young he was. No more that nineteen. Didn't
say a word. Let Tiny in. No questions. I waited in the car. He was
there hours. I got vacant. Fell asleep on the steering-wheel. He

woke me when he returned. Trembly. Looked like he'd been weeping. *(pause)* After that we'd go for longer. Out 'til the small hours. Drive him back and no Delores in her dressing-gown. Open up to an empty house. He'd wave at me from the doorstep.

HONEY   Fine fable.

MOON   No.

HONEY   You drive home and –

MOON   No more jobs after that. He just talks more and more. How they first met. Sweet stuff. Then the night after I confront scooter boy on the Vespa he tells me something else. Tells me all hook line and sinker –

(Lights come up on the duck and it quacks. Both their heads turn)

MOON   You hear that?

HONEY   Yes.

MOON   It's coming from the back wall.

HONEY   Could be.

MOON *(shouts)* It is going to kill me!

HONEY   The house?

MOON   No. The duck! The flaming quack quack.

HONEY *(walking over to the wall)* Which one?

MOON   It's an omen. A warning. *(talking to the ducks)* Alright Donald. You got it. Whatever you want.

HONEY   Donald?

MOON   And that one's Daffy and that one's Jemima.

HONEY   Jemima?

MOON   Donald. Daffy. Jemima.

HONEY   *Jemima?*

MOON   Puddleduck. Beatrix Potter.

HONEY   Finish the fucking fable!

MOON   No.

HONEY   Right. I'm going home.

MOON   You wouldn't.

HONEY   You can't feed me half a cake!

MOON   Please –

HONEY   Fucking feed me!

MOON   I'll rustle you up some booze.

HONEY   Feed me or I'm out the door.

MOON   They wanted kids. She never got pregnant. They did all the tests money can buy. Tiny doesn't make much cream and when he does don't pasteurize. Hits him bad. Gets depressed. Gets stressed. Doesn't get stiff much after that. Tried different things. Put in some romance. Get back the sex. Games. Fantasies. Dressing-up. Dressing-down. Till they hit forty. Run out of steam and he can't get a hard-on at all! Scooter boy's half the problem solved. Delores gets him five nights a week. Tiny's choice of lover. They set it up. He pays. I'm the other half. The off-loader. Delores's choice of driver. They set it up. She pays. He dreams his dreams. I give it reality. Anything he likes. Gangsters, guns, crispies, cuts. Drive. Drive. Drive him anywhere. Keep him from losing his noodles. Pays me well. Treats me right. Says if anything comes out. He'll know it's me and that's the bitter end.

(Light comes up on all the ducks which quack. Honey goes over to all three and takes them down. Pause)

HONEY   The doorbell. The phone. The wind. The cough. The scar.

MOON   Rigged up.

HONEY   The razor. The handcuffs. The 'do's and don'ts'.

MOON   There'll be more stuff. The place will be crammed with them.

HONEY   Why?

MOON   Fragments of his dream.

HONEY   He scares to keep you faithful.

MOON   To keep the dream alive.

HONEY   And yours.

MOON   What?

HONEY   Your dream too.

MOON   I haven't got sex problems!

HONEY   We're all guilty as each other. I'm a pop star with dyed blonde hair slicing through the fans like a hot knife through

Vienetta. Delores gets a massage once and a scooter boy five
times a week. Feeling like she's twenty-two with sex that never
sleeps. And Tiny with a cock that don't cock and too much T.V.
giving himself an Oscar with the role of a lifetime. We're all in it
together. Their names – Tiny and Delores?

MOON   Gordon and Lorraine.

HONEY   Gangster and ex-chorus girl?

MOON   Landlord and housewife.

HONEY   This house – *Maison Splendide?*

MOON   Definitely.

HONEY   The *house* is still the dream.

MOON   I've fed you all the cake.

HONEY   Yes. I liked it. Filling. Pleasing. Tasty.

MOON   Still want to go home?

HONEY   No. I want to celebrate.

MOON   What?

HONEY   The house. The garden. These four dreamers. They
could have got adoption. A.1. Kidnapping. But they became
anyone they wanted. We're still housesittees under contract.
We're still going to hoover up and make the bed. Like we never
knew the difference. I am Honey. You are Moon. They are Tiny
and Delores and Buckhurst Hill is still sweating away under the
heat of the August stars. *(picking up the paper and takeaway)*
Let's begin at the beginning.

*(They both strike up the same position as at the beginning on the
sofa. Take-away and newspaper in hand. Silence. Honey begins
to place her take-away on the floor)*

MOON   I said no.

HONEY   Don't want anymore.

MOON   It'll stain the carpet.

HONEY   Can't finish it.

MOON   Chuck it in the rubbish.

HONEY   You told me not to move!

MOON   Don't.

HONEY   How can I find the rubbish?

MOON   Give it here.

HONEY *(passing her the takeaway. Moon juggles the paper in one hand and the container in the other. Eventually she places them both on the floor)* Smart.

MOON   That's it.

HONEY   I wanna explore.

MOON   We're house-sitting not on *Star Trek*.

HONEY   You're here regular – I wanna look!

MOON   Sit still – you'll break something.

HONEY   I got to move sometime.

MOON   I'll get you everything.

HONEY   Everything?

MOON   Yes.

HONEY   What about a Snowball?

(Moon rises and goes over to the trolley. Honey shuffles on the chaise longue, looks under it and pulls out one of the cardboard boxes. She prises it open and begins to take out a spangly dress. Moon spins around)

MOON   What you doing?

HONEY   Nothing.

MOON   Put it back!

HONEY *(sings)* *'You can tell by the way I use my walk'* – Quite pretty – a bit seventies – *Saturday Night Fever*.

MOON   I'm gonna count to three. One . . .

HONEY *(sings)* *'I, I, I, Stayin' alive, stayin' alive . . .'* *(begins to put on the dress)*

MOON   . . . Two . . .

HONEY   Quite tight . . .

MOON   . . . Three –

HONEY   Come any nearer and I'll rip it. It'll be easier to fold than to stitch.

MOON   Put it back.

HONEY   *When* I've had a play. Back off or I bite. Yum. Yum.

MOON   O.K.

(Moon watches her putting on the dress which pinches a little but looks good. Honey then puts on her shoes by the door and stands looking at Moon)

HONEY   What d'you think?

MOON   Groovy.

HONEY   Can't reach the zip.

(Moon goes and does her up) I still wanna Snowball.

MOON   Got this out now.

HONEY   Can't have two toys at a time?

MOON   No.

HONEY   Well?

MOON   Changes you . . .

HONEY   For better?

MOON   Different. How d'you feel?

HONEY   Dreamy, like a Walnut Whip –

MOON   Chocolate and cream –

HONEY   What the girlie likes.

MOON   Sweet stuff.

HONEY / **MOON** Must have a tooth for it.

MOON   When we got money you can wear what you want.

HONEY   There's another box under there.

MOON   Yeah?

HONEY   Maybe something better.

MOON   That's two toys.

HONEY   Promise I'll clear up. *(dives into the box and pulls out a white suit, again in seventies' style)*

MOON   That's Tiny's.

HONEY   Must be.

MOON   No don't.

HONEY   Rock and roll.

MOON   He'll go ballistic.

HONEY   Try it.

MOON   Not my style.

HONEY *(sings)* '*You can tell by the way I use my walk . . .*'
(lunges at Moon and starts to take off her clothes and dress her up. Moon is totally compliant) He won't mind us borrowing it. Like the money he'll get it back. That's his business. Got to start letting go. You're walking coronary. Whatever we disturb – we put back. Whatever we use – we replace. We're not in a museum, we're in *Maison Splendide* – let's get living.

MOON   It's taking the piss.

HONEY   It's us . . . and you look dandy.

MOON   Yeah?

HONEY   Umm, how do you feel?

MOON   Kinda flarey, kinda darey, kinda tip-top –

HONEY   Better.

MOON   Get some of this! *(giving attitude with the suit)*

HONEY *(linking arms)* What a pair!

MOON   We'll knock 'em dead one day. Mobile phones. Customised number plates. Holiday time-shares . . .

HONEY   Don't want you hurt.

MOON   Talk soft.

HONEY   Coming home with your face on your shirt.

MOON   I'm smart.

HONEY   So am I.

MOON   That's why we gonna cut through. Out of the rented room . . . into the maisonette.

        (pause)

HONEY   I don't know what I'd say. If you asked –

MOON   What?

HONEY   How long 'ave we been going?

MOON   Known you since school.

HONEY   Never crossed your mind?

MOON   Tie the knot?

HONEY   Yeah.

MOON   We don't need a bit of paper. We need the wad of crispies else we'll always stay at the bottom – when we should be at the top.

HONEY   All I hear is money and thinking big. Take a load
     closer to home. I'm talking.

MOON   I hear you.

HONEY   What d'you call me?

MOON   Honey.

HONEY   Why?

MOON   'Cos your tooth is sweet and you love it on your
     toast.

HONEY   What do I call you?

MOON   Moon.

HONEY   Why?

MOON   'Cos I work nights and my eyes look like stars.

HONEY   Put them together what you got?

MOON   Gold and silver.

HONEY   And the best holiday after the business. Propose!
     Down on your bended.

MOON   I ain't doing that!

HONEY   Alright. *(gets down and holds out her hand)* Please
     be mine.

MOON   You'll spoil the dress.

HONEY *(shouts)* Get on with it!

MOON   I'm yours.

HONEY   Right we need a guest list, a couple of witnesses,
     someone to do the honours, speeches, and a party complete with
     catering à la carte, bubbly, live band and prezzies galore.

MOON   Where we gonna get all that?

HONEY   Use your noodle! *(dashes over to the wall and pulls
     off the flying ducks and places them on the floor)* The guests.

MOON   Who are they?

HONEY   My mum and dad and your brother Len.

MOON   Len won't come.

HONEY   Why?

MOON   He hates vol-e-vants.

HONEY   There'll be other stuff.

MOON   What like?

HONEY   Steak Diane.

MOON   That's better. He likes it well done, mind. Blood makes him squeamy.

HONEY   Anyway he's your only family – he don't make it and you're all out of guests . . . Right, witnesses . . . there ain't much here.

MOON *(pointing to the boxes)* Use the cardboard.

HONEY   Yeah – take a box each. Who can they be?

MOON   Delores and Tiny.

HONEY *(places them on the floor)* Delores. Tiny.

MOON   Right. What about the cadeaux?

HONEY   What?

MOON   The pocket-burners, the from me to you's –

HONEY   Yes, and I need a bauble for the digit. *(she waggles finger)*

MOON   Smart.

HONEY   Find something. *(picking up the newspaper)* Wrap it in that and give it to me.

MOON *(looks about)* I don't know.

HONEY   Use those starry brights –

MOON   Shut yours. Can't get a cadeau when you know what it is. *(she shuts them)* No cheating.

HONEY   O.K.

MOON *(she goes over to the drinks trolley and pulls out the bottle of Avocad. Wraps it in the newspaper. She undoes the lid and pulls off the bottom of the bottle's lid and holds it in her hand for a ring)* All done. Your turn. *(she clamps shut eyes)*

HONEY *(lifts up the cushions on the chaise. One makes a noise, she opens it up and finds a wad of notes)* Crispies – never seen such a wad –

MOON *(opening eyes)* What you found?

HONEY   Shut 'em.

MOON   Leave it!

HONEY *(looking at money)* We're stealing presents – but we put them back – they're just for the occasion.

MOON If there's one missing, she'll know – Delores's got a Xerox head.

HONEY Relax!

MOON They can't put too much through the bank –

HONEY *(wraps it up)* Should have a safe then! Crispies in the cushions!

MOON Are we fixed for prezzies?

HONEY *(going to the Karaoke machine)* Absolutely. Help me with this –

MOON What for?

HONEY Gonna do the honours.

MOON The boogie box?

HONEY Yes. Grab a mike and shoot some breeze.

MOON What kind?

HONEY Sweet stuff. Privatisation.

MOON Out with the Kleenex.

HONEY Three things for me. Three things for you. On why we're still together. Hopes and promises. *(she turns on the music score – Barry White's: 'You're the first, the last, my everything')* Take it away –

MOON *(unsure at first. Honey swings all the time)* I am with you. Because when I was kipping in the back row of form six, you poured acid over my skin and I couldn't wash it off for weeks. I hope you'll be there when I'm ancient and slowly losing my noodles. I promise you harmony throughout our days ahead and a fat wad of crispies if I push the daisies up before you.

HONEY I am with you. Because I found you kipping in the back row of form six and I gave you starry brights to see me with and I couldn't close my curtains for weeks. I hope you'll always be mine even when my bonanzas are down to here *(indicates with hands down to waist)*. Even when my bonanzas are down to here *(indicates her knees)*. I promise to make you toasty when it's cold and a Beechams if you end up getting one.

HONEY / MOON *(sing) 'You're the first, the last, my everything.'*

HONEY   Is there anyone here who knows anything that should stop this couple getting together this instant, speak now or forever keep your motor in the garage because from here forth they are now pronounced –

MOON   Married.

HONEY   Married! Slip on the ring.

MOON *(slips it on Honey's finger)* Like a dream.

HONEY   Chocolate and cream.

MOON   Sweet stuff.

HONEY   What the girlie likes.

HONEY and **MOON** Must have a tooth for it!

They kiss and then hand each other the presents. Moon goes over to pick up the take-away in the tinfoil and throws the rice over their heads. The doorbell rings. The telephone rings. The ducks quack. The sound of coughing and wind. Lights down.

The end.

Laura Bridgeman

Trained as an actor at East 15 and the National Youth Theatre and currently writes under commission and for her own company **girl/boy.** Her previous productions include **Billie Blue** (The Oval House Theatre Downstairs) 1995, **Medicine Girl** (Guinness Ingenuity Award. The Etcetera One Person Play Festival) 1996, **Junk** (Gay Sweatshop commission for Club Deviance tour) 1997, **Loonatik** (girl/boy commission, funded by The London Arts Board for The British Festival of Visual Theatre) 1997 and **Heathens** (Wild Lunch 2 reading for Paines Plough writers group) 1998.

Current commissions include **45** (The Arts Council New Writing Department) 1998 and **Etiquette** (B.B.C. Radio 4 drama) 1998.

In the Fields of Aceldama

by Naomi Wallace

In the Fields of Aceldama

Notes:

The play is set on a small farm in Kentucky. The stage design is minimal and not realistic. The scene and time changes should be signalled by lighting. The use of typical farm instruments or props such as pitchforks, hay, old tyres etc. must be avoided. (The exception is the sack of grain that represents Mattie's mother during the suffocation scene). Any inclination to work from clichés such as 'backwoods America' etc. should be strictly avoided. The stage floor should not look 'farm-like' or 'real' in any sense. Wooden boards that criss-cross at sharp angles might be effective. These boards might suggest the furrows in a field but be made of a material that counterpoints this same idea. The lighting should be neither 'poetic' nor 'dramatic'.

The three characters are on stage at all times. The characters exist in their own right, but also in a sense, only in Mattie's mind. The 'Enemy' referred to in the play is whatever people or nation in the world happens to be at odds with United States foreign policy.

Naomi Wallace

In the Fields of Aceldama

by Naomi Wallace

First produced by London New Play Festival in 1993 at the Old Red
Lion Theatre, Islington.
Directed by Jessica Dromgoole.
Designed by Naomi Wilkinson.

Mattie mother, mid-thirties   Anna Clarkson
Henry her husband, mid-forties, balding   Ian Bailey
Annie their daughter, 17 years   Maureen Purkis

SCENE 1

*A small farm in Kentucky. In the present time. Dark stage. The sound
of a child's xylophone is heard, undercut by the sound of sawing,
which occasionally takes on the skewed sound of a helicopter.
Whispering begins, which starts softly, then builds. Then silence.*

ANNIE *(chants)* Worm, Worm, go away.

MATTIE   Not that one.

ANNIE *(chants)* Come again another day.

MATTIE   Play the game, child.

ANNIE   No.

MATTIE   Play the game, little Yankee.

ANNIE   Dark, dark go away.

MATTIE   Always hiding. Always hid.

ANNIE *(sings)* 'This is the way the Ladies walk
    Clippety-Clop, Clippety-Clop'

MATTIE   Not that one either.

ANNIE   Alright. Who's there?

MATTIE   Good girl. But let me knock first. *(raps on the stage,
    twice, loudly, in the dark)*

(Again the sound of the saw. This time we notice Henry's shadow and that he is the one sawing. But we only hear the sound and see the motion of sawing; there is no saw. We hear Annie's voice in the darkness)

ANNIE   Who's there? *(frightened)* Who's there? *(shouts)* Who's there?

Lights up. Mattie comes out of hiding, pulling a metal tub.

MATTIE   Oh quiet down child; I made you the dress.

ANNIE *(she is wearing a clean, white, plain nightgown which she wears for the entire play. She is barefoot. The 'sack' Mattie dresses her in is 'seen' by the two of them, but not by the audience)* For the dance? *(she stands on the back of tub)*

MATTIE   You'll be the prettiest potato on the dance floor.

ANNIE   But it's a sack.

MATTIE   Now it's a dress.

ANNIE *(threatening)* I'll wet my pants!

MATTIE   I'll break the neck off your puppet.

ANNIE   But it's a sack.

MATTIE   There's no need to be looking too pretty for those little soldier boys.

ANNIE *(sincerely)* Am I pretty, mother?

MATTIE   Spread your legs so I can pin it.

ANNIE   Ouch. You pricked me. *(beat)* Ouch!

MATTIE   Stop whimpering. This will break you in. Hold still.

HENRY *(sneaking near to spy on them, sings)* Los soldados se rebelaron durante la batalla . . .

ANNIE *(finishes song)* . . . y el lugarteniente se suicido.

MATTIE *(harshly)* Get in the tub. Now!
(Annie runs away. Mattie climbs in the tub and speaks with a girl's voice. She is reliving an experience she had as a child)
I won't take a bath without my underwear on. I won't let you see my privates! *(her own voice)* But you're only twelve years old. What have you got to hide?

Lights dim on Annie and Mattie, who moves into the shadows. Lights up on Henry who sneaks nearer, confiding to the audience.

HENRY *(whispering)* I never touched the child. But a person has a right, you know. She was mine too. This is my leg *(clutches leg)*. I have a right. This is my ear *(pulls it)*. She was my kid. *(beat)* This is my land.
(Henry now speaks to Mattie who moves to an area that represents the 'stall.' She begins to talk to the horse, which we do not see but imagine is there. She speaks not in a cute way, but with serious affection. He follows her and waits outside the stall) I've been thinking seriously again and I think its time.

MATTIE   It's not time yet, Henry.

HENRY   I think it is. It's time.

MATTIE   I said it's not.

HENRY   It's for your own good, Mattie.

MATTIE   It's not Sunday today, Henry. You're still in your suit.

HENRY   Maybe today. Maybe tomorrow. You never know when I might be called up to fight.

MATTIE *(talking about the horse)* I gave her a handful of those dried apricots this morning. It sweetens her breath like nothing else will.

HENRY   Where's your body, Mattie? Why don't you put on a dress like you used to and let me see your shape?

MATTIE   Pants protect the knees. I can't drive the tractor in a dress.

HENRY *(stamps foot angrily a few times until Mattie turns slowly around)* Move out of the way. I'm taking that horse off this farm.

MATTIE   Take off your jacket and get back to work.

HENRY *(changing approach)* Knock, knock . . .
(Mattie looks at him but doesn't respond)
Knock, knock . . .

MATTIE   No-one's home, Henry.

HENRY   Knock, knock, knock, knock . . .

MATTIE *(reluctantly)* Who's there?

HENRY *(triumphantly)* Owl.

MATTIE   Owl who?

HENRY   Owls about a rub, darling? *(he rubs his bald head. Mattie can't help chuckling)* Tickle, tickle.

MATTIE   Not there.

HENRY   Where not there?

MATTIE   Your guess.

HENRY   In your ear?

(Mattie shakes her head 'no') Above the knee? Where you pee? *(Mattie laughs, still shaking her head 'no')* Now you do one.

MATTIE   Uh-uh.

HENRY   Do one of those you and Annie did together.

MATTIE   Nope. Those were between me and her.

HENRY   I bet you forgot them.

MATTIE   I haven't forgotten any.

HENRY   Sure, sure.

MATTIE *(offensive)* Knock, knock . . .

HENRY   Who's there?

MATTIE   Knock, knock . . .

HENRY   I already said: 'Who's there.' *(louder)* Who in the hell is there?

MATTIE   Kent.

HENRY   Kent who?

MATTIE   Kent get it up, can you?

HENRY   Lulu taught you that one, not Annie.

MATTIE   Bang, bang.

HENRY   Who's there?

MATTIE   Harry.

HENRY   Harry who?

MATTIE   He doesn't like it hairy, he likes it shaved. *(to audience)* Do you? Do you like it shaved?

(Henry slips unnoticed past her. When Mattie sees the trick, she grabs a long stick, which serves as both a hoe and broom, and whacks him on the behind with it) Get away from that stall or I'll drive this blade right through your head.

HENRY   Put that down, Mattie. You're mixed up.

MATTIE   Mixed, mixed.

HENRY   You aren't like you used to be.

MATTIE   Used to be.

HENRY   Like when I met you. You were lively as a cricket.

MATTIE   Cricket, cricket.

HENRY   It's been two years. That horse reminds us too much.

MATTIE   I like being reminded.

HENRY   But it's no good, Mattie. You're still a young
woman.

MATTIE   A young woman.

(This monologue should be told without any 'emotion'. It is told in a detached manner so that the language will be foregrounded and 'speak' for itself. There might also be an enjoyment for the simple fun of telling a story and being in command of the story)
I was sweeping the porch when the horse came galloping back from the field, alone. I thought: 'that damn animal has thrown her again'. So I screamed: 'Henry! Henry!' and I dropped the broom and started running out to the field where the horse came from . . . *(becomes exhilarated in telling the story)* So I ran and I ran and up ahead I'd already spotted, way in the distance, that shape on the ground. I remember the running, the thrill at how fast my feet were speeding over the ground, all the while screaming: 'Henry! Henry!' but he was slow and struggling and panting behind me. *(speaks more slowly now, but with awe rather than any visible pain)* And then I came to it, that shape on the ground, and I dropped to my knees *(does so)* and there she was, lying there like she was napping.
(Upstage Annie gets on swing in the shadows and begins to swing and hum softly)
Except for one thing – a trickle of blood that ran from her nose. I wiped it with my apron. *(now she speaks directly to the dead child we can't see)* It's time for supper, child. It's time for supper and tonight you're gonna eat every one of those peas. *(beat)* Child, don't push me. I've had a hard day. *(starts to get angry)* You're being naughty again and testing my patience. *(she slowly raises her arm to slap the dead child we can't see. She speaks*

with strength, not hysteria) So I slapped her and slapped her again, hard, and again even harder. And again and again.

HENRY   Stop it. Stop it. She's dead, Mattie. Look at her face. Look at it. Can't you see she's dead?

(Annie comes up behind Mattie. Lights change. Annie begins to search through Mattie's hair for lice. Mattie enjoys this, closing her eyes and smiling. Annie does a thorough job and also seems to enjoy it)

ANNIE   If you'd wash it with a dandruff shampoo it might help. *(beat)* Hand out.

(Mattie holds up her hand and Annie puts the bug she's found in it)

MATTIE   Lice love shampoo, child. The more you give them the fatter they get.

ANNIE   I don't like picking Lulu's hair.

MATTIE   You pick mine.

ANNIE   But her hair comes out with the bugs. And her head bleeds.

MATTIE   She's my mother. You'll pick her when I tell you to.

ANNIE   I want a horse. *(beat)* Arms up.

(Mattie raises her arm over her head and Annie kneels next to her and searches under her arms for lice. Mattie does not shave her armpits anymore)

MATTIE   She's your grandmother. She tells you bed-time stories.

ANNIE   There's one for sale out in Jefferson. The owner said he'd trade it to us cheap, for our old plow. *(beat)* I never understand a word of her stories. She tells them in Basque.

MATTIE *(amused)* A horse for a broken plow. Hmmm. Must be some horse.

ANNIE   It's got white hooves.

MATTIE   Lulu's giving you the sound of it and that's better than the story. You don't need to know the words.

ANNIE   I want to have it.

(Mattie just smiles) I'm going to have it.

MATTIE   Give me a kiss.
(Annie kisses her on the mouth. Mattie doesn't respond)
Not there. On the neck, where I like it.
*(Annie bites the side of Mattie's neck playfully, but hard enough
to make Mattie flinch)* Alright. Little dog wants to play. *(she
jumps to her feet)* Let's play. *(she circles Annie, snapping at the
air. Annie shrieks with delight at the game and responds in kind
so that the two of them are crouching and circling each other,
snapping and growling)*

Lights dim on them and come up on Henry. Annie runs off.

HENRY   But it's been two years since you rubbed it, Mattie.

MATTIE   More than two years.

HENRY   But that's why I married you. You were the only one
who ever cared to rub it.

MATTIE   It's got a cheesy smell, Henry. I can't stomach it
anymore.

HENRY *(to audience)* When we first met I was shy about it, hid it
under my cap. But on our first date she knocked that cap right off
and took to rubbing my bald head with her palm like it was an
Aladdin's lamp. *(rubs his bald head vigorously)* It made me feel
special in a way I never had before.

MATTIE   I was silly. I polished what came my way.

HENRY *(to audience)* When she finally kissed me here, on this bald
spot –

MATTIE   I was being polite. That's how I was brought up.

HENRY *(continuing)* I just had to ask her to marry me, right then
and there.

MATTIE *(speaks to Annie, though we don't know who she is
speaking to as Annie is elsewhere on stage)* If you stop that
squirming I'll finish the story now.

HENRY   I've been to the Priest and he says you should start
coming to church again.

MATTIE   I stopped irritating the Lord. He's stopped irritating
me.

HENRY   Then you won't rub it?

MATTIE   I rubbed it once and it got me married. I rubbed it again and it got us a child.

HENRY *(whispers)* Buckwheat . . . bulgar . . . pomegranate

MATTIE   It's too late, Henry.

HENRY *(coaxing)* Basil spring . . . cumin seed . . .

MATTIE   Pot's been stirred. Leave it be. *(she plops down to take off her boots)*

HENRY *(following)* . . . black-eyed pea . . .

MATTIE *(ignoring)* I never could wear a size nine.

HENRY   That's because you're a size ten.

MATTIE   I'm a size nine, just like my mother, Lulu.

HENRY   She was a ten too. *(he moves off)*

MATTIE   She was a ten in the old country. Not here. When Lulu got to America she made up her mind about life: 'If I'm going to be an American then I'll have to wear small shoes.'

HENRY *(speaks from shadows)* She had peasant's feet.

MATTIE   Before she died she made me promise to get her a pair of those expensive soft leather shoes, in size eight, so she'd look grand at her funeral. I had to break her toes to get them to fit. *(beat)* Snap, snap, snap. Just like snapping beans. *(jumps up and speaks excitedly to audience)* You remember that Basque song your grandmother taught you? Sing it. *(shouts)* Sing it, I tell you.

(Silence. She now approaches Annie, whose back is turned to her. She speaks to Annie as though Annie were Lulu)

How many times have I got to say it, mother? We'll get the money somehow and build you that little room on our cabin. You'll come live with us. *(beat)* Stop worrying. Henry's a good man. He tells me I'm sturdy. I like being sturdy. *(beat)* No, no. All he's ever been to me is gentle. *(beat)* I want to marry him. *(beat)* The other day he picked a scab off my elbow and I didn't feel a thing. Maybe it's not your ordinary kind of love, mother, but I believe in it.

(Annie moves away shaking her head)

We're going to give you as many grandchildren as I've got toes. *(beat)* Damn it, Mother, be happy for me!

Lights now dim on Mattie, who moves off into the shadows and begins digging. Lights up on Henry who is sitting on the tractor /sawing block, having a good time. He is apparently at a bar. He uses his hands as puppets to present the different voices.

HENRY   **Voice one** Hey, music's too loud!
Voice Two What's up yours, buddy? You don't like Western music?
Voice Three Some kind of a Commie, are you?
Voice One *(sings)* And it's one, two, three
                    What are we fighting for?
                    Don't ask me, I don't give a damn.
                    Next stop is –
Voice Three Big Saddam! *(beat)* Yeah!
Voice Two Where's you're American flag, bub?
Voice Three Love it, cowboy, or leave it.
Voice One *(chants)* Support our troops!
Voice Two *(sings)* Tie a yellow ribbon round the old oak tree . . .
Voice Three Let me buy you a beer, partner. So what colour's your flag?
Voice One *(sings to the tune of 'Rawhide')* Burn it, burn it, burn it. Keep those babies burning.
Voice Three Rawhide!
(now he speaks to the audience as though he were seducing someone in the audience) Ah, come on you sweet, green thing. Mattie knows. She doesn't mind, ever since the accident. Ten dollars? That's money I don't have. Alright. Alright, you pretty, little green bean, get in. *(he swings up on the block as though it were a truck and helps imaginary lady up on his lap. He pretends to drive a while, whispering in her ear, laughing. Then breaks suddenly. Sternly)* Get out. I said: Get out.
(Dim lights up, upstage left, on Annie, who stands facing the audience)
Take off your clothes. Go on. I paid you. *(shouts)* Do it!

(Henry watches imaginary woman undress in front of him. He is unaware that Annie responds to his words. She shakes her head in refusal) Now throw me your clothes.

(Annie doesn't move, but he catches the imaginary clothes in his arms, then climbs back on block) See you in town, grass-hopper. Have a nice walk.

(After some moments pretending to drive, there is a silence, then he begins to laugh at the joke he's played. He slowly gets down off the tractor and addresses the audience again. Annie, crouches and turns her back to the audience. He circles the imaginary woman)

Hey, I was just fooling. *(silence)* Will you look at me? I said, I was just fooling.

(After some moments he begins to search in his pockets until he finds his pet mole. Slowly he pulls it out of his pocket, calls) Mattie. It's dead again.

(Lights dim on Annie. Mattie speaks from the shadows)

MATTIE   I told you not to leave it in your pocket.

HENRY   Drowned.

MATTIE *(comes into light)* You know I wash on Fridays.

HENRY   Drowned. Just like the last one.

MATTIE   Next time, take the mole out of your pocket before I put your shirt in the wash.

HENRY *(fingers mole in his hand)* Tickle, tickle.

MATTIE *(comes into light)* Where?

HENRY   Not you. Her. *(points to mole)*

MATTIE   Go catch another one. *(beat)* I'm stocking the supplies for you so you'll have enough to eat.

HENRY   It's not that easy. They're delicate. You can only give them little bits of daylight at a time.

MATTIE   Even if you can keep one alive for more than a couple of weeks, even if it learns to live in the open air, it'll still be in the dark. Cause it's blind, Henry.

HENRY   You can't leave me, Mattie. *(beat)* Did you know wives that leave their husbands grow big feet?
(Mattie stares at her feet) The size of buckets.

MATTIE   Then I won't have to buy new shoes.

HENRY   The size of bathtubs.

MATTIE *(musing)* You know, I've never been past the Oldham county line?

Lights change. Mattie and Henry are courting.

HENRY   Let me smell you, Mattie.

MATTIE   Don't talk like that. You shouldn't put it to words. *(she pulls his head between her breasts and he breathes deep. Then he slides down to her belly. As he moves lower she moves away)*

MATTIE   Not there.

HENRY   Where not there? Above your knee?

MATTIE *(laughs)* Where I pee?

HENRY   I bet you're smooth as a girl down there.

MATTIE   Am not.

HENRY   Bet you are.

MATTIE   I'm not a girl, Henry.

HENRY   I bet you got buttercups on your panties.

MATTIE   You're not marrying a girl.

HENRY   We'll see.

MATTIE   Daddy won't give us the field with the pond.

HENRY   Why not?

MATTIE   He won't say.

HENRY   Did you ask him nicely?

MATTIE   Of course I did. He pulled my ear so I spat at him.

HENRY *(grabs her by the hair roughly)* This is important to me, Mattie. I thought you understood that.

MATTIE   I hit him with a wad just below his Adams.

HENRY   I want that piece of land. Ten years from now it will make a difference. *(beat)* Ask him again. Show him some respect.

MATTIE   Oh, to hell with his dirty old piece of land! Tell him you'll marry me without it.

HENRY   I need that piece of land.

MATTIE   You know, I promised Mother that as soon as we get up the money we'll build her a room on the cabin.

HENRY   If I had it I could sell it ten years from now for twice the money.

MATTIE   She can come live with us and I'll buy her some expensive dentures so she won't have to sip her bread through a straw.

HENRY   Let your Daddy buy her her teeth. He knocked them out.

MATTIE *(notices his shoe-lace is untied, kneels to tie it)* When I think about how it's going to be, all of us living together in your house, I get this feeling like a hand is opening up inside me and it's snapping its fingers from the joy of it.

HENRY   That's my hand you're hearing. Just listen.
(he begins snapping his fingers. Mattie pulls his hand against her ear. When she catches the rhythm of it she gets up and stamps her feet in accompaniment. She does a movement in between a military step and a dance as Henry sings)

> Hup, two three, four
> Liberty's what we're fighting for.
> Hup, two, three, four
> Spreading peace from shore to shore.
> Hup, two, three, four.
> Standing by the U.S. Law.

(speaks to Mattie) You should join up with me, sweetheart. You'd keep our spirits high. *(beat)* Come on over here.

Lights change and Mattie now moves to an area designated as a garden where Annie is making holes with a stick. Mattie kneels to join her. Henry remains in the shadows, he spies on them, crawling on his belly. Mattie makes the hole and Annie drops in the seed. The actions can be mimed.

MATTIE *(enthusiastic)* So I made Paul climb up the rope to the loft first, so he wouldn't get a peak at my panties. *(smacks Annie in the head, though it shocks neither of them)* Don't put two in. One seed per hole. *(continues)* Pretty soon we were both as itchy as goats. You haven't got any hair, he said, when I took off my panties. I was only ten, you know. *(breaks off)* Stop picking at that scab. Don't smear it on your clothes. Here, wipe it on my apron.

(Annie smears it on the ground)

Then my sister was down below yelling for me. You see, Paul was her boyfriend, not mine. But she never knew. Ha!

(Annie gets up and begins to brush Mattie's hair with her fingers. She begins gently but slowly becomes more rough)

My sister Tara thought she was the prettiest girl in Oldam Country. She used to take her clothes off in front of me and say: 'I've got tits and you don't.'

(Annie begins to echo Mattie's words)

ANNIE   Tits and you don't.

MATTIE   She called me Princess Toad and made me kiss her toes.

ANNIE   Kiss her toes.

MATTIE   Her feet smelled like liver. But I got her back, oh yeah.

ANNIE   Her back, oh yeah.

MATTIE   Paul liked me and she never knew. The bitch.

ANNIE   The bitch.

MATTIE   Tara thought I was so stupid she had to show me how to do it. Just like my Father, my sister would make me watch her.

(Annie is now jerking hard on Mattie's hair but Mattie doesn't notice)

ANNIE   Watch her, watch her.

MATTIE   She'd put a tune on the radio and then she'd start brushing her hair.

(Annie moves off into the shadows and begins to slowly move to a rhythm she hears in Mattie's voice)

Tara had some long hair too. Then she'd undress and brush her hair some more.

(Annie begins to hum, and touch herself as a child might, who is exploring her body for the first time)

She'd start going over her body with the brush, brushing it up and down her skin. It made me sick to watch her moaning and groaning and brushing and brushing. And then she'd marry the brush.

(Annie freezes)

That didn't take long.

(Annie collapses on the floor)

And when Tara was finished she'd call me a dirty little girl for spying on her.

(spits on girl's back. They are motionless a few moments)

How much?

ANNIE *(springs up and is playful)* Much.

MATTIE   Show me.

ANNIE *(stretching out her arms wide)* This much.

MATTIE   Is that all? If you can't show me a better *much* I'll have to tickle you again.

ANNIE *(happily playing the game)* This much I love you. *(stretches exaggeratedly)*

MATTIE   Alright, you asked for it. *(she grabs Annie and begins to tickle her until Annie collapses and Mattie straddles her, still tickling)*

ANNIE   Stop it. Stop, Mother. Stop or I'll go. I swear it. *(beat)* Shit.

(Mattie quits tickling) I went.

MATTIE   Of course you went, child. You're my baby, aren't you? Come on, I'll change your pants.

ANNIE   Can we pick blackberries after supper?

(Mattie nods, helping Annie to her feet. Mattie notices the wet spot on the stage and bends to touch it, then licks her finger, as though testing the urine for something)

Mother! You promised you'd quit that!

MATTIE   You still got a healthy taste child. Hmmm. Possibly a little short of Vitamin C.

Annie playfully smacks Mattie's head. Both laugh. Lights dim on them, up on Henry.

HENRY   I saw a birthmark on my wife's neck the other day that I never noticed before, in all these years. *(beat)* She's holding out on me. *(jumps up and speaks in the direction of the stall)* Yeah, chew those oats slow, nice and slow. Enjoy yourself. You haven't got much longer, pal.
(he turns to the audience to speak. Annie moves about the stage, hiding and interrupting Henry by finishing sentences for him. The lines overlap slightly. He does not seem to notice)
I get this dream sometimes and I'm lying on top of the dirt and below me I hear 'knock, knock' I open my mouth to say 'who's there?' but no sound /

ANNIE   comes out. So the knock, knock tries again but I still can't get the /

HENRY   'Who's there?' out. So the knock, knock, gets louder and angrier /

ANNIE   but I can't make a sound to answer it /

HENRY   and I get so wild I can't breathe.
(Annie moves again into the shadows. Henry feels his pockets in a panic, but finding the mole there, relaxes)
But it takes patience, you know. You've got to sit down and wait. Annie would sit in the yard for hours *(in the shadows Annie moves and squats, as though watching for a mole)* until one came up close enough to the surface. Then she'd shout –

ANNIE *(whispers)* Daddy! Daddy! *(continues whispering 'Daddy, hurry up. I can see it move' etc. while he speaks)*

HENRY   and I'd drop what I was doing and come running with the shovel. She'd tell me exactly where to slide the blade so I wouldn't hurt the little fellow. She had one tamed so good it ate roots out of her hand. One day she was at school and I decided to surprise her with another one and I waited and waited, Mattie yelling at me to get back to work.
(Annie quits whispering)
Then I saw the dirt move, once, twice – I grabbed the shovel and dug like mad. *(beat)* Cut the mole clean in two. Well, one half lay dead at my boot while the other half kept on digging to get back under the dirt. I buried both the pieces in a hole. Mattie saw it all.

I was sure she'd tell Annie, just to see the child cry, but she didn't. I'm thankful to her for that.

(Mattie appears upstage, pushing the swing . She swings it harder as Henry speaks. Lights on Henry and Mattie now) But I've still got patience. And slow by slow things will be getting better. *(chuckles)* I've seen some good signs lately. *(Mattie suddenly stops the motion of the swing. There is no movement now on stage. Then Mattie calls out, as though to someone at a great distance, though she does not face in Annie's direction)*

MATTIE   Annie . . .

(Annie is startled at the sound of her name but Mattie does not see her)

HENRY *(to audience)* When I met Mattie she was almost eighteen. I married *her* and not somebody else. That's got to mean something.

He begins to sing, and lights change. He and Mattie are courting.

HENRY *(sings)* My darling is my baby
                    My darling is my girl
                    I'm gonna put her in my jet
                    and take her for a whirl

(he finds Mattie sitting and he takes off her shoe as he sings and plays a game with her toes. She enjoys the game. Then he bends back a toe until she gasps)

HENRY   Love me true, Mattie?

MATTIE   Hey!

HENRY *(bends her toe further)* Are you going to be a faithful wife?

MATTIE   Of course. Ouch.

HENRY *(bends her toe harder)* Hope to die?

MATTIE *(shouts)* Hope to die. *(he releases her. She rubs her toes)* My toe will swell.

HENRY   No it won't. *(beat)* I was only fooling. *(he takes her leg again and lies it across his lap. He picks a scab on her knee as they talk)* I should join up, Mattie. Everybody else is.

MATTIE   So . . . you're not a copy-cat.

HENRY   I could make some decent money. More than I make from this farm. *(he picks her scab more roughly)*

MATTIE   Your feet are no good. *(beat)* Not so hard.

HENRY   Doesn't a patriotic man mean anything to you?

MATTIE   Marrying me will be patriotic. Ouch!

HENRY   I was in town the other day and a man I've known as my neighbour all my life, asked me why I wasn't doing my duty like other men.

MATTIE   What's the use of picking off a scab if you make it bleed again?

HENRY   He spit on my boot. *(beat)* I want to get married now. Why wait six months?

MATTIE   Lie down. *(beat)* Lie down.
(Henry lies down and Mattie rubs her bare feet on his head. This is what he likes best)

HENRY   Feels like I'm flying. Like I'm an airplane and you're loading my guns.
(Mattie giggles. Then he suddenly turns on all fours. She jumps up) And now that my guns are loaded, what are you going to do about it?

Mattie runs off laughing. Annie comes from the shadows.

HENRY   Where's your mother?

ANNIE   At the store.

HENRY   OK then, but don't tell her I taught you. Let's do the slow one first. *(he takes Annie in his arms)* Hum a little something, so we feel the mood.
(They turn slowly, awkwardly, Annie hums. After some moments, Henry joins in the humming)

ANNIE   It's too tight.
(Henry doesn't respond) Too tight. Let go.
(Henry releases her abruptly. She stumbles)

HENRY   Use that tone again and I'll swat you.

ANNIE   It hurt my ribs.

HENRY   See my leg? *(grabs it)* It's mine. My arm? *(grabs arm)* The same. Your ribs are mine. Your leg is mine.

ANNIE   Then what of me is mine?

HENRY *(ignores her question)* What you got there is just a loan. Don't forget it. Well . . . Now what did I tell you to remember at the dance?

ANNIE   No touching.

HENRY   No touching, picking, plucking or poking. These are dangerous times, honey. Don't forget there's a war on. If we don't watch out for each other, foreign things are going to take over. Foreign bodies. *(kinder)* Ah, don't look so down, grasshopper. Sit on my knee. Come on.
(Annie does so, reluctant but also relieved) Now, who was your first and favourite horse?

ANNIE *(cheering)* Daddy!

HENRY   Well then!

ANNIE   Thunderbird was its name.
(Henry begins to buck his legs about. Annie balances)

HENRY   Catch hold of that streak of lightning, girl . . . straight into battle . . . My Annie sure can ride!

Lights dim on them and up on Mattie, alone, stage right. She is whittling. In the shadows we see the bucking of the horse game continuing.

MATTIE   None of the women from the Basque country ever shaved under their armpits. Mother said their men thought it was sexy. *(beat)* My mother, Lulu, she came over from Spain some years after the Big War and met Father. At the wedding his sisters dressed her. One of his sisters fainted when she saw Mother's soft black hair poking out from under her arms. *(beat)* Father had to find a razor to shave her with. They had to do a rush job so as not to hold up the ceremony too long. *(beat)* When I was sixteen, Lulu gave me the dress she married in.
(Annie now finishes Mattie's thoughts for her)

ANNIE *(whispers)* Where the pits of the arms had been, the cloth was stained brown with the blood.

(Mattie is startled by Annie's voice, then she kneels and knocks on the stage floor. She listens – no answer. She knocks twice again, harder. This knocking wakes Henry. Frightened, Annie runs and hides. From the other side of the stage, Henry now begins to knock aggressively in answer)

MATTIE *(frightened)* Who's there?

HENRY *(whispers)* It's Lulu.

MATTIE   No!

HENRY   Yes, yes.

MATTIE   Mother? Is that you?

HENRY *(sings to the tune of 'skip-to-my-Lou.')*
        I'm Lulu, turning blue
        I'm Lulu, turning blue.

MATTIE   Quiet! . . . Hush!

HENRY *(sings)* Lulu, how do you do?
        I'm turning blue, my darling . . .

MATTIE *(drops to knees. angrily)* No! No!

Lights dim on Mattie, who remains on her knees and then crouches over a sack of corn as though it were a body. Lights up on Henry, who stands up and stretches as if from a good nap. He sniffs the air.

HENRY   It's getting stuffy out here. Must mean rain.
(Annie comes out of hiding now and into the light. She approaches Henry, who now speaks to her as though she were Mattie) We just can't afford to keep Lulu anymore, Mattie.

ANNIE   She's my mother.

HENRY   She's forgotten the little english she knew. All she can talk is gibberish.

ANNIE   Basque, not gibberish. Basque.

HENRY   Lulu eats too much, Mattie.

ANNIE   I'll eat less.

HENRY   I'm going to have to put her in one of those homes.
We'll find one that's got good linen.
(Annie stares at him some moments, then moves off)
But she's not even a lady anymore, Mattie. She's got a beard.
*(While Henry speaks the following, Mattie smothers the sack,
first gently, then powerfully, as though it were a body, all the
while half- singing, half-chanting the tune)*
MATTIE   Lulu, what'll we do?
          Lulu, I'm here with you.
          Lulu, you're turning blue,
          it's the best thing for my darling.
*(When the deed is done, she gently covers the sandbag with her body
as though shielding it from harm)*
HENRY *(calling after Annie)* Lulu doesn't even know she's here.
(to audience) And she watches me, with that foreigner face of
hers. Whenever I get near Annie, Lulu starts to screech and
scratch with those foreigner words of hers like you've never
heard before. *(imitates how he hears her language, now speaking
to audience)* Que le vamos a hacer? Que le vamos a hacer? And
that look of hers. It makes you feel like you're choking, like
you're down there under the ground. *(shouts after Annie)* She's
going to one of those homes. On that I swear!

MATTIE *(whispering)* You're staying here with me, mother. I
won't let them take you away from me. Shhhh. Hush. There,
there, you can rest now. *(continues comforting the sack. As Henry
speaks the following, Mattie tears open the sack and spills out the
grain. She runs her hands through the grain, spreading it out on
the floor. If possible, the grain should disappear through slats in
the stage floor. As Henry speaks, we also hear a pounding, like a
helicopter which builds as he speaks)*

HENRY   But I've always done my best, for my family, and for
this country. I would have gone to one of the wars but they
wouldn't have me. I've got a bad balance because of my flat feet.
They say this new war is the war that's going to stop foreign
things from taking over. For *good*. The President says this war is
going to put some order back in the world. *(beat)* Like the Arabs.
They say we've got to bomb them so they know who's boss.
(beat) It's the things we don't know about, that we've got to stop.

Sometimes I dream I'm flying one of those sound-breaking jets and it makes me feel like . . . like . . . an artist because the patterns I'm blowing on the ground look like . . . like . . . quilts. *(beat)* When I was a kid I wanted to get a plaque on the door of the town hall that's reserved for special citizens. I wanted to do a good thing so when I went into town people would point and say: 'That's him! That's the one with his name on the door!' *(takes the mole out of his pocket, zooms it about like an airplane. The pounding stops. He tickles the mole. It bites him. He smacks it and puts it back in his pocket. Lights change. He notices Mattie)* You've got to close your eyes when we do it or it makes me lose my will. You've got to be thinking the same thing I am, not about something else, or it won't work.

MATTIE   The radio says the enemy hide in holes under the ground.

HENRY   Just close your eyes like a proper woman. *(beat)* Remember when those words used to make you crawl for it?

MATTIE *(continues)* and our boys drive right over their heads, never knowing there's somebody down there breathing, right below their treads.

HENRY   Sweet potato . . . leeks . . . brussel sprouts.

MATTIE   You fucking yankee bastards! Trespassing again. We're going to reach up through this sand, grab you by the ankle and pull you down here with us. We'll pull you down here and smother you. *(yells)* We'll smother you! *(grabs Annie's ankle and pulls her off her feet)* I got one ! I got me a real GI! *(Henry now begins to march, flatly singing the following, continuing until the end of the scene)*

HENRY   And it's, one two three
          What are we fighting for?
          Don't ask me, I don't give a damn
          Next step is, bomb Saddam.

MATTIE *(raises arm as if to strike Annie, but then sits down and puts Annie's feet gently in her lap. She caresses her feet)* Peasant's feet, child. Just like your grandmother's. The boys won't like it. We'll have to break them down to size. *(beat)* And this little piggy went crack, crack, crack. *(passionately kisses Annie's feet)*

HENRY   And it's, five, six, seven
Open up the pearly gates,
Well there ain't no time to wonder why
Whoopie! We're all gonna die.

As Henry finishes the last lines of his song he lies down on his belly. Annie breaks away from Mattie. Lights change and Annie is walking on Henry's back.

HENRY   Keep the heel on the bone.

ANNIE   My girlfriend is waiting.

HENRY   Hup-two, Hup-two. Just like a trooper.

ANNIE   She'll leave without me.

HENRY   Hear them popping back in place?

ANNIE   I've got to go.
        (she jumps off but Henry grabs her leg and holds on)

HENRY   I was talking to Mr. Leet the other day. He says you're a hardy girl for sixteen.

ANNIE   Let me go.

HENRY   He's not an old man. Just barely forty.
        (Annie struggles but cannot free herself)
        His wife has been dead for eight years.

ANNIE   One of his eyelids is torn.

HENRY   A real polite man.

ANNIE   He's got hair in his nose.

HENRY   A sense of humour too.

ANNIE   I've seen him pick the wax out of his ears.

HENRY   He might be willing to sell me his north field.

ANNIE   and feed it to his cat.

HENRY   The field with the lake. There's bass in there as big as my thigh. If I had that piece of land I could make something of this farm. I could be a respectable citizen.
        (Annie manages to twist free)

You be polite to him, you hear me?
(Annie runs off. Henry picks at his ear and looks at it)
But I've got to admit it, feeding it to a cat just isn't polite.

*Lights change, then come up on Mattie and Annie standing closely
side by side, holding hands and facing the audience.*

HENRY *(from shadow)* You can't just go to school with her, Mattie.
You're too old. They'll laugh at you.
*(As Mattie speaks, Annie begins to pull her hand away from
Mattie's grasp and Annie moves away)*
MATTIE *(like a grade-schooler)* Me? Yes. I know the answer Mrs.
Prune. The names of those capitals are . . . Charlie and Robin.
This is Annie's favorite story. For twenty-three years those horses
pulled the plow side by side. Charlie died one winter in that field.
I found him covered with frost. A trickle of blood ran out of his
nose into the snow. Robin went crazy because Charlie wouldn't
get up. The next day Robin lay dead right next to him. Father said
Robin died of a heart attack. Me, I knew different. Animals still
have it in them to die of grief. *(laughs)* What's that, Mrs. Prune?
The first explorer? Think I don't know? It was Lulu. She was
here before any of you. *(rudely)* And don't think she gave it up
easily. Three men had to hold her down while my Father shaved it
off and –
(Annie finishes Mattie's sentence for her)
ANNIE   it never grew back like how it was before. In August,
when it's hottest, the scars still burn.

Lights change. Annie is searching for Mattie, who runs to hide.

ANNIE *(pleads)* Where are you?
MATTIE   You don't love your mother.
ANNIE   Come out.
MATTIE   If you did, you'd find her.
ANNIE   Rain, Rain, smash and spray
          Wash the heavy mud away

ANNIE   Mother? Mother?

Mattie appears from hiding, waving a pair of girl's panties on the end of a broomstick.

MATTIE   Lookie what I found.
(*Annie turns away*)
Looks like my little soldier messed her pants. Bloody, bloody. *(nears Annie and taunts her with a stick)* Thought you'd hide them in the loft. Thought I wouldn't find out, didn't you? *(louder)* Didn't you?
(*Annie breaks away and Mattie chases her with panties until she pins her against the fence*)

ANNIE   It's not my fault.

MATTIE   Of course it's your fault. *(she gives Annie's hair a hard pull. Annie is stunned a moment, then kicks Mattie hard)* Ah! Kicks like an angry little soldier too. *(she strikes Annie across the face)*

ANNIE   Not in the face. The boys don't like it.

MATTIE *(amused)* The boys don't like it?

ANNIE   They tell me I'm pretty, except when my eye swells shut.

MATTIE   So I guess that means no more scratching games either?

ANNIE   I'll play the scratching games, just not on the face. *(holds out arm)* We can still do it on the arms.
(*Mattie scratches down Annie's arm. Annie hardly winces. Then Mattie rolls up her sleeve and holds out her arm. The scratching is done violently yet sensuously*)

MATTIE   Give me the war-mark, child.
(*Annie returns the scratch*)
Why do you care what the boys think?

ANNIE   All the girls care.

MATTIE   Oh, they *do*, do they? And all the girls like to please? Those blue-eyed yanks just want to own you, child, and the piece of ground you're standing on. *(walks Annie downstage and* *points)* See those fields? Your grandmother, Lulu, called them Aceldama, the blood fields, because my father lent her to his neighbour, for one night plus fifty dollars, in exchange for that piece of land. When it rained, she said the mud turned red. *(takes Annie's hand)* There are better things a girl can do with her body than give it over to a boy who can't tell her pleasure from a hole in the ground. *(walks into shadow)* Come on, Mattie will show you how.

(Annie follows but then moves off and lies against the grave-slab that rises up from the floor. The slab should not be 'grave-like' but just a piece of the stage-surface)

ANNIE   When I woke up it was dark. I heard scratching and crunching sounds. Then I knew I was in the ground and the bugs were coming in to familiarize themselves with me. But it's a comfort in some ways. I never get hungry. And she comes and stands over me.

(Sounds of Mattie knocking with spade in garden)

But lately she's been up there hitting the dirt so hard I'm afraid she's going to break through the top and pull me out of here by my hair. I keep yelling up to her to go on, to get the hell out of here, as far away as she can run, but she won't listen. *(stands, awkwardly trying to cover herself as though she were naked. Angrily she confronts audience)* Stop it. I don't like it. *(rudely)* Just like you are now, they watched and watched and stared. *(shouts)* Close your eyes. Just listen. *(softer)* Just listen. *(gutsy)* Before that damn horse threw me I had a boyfriend. He was just back from Iraq and hadn't had a girl before. I let him mess around under my skirt because I felt sorry for him on account of him missing a piece of his chin. Ha! But he couldn't do it right so I sent him home and did it myself and it felt a whole lot better. I never told her though. Even though she was right about how a girl should please herself, I never gave her the satisfaction of knowing it. *(beat)* I'll be eighteen in August. Then no-one can tell me what to do.

Lights dim on Annie, and up on Henry and Mattie.

MATTIE   I've heard that before.

HENRY   I mean it this time. If you leave, I'll kill my mole. It's the biggest one I ever caught. Annie would have been impressed.
(Mattie ignores him)
Alright. Better than kill the mole, I'll marry the damn thing. *(hums wedding ballad)* But what about the plans we had, Mattie? To move away together. To start new. Without. . . without . . .
(Mattie puts new laces in her boots)

MATTIE   without Annie? *(laughs)*

HENRY   There was a lot of good between us. Can't you try to remember it?

MATTIE   What's the use.

HENRY   Remember when we were first married and I'd come in from the fields with a crooked back? I'd lie down on the kitchen floor *(walks as though he were balancing)* and you'd walk barefoot up and down my back, like this, to straighten me out?

MATTIE   The most travelling I ever did in my life was on your spine.

HENRY   And afterwards I'd check your toes for splinters. *(runs his finger down her spine)* You never wore shoes back then and if I found a splinter in your foot I'd suck on it 'til it came out.

MATTIE *(interrupts)* I never got splinters!

HENRY   I pleased you then, Mattie.

MATTIE   No.

HENRY   Had you grunting.

MATTIE   I got to get some fresh air, Henry. My throat's stuck up.

HENRY   Grunting like a pig.

MATTIE   I can't breathe.
(Henry grabs her boot and taunts her with it)

HENRY *(pig call)* zooie . . . zooie . . .

MATTIE *(coming after him, now teasing)* Yeah, I remember. I remember one day the old sow just quit grunting. She quit grunting. Remember?

HENRY   Oink, oink.
(They embrace and kiss)

MATTIE   Why? Cause she found out she could do it herself a whole lot better than that old boar could, with his shove and poke it.

HENRY *(shoves her away)* You went dead from the neck down after the accident.

MATTIE   Before then, Henry.

HENRY   If you leave, I'll cut off my ears.

MATTIE *(moves off)* How 'bout your scalp?

HENRY   I could learn to fly a Stealth fighter. I could make you proud. *(pretends to be an airplane)*

Lights change and come up on Annie who is squatting and pissing. Mattie joins her. They both piss as they talk.

MATTIE   But the county fair isn't a place for a girl.

ANNIE   My girlfriend is going.

MATTIE   You and me. We'll do something fun.

ANNIE   Throw me a rag.
(Mattie throws her a rag. Annie wipes)

MATTIE   We'll do something special.

ANNIE *(throws rag back to her. She wipes)* Whether you say so or not I'm going this week.

MATTIE   If you're gone more than an hour I'll tear your dress.

ANNIE   Hurray!
(Mattie now uses the rag to wash Annie. She washes Annie's limbs as easily as if they were her own while she speaks. She also cleans behind Annie's ears)

MATTIE   The first time I saw your Father was at the county fair. I felt a pity for him on account of his bald head. I thought to myself: someone should do a good thing and marry that poor man. So I did. But I liked him too. He knew how to tickle me where I liked it. And he promised he'd buy Lulu some expensive teeth. *(moves to wash between Annie's legs. Annie squeezes them shut)* Open your legs. *(Annie resists)* Open your legs.

(Annie grabs the cloth from Mattie, and shoves it in Mattie's mouth)

ANNIE   Remember when Grandma Lulu's teeth disappeared, right after she died? *(beat)* I stole them.

(Mattie struggles but Annie pins her down and stuffs the rag further into her mouth)

I stole them and traded them to a girl at school for a pair of silk socks, the kind with the ruffles at the top. I wore them to school and you never knew 'cause I hid them before I got home.

(Mattie breaks free and spits cloth out)

MATTIE   That was a dirty thing to do to your grandmother.

ANNIE   She wouldn't be eating in her coffin. That's what I figured.

(Mattie begins to laugh. After some moments Annie joins in. Then Mattie quits)

MATTIE   Well, I'm glad you didn't keep it a secret. *(beat)* One hour at the fair. No more.

ANNIE *(crosses herself)* And hope to die.

MATTIE *(picks up rag, spits on it and tosses it to Annie)* Wash your own self child.

(Mattie moves away. As Henry and Mattie begin talking, Annie begins to chase a horse that we can't see, upstage)

HENRY   But why give her a horse? Why not a pony, or something she can handle? That animal is wild.

MATTIE   She'll break it in.

HENRY   Don't say I didn't warn you.

MATTIE   It will get her away a bit.

HENRY   A horse is going to get her away?

MATTIE   Away from us.

HENRY   What the hell?

MATTIE   She's like Lulu was, Henry.

HENRY   No. She is nothing like Lulu was. *(beat)* Something foreign has gotten inside you, Mattie.

MATTIE   The child's turning blue.

HENRY   We can't afford that horse.

Lights dim on Henry and Mattie and up again on Annie who is calling for help with the horse.

ANNIE Mother! Just give me a hand. I can't catch the damn thing! *(she talks to the horse)* Come here, baby. Come on. We did it yesterday. It's not that bad. I'll just slip this over your neck and . . . *(leans to grab its neck but misses)* Damn. *(beat)* Daddy! Scare him over this way. *(beat)* Not that way, back to the fence . . . *(to horse)* That's it. Come here. Shhhh. That's it. . . . *(misses horse again)* Shit! *(begins to follow horse further upstage)* Alright. Alright. But you're going to pay for making me chase you.
(Lights dim on Annie. We hear her voice from the shadows)
God damn it, I got him!

Lights change. They come up on Henry and Mattie.

HENRY Give it another try, Mattie. Work with me.

MATTIE Once was enough.

HENRY But it can't hurt to try again. Just one day.

MATTIE *(nears Henry and takes his face in her hands)* Now Henry, what happened the first time I went out to work in the fields with you? *(turns him so he must face the audience to tell his story)* Speak up. Tell it like it happened.

HENRY Well, after the accident . . .

MATTIE Go on.

HENRY Well, after the accident you went out into the fields to work beside me, your husband, and you drove the tractor, mended fences, almost better than a man.

MATTIE And how did I like it?

HENRY You didn't.

MATTIE *(smacks his head)* And I was amazed, wasn't I, Henry?

HENRY Yes, you were amazed, at . . . *(falters)*

MATTIE at the power.

HENRY   At the power of . . . your body: lifting fence posts like they were broomsticks, pitching mounds of hay from the loft . . .

MATTIE   And had I forgotten about the accident?

HENRY   Yes.

MATTIE *(slaps his head and repeats her words with infinite patience)* And had I forgotten about the accident?

HENRY   No. No, you hadn't forgotten, but the work did you good. And we lived happily ever after.

MATTIE *(sternly)* Henry!

HENRY   OK, OK, but then Henry doesn't want her to help. He figures she'll quit in a month or so but she keeps up with him. Her hands get all swollen up and her hair all knotted up like a dog's, and she stinks like –

MATTIE *(interrupts)* Enough! *(beat)* Then what does Husband Henry do?

HENRY   Husband Henry isn't a hero anymore. He just quits working and sits on the porch.

MATTIE   And when does he go back to work?

HENRY *(inaudible)* Only when she quits.

MATTIE   Speak up! We can't hear you.

HENRY *(louder)* Only when she quits working and stays at home . . . like a decent woman.

MATTIE *(pats his arm)* Was that story so hard to tell?
(Silence for some moments)

HENRY   I called the vet today.

MATTIE   Oh? One of the calves sick?

HENRY   Nope.

MATTIE   Chickens got the lice again?

HENRY   Nope.

MATTIE   Then why is he coming?

HENRY   Just let it be.

MATTIE   Don't start playing the fool again.

HENRY   He's coming to get it, Mattie. The horse will be gone by morning.

MATTIE   If anyone so much as touches that animal I'll –

HENRY *(interrupts)* It's got to be done. For both our sakes.

MATTIE   I won't have some stray dog eating my memories out of a bowl.

HENRY   The vet found a nice family, with kids, who'll pay for it.

MATTIE   I won't have some snot-nosed brat riding *her* horse. The horse will go to the meat-packers first.

HENRY   Fine. Then I'll tell the vet to call them.

MATTIE   I'll choose when and how that animal goes and that's nowhere for now. When I'm gone somewhere else, well, then I won't give a damn.

HENRY   The horse killed her, Mattie. Kicked her dead.

MATTIE   Quit using that word 'dead.' After a lot of years she'll just go to dust, and then there will be nothing where we laid her down. And if there's no body there can be no death.

HENRY *(starts to laugh, then is angry)* When it got rough between you two she'd come out to where I was working. *(beat)* Oh yeah, you didn't know that. You always thought she was off alone, like you wanted her to be, riding that horse. *(Mattie listens stunned)* Well, I'd pull her up on the tractor with me and we'd ride back and forth across the field. Sometimes she'd steer. And then I'd cut the motor and she'd tell me what she'd learned in school that day. She was sharp as a tack. She'd tell me things she learned in history class. She was really keen on the wars, about the Koreans, the Vietnamese, the Iraqis . . .

MATTIE   The Iraqis?

HENRY   Yeah , and them hiding in their bunkers under the ground, and whole families, whole villages, hiding out under the surface. She always wanted to talk about the bombing, about the enemy suffocating down there with no way out.

MATTIE *(bewildered)* Suffocating?

HENRY   And all those kids burnt up in that shelter . . . kabam, kabam . . . fried like bacon . . . while they slept. *(nears Mattie threateningly)* We had our talks. We had our secrets together. Yes we did, Miss Mattie.

(Mattie shakes her head in denial)

I bet you didn't know she told me about that boy she was planning on kissing?

MATTIE   You're lying!

HENRY   Oh yes. But I made sure she knew what was a sin and what was clean and smart. A few days before the accident she asked me if it would be alright if she kissed the boy. I told her it would be OK, as long as it wasn't on the mouth.

MATTIE *(struggling)* I bet she didn't tell you when she got the curse!

HENRY   Nope. But I wouldn't have expected her to. That's woman's talk.

MATTIE *(regaining composure)* Ha! Well, she told me . . . She had no secrets from me I can tell you.

(Henry laughs quietly)

And I had none from her. I told her all about those other boys that had me before you. I told her all about it right down to the last detail.

(Henry shakes his head with disgust)

I even told her about our first night together. About how I laughed –

HENRY *(shocked)* You wouldn't have dared!

MATTIE *(she laughs with delight)* Oh, yes I did. I told her all about that filthy wedding joke!

(Henry swipes at her but misses, then she approaches him seductively)

About how it wouldn't *work* for you, about how I had to do things to help you.

HENRY *(screams)* Stop it! You're lying. She never knew.

MATTIE   How you made me scratch you and slap you.

HENRY   She never knew! Girls never know about their fathers.

MATTIE *(silent some moments, then seems defeated)* No, she never knew. That was my one secret. I told her everything but that. I made up her brain, strand, by strand. And I taught her the scratching game.

HENRY   Yep. You taught her the scratching game. *(beat)* She held us together, Mattie.

MATTIE   Nope. She kept us apart. Just apart enough to keep us together.

At this point Henry also begins to speak. The voices slightly overlap. The voices are in harmony, not clashing. And the sound of the voices, their rhythms, are as important as what is being said. Mattie and Henry are oblivious of one another in this union.

MATTIE   And to imagine she never even got to kiss that boy. And there was a war on then, the Yankees were coming and we were the Enemy so we had to run.

HENRY   Now and then I'll be out in the field and I'll cut the engine and just listen to the places where her voice used to be.

MATTIE   I'd take Annie up to the loft to hide her from the soldiers and I'd tell her about Paul

HENRY   And how they used to fight! but she always wanted to hear about those two horses, Charlie and Robin. Annie would go off to school covered with black and blue marks.

MATTIE   But I'd say to my father: I won't watch you, but he'd make me watch . . .And then I got my period.

HENRY   Mattie would be in the house like the queen of Sheba.

MATTIE   I was ashamed so I hid my panties but Lulu found them. swabbing her scratches with alcohol. She hung them on the end of a broomstick and she chased me through the yard. She was crazy for those games. Until I fell down on my knees.
(A moment of silence)

HENRY   Maybe I should have put a stop to it.

MATTIE   She was my Annie.

HENRY   Maybe I could have made it work.

MATTIE   The one sweet thing in this world that was mine.

HENRY   Maybe if we'd had another –

MATTIE   And I was hers.

HENRY   Another child.

Lights change. Henry begins to stalk Mattie from the shadows.

HENRY   But it doesn't take that long to heal up, Mattie.

MATTIE   Just a few more days.

HENRY   It's been two months since Annie was born.

MATTIE   I'm a mother now.

HENRY   You promised you'd make it smooth again, how I like it. *(throws a small, sharp object at her feet that could be a knife)* Do it!
(Mattie shakes her head 'no') You've done it before.

MATTIE   I've got a child to think about now.

HENRY   But I shave my chin for you. *(beat)* Then I guess I'll have to shave you myself. I can make you a little girl again. Smooth as a baby, smooth as our own little girl.

MATTIE *(firmly. No longer afraid)* No. Henry. I'm not a girl.
(Lights change as Mattie sings)
               Lulu, what'll we do?
               Lulu, we're turning blue
               Lulu, we're finally through
               it's no fiddle-sticks my darling.
(From the shadows Annie softly hums as a backdrop to their conversation)

HENRY   This isn't about her anymore. It's about you and me. We're still here and we're all we know. *(pounds his chest)* You see this? This is live flesh. *(louder)* We're still here! That's got to mean something.

MATTIE *(flatly)* It's no fiddle-sticks my darling. *(beat)* It's time for me to go, Henry. I'm headed back to the old country, Henry. Where I was born.

HENRY   But you were born here. Your mother was born over there, not you. *(to audience)* Lulu was the foreigner.

MATTIE *(Annie stops humming in the shadows)* Remember that Christmas I won the city bingo-game and I was going to use the money to take mother back to her home in Spain so she could die there? *(nears his face and sings flatly)*
               Los soldados se rebelaron

durante la batalla
y el lugariente se suicido.
You know what that meant? *(laughs)* What she was always
singing? *(speaks)* The soldiers, they revolted during battle and the
lieutenant committed suicide. Well, after you finished breaking
my arm, you swore you'd break both of Annie's if we went. You
were afraid we wouldn't come back.

HENRY   So a man likes his wife to stay around.

MATTIE   So tell me, how much is around, Henry? *(shouts)*
How much is around?

HENRY   If you leave, I'll join the army. I'll go up in a bomber
and I'll never come down.

ANNIE *(from the shadows, she spies on them and sneaks closer.
Hissing)* I won't be your soldier.

MATTIE   Listen!

HENRY   What?

MATTIE   What?

HENRY   Listen!

ANNIE   What?

MATTIE   What?

ANNIE   Listen.

MATTIE *(to Henry)* I won't be your soldier.

ANNIE *(moves closer. Mattie and Henry aren't aware of her but
Mattie hears 'something' as she unconsciously receives her
daughter's words. Whispers)* I've stopped obeying orders . . .

MATTIE   I've stopped obeying orders, Henry.

HENRY *(irritated)* Always this nonsense. Just like when I met you.

ANNIE   But I was a smart girl . . .

MATTIE *(to Henry)* I was a smart girl when you met me.

ANNIE   Sharp as a tack.

MATTIE   Sharp as a tack.

ANNIE *(calls)* Mother!

MATTIE *(calls)* Mother!

ANNIE   I can't breathe.

MATTIE *(to Henry)* I'm turning blue. You hear me. I can't breathe anymore. *(beat)* They ripped off the hair under my arms, Henry. On my wedding day.

HENRY   But that was your mother Lulu, not you!

MATTIE *(powerfully)* They broke my feet so my shoes would fit.

HENRY   That wasn't you.

MATTIE   We smothered her, Henry. We smothered her.

HENRY *(shouts)* No!

ANNIE *(whispers)* That's no fiddle-sticks my darlings.

Lights dim. Henry moves downstage and begins planting. Annie stands as though a statue. Mattie is on all fours, cleaning and brushing the area around Annie's feet.

MATTIE   When you were a baby your toes were like peas, so perfect and so small. *(jumps up, but Annie doesn't flinch. Shouts)* But you had to keep secrets from me, didn't you? Why? Why? Hiding your privates, not telling me when you got the curse. And just to spite me you let that horse get wilder and wilder until . . . If you'd been my son I'd have sent you off to fight the Enemy. They'd have taught you a lesson.

ANNIE *(chants)* Hurrah for my boys!

MATTIE   You think those boys are gonna set you free? *(shouts in Annie's ear)* Run! Run!

(Annie doesn't flinch) After Lulu died, I was so alone with your father, child. I needed your secrets. I needed them 'cause I didn't have anymore of my own. *(beat)* I want you to know that I can hear you . . . now . . . I can hear you even though . . .

(Silence. Mattie moves off and gathers some articles, putting them in the emptied sack, getting ready to leave)

HENRY   When I was a kid I wanted to get my name on a plaque on the town hall door, the one reserved for special citizens.

(Annie echoes his words. We hear a staggered monologue although the 'him' and 'he' of the monologue become 'her' for Annie)

I wanted to do a good thing so when I went into town people
would point and say: 'That's him! The one with his name on the
door.'

*(Mattie takes the bundle she's packed, ties her boots, again. She
is ready to leave. Annie is still motionless. Then Mattie nears
Henry and critically watches how he is planting to make sure
he's doing it right)*

MATTIE   Don't put two in, one seed per hole.

*(Henry continues planting. Mattie runs her hand over his bald
head tenderly. Then she moves off, once she is satisfied he is
doing the planting properly)*

That's it. That's it. You'll do just fine.

*Lights dim on Henry. Mattie looks Annie over a last time. Annie is
still like a statue. Then Mattie begins to exit. Annie's voice halts her.*

ANNIE   Knock, knock.

(Mattie freezes but doesn't turn)

(louder) Knock. knock.

MATTIE *(turns only her neck to look back at Annie)* Who's there?

ANNIE   Annie.

MATTIE *(beat)* Annie who?

ANNIE *(as though she is trying to say something else but can now
only speak in games. A sense of farewell in her tone)* Annie news
comes your way, you send it back to us.

*Mattie holds her gaze on Annie for some moments, then she strides
away. Blackout – just before Mattie walks offstage.*

The end

Naomi Wallace

Graduated in 1993 from the University of Iowa. Her first play, **The War Boys** (Finborough Theatre) in 1993 was followed by **In the Fields of Aceldama** and her children's play **The Girl Who Fell Through a Hole in Her Jumper** (co-written with Bruce McLeod) produced in the London New Play Festival in 1993 and 1994 respectively. Naomi also co-wrote **In the Sweat** with Bruce McLeod for the 1997 BT/National Connections.

Naomi's poetry has been published on both sides of the Atlantic. She has won the National Poetry Prize in America and in 1995 her first poetry collection **To Dance a Stony Field** was published in the UK by Peterloo Poets.

In the Heart of America premiered at the Bush Theatre, London in 1994 and the US premiere of **One Flea Spare** was at the Humana Festival, 1996. **In the Heart of America** and **One Flea Spare** have both been Susan Smith Blackburn Prize winners; Naomi is the only writer ever to have won this award twice. **One Flea Spare** went on to the Joseph Papp Theatre in New York, winning an Obie Award.

Naomi's Mobil Playwriting Competition prize-winning play **Slaughter City** received its World Premiere by the RSC in January 1996 and its US premiere shortly afterwards with The American Repertory Theatre.

In 1997 her stage adaptation of William Wharton's classic novel **Birdy** opened in the West End and her first feature film **Lawn Dogs**, directed by John Duigan, was released, having won the Best Screenplay award at the Sitges Festival.

Two Horsemen

by 'Biyi Bandele

Two Horsemen

Notes

A room somewhere: a dirty, scrap-filled room whose only claim to fame is a broken-down bed, a battered coffee-table and two cane chairs that have certainly seen kinder days. A kerosene stove. Pots and plates. A hurricane lamp against the wall. Beside this, a dead old clock. Shirts, trousers, books and newspapers flung carelessly everywhere. A coin-operated telephone is situated by the door.

Two Horsemen

by 'Biyi Bandele

First presented at the Gate Theatre on 27 July 1994 as part of the London New Play Festival.
Directed by Roxana Silbert
Designed by Naomi Wilkinson

Banza   Leo Wringer

Lagbaja   Colin McFarlane

ACT ONE – Rain

The lights come up on the room. It is early evening. Banza and Lagbaja are sitting stone-faced, looking intently at each other, as if studying specimens in a laboratory glass case.

BANZA   It rained yesterday, did you know that?

LAGBAJA   Really. I didn't know that.

BANZA   You didn't know that it rained yesterday?

LAGBAJA   I must've been too busy at my sweeping to have noticed.

BANZA   You sweep?

LAGBAJA   Streets, sure, that's my job. Always been my job. Twenty, maybe thirty years now. A family trade actually.

BANZA   Cleaning streets?

LAGBAJA   Handed over from one generation to the next.

BANZA   Well, my friend, it did rain yesterday.

LAGBAJA   Was the ground wet?

BANZA   Cats and dogs. But mostly water. You should've seen it. Mud everywhere. In the streets, under the bridge, at the beer parlour, the church . . .

BANZA   Cats and dogs. But mostly water. You should've seen it. Mud everywhere. In the streets, under the bridge, at the beer parlour, the church . . .

LAGBAJA   Oh no! Not there as well. Please don't you ever say that again, not even in jest – mud in the beer-parlour!

BANZA   Well, it happened, and that's it, whether you like it or not.

LAGBAJA   You were there? You saw it?

BANZA   I was there, I saw it. Mud in the beer-parlour. Never seen the like of it in all my life. This disgusting, utterly disgusting carpet of mud in the beer-parlour. Of all places, for christsake. I almost threw up.

LAGBAJA   Ah, that explains it then.

BANZA   What?

LAGBAJA   The beer, last night. Tasted like mud. I could've sworn it. I almost puked.

BANZA   Well, for one thing, it wasn't like you to be so sad after such a fine day at the beer-parlour. And when you burst into that fit of drunken laughter – that was when I said to myself, I said to myself, something must be wrong with Mensa.

LAGBAJA   And something was wrong with me, old friend. My beer tasted like mud. That's what was wrong, like mud, my friend!

BANZA   I was about getting around to asking you what was the matter – being the good friend that I happen to be . . .

LAGBAJA   . . . and realising too, I suppose, that a friend in need . . .

BANZA   . . . is a pain in the neck. Moreover, that's when you farted. And everyone ran for cover.

LAGBAJA   Me, fart? *(indignantly)* I'll have you know, sir, that I take exception to such blatant defamation of my character, such cold-blooded campaign of calamity –

BANZA   Calumny.

LAGBAJA   – That too . . . on my person.

BANZA   Hey, hey. Don't get worked up over nothing. You farted, and that's all. No big deal. I used to be quite – prolific myself. At farting. It was my speciality in primary school . . . but, come to think of it, it wasn't really my fault. My old man's idea of a balanced diet, you see was . . .

LAGBAJA\BANZA *(together)* . . . mashed beans for breakfast, bean-cake and garri for lunch, and mashed beans again for supper.

BANZA   Balanced, my foot, you might say. But you should've seen me in those days. Round like a ball. They used to call me Michelin – and I'd wave – and then break wind. I was so good at it no one ever knew I was the one. *(he moves around as he speaks)* But one day, I pushed my luck too far. It was during an arithmetic lesson, I remember. The mistress said 'Class, what are two plus two?' and we answered –

LAGBAJA   'Two plus two are five.' *(pause)*

BANZA   Erm, yes. And she was so pleased with us, with our precocious intellect, our superb arithmetic, and was, in fact, heaping praise on us when – I broke wind. Booooom! A cross between a rotten egg and a decomposing dead body. The teacher – Mississ Shorum we used to call her on account she was married to this man called Mr Aaron, which in our barely weaned mouths came out simply as 'Shorum' – came to a dead halt in front of the class. *(mimics)* 'Wish of you messed?' she asked slowly, casting her stern, furious eyes on our frightened little faces. 'I said, who messed? Ta lo so?' No one said a word. I dared not breathe. I was trembling in my seat. 'Ah, so you're not going to confess, abi. Well, I am going to find the culprit today-today. Oya, all of you, useless children, stand up.' So we all got to our feet. And – you won't believe this – what she did next – she embarked on a sniffing exercise: she would drag a child up from his seat, raise his arms close to her nose and sniff. Satisfied you weren't her man she'd put you back on your seat and go on to the next suspect. One by one she went round the class, sniffing one arse after the other, but it seemed her culprit would never be caught. That is until she came to yours truly. I'd been trembling before she came to my desk, but the moment she came, the trembling stopped. The same routine: she pulled me by the trouser, lifted me up to her nose-level and sniffed. Luckily for me, the stench of the 'blast' had been blown away by the wind long before she came to me, so I was quite confident I was going to pass the scrutiny. But I made this assumption without including my buttocks – and it turned out to be a terrible oversight. I was right up there in the air, confidently defying gravity courtesy of Mississ Shorum, happily bearing the supreme humiliation of having my arse sniffed at, when I heard the terrible, utterly horrible sound come out from none other than – my arse! It was like the sound of a car with a bad silencer. You should've seen Mississ Shorum that morning.

LAGBAJA   What did she do to you?

BANZA   Do? For the next five minutes she wasn't in any position to do anything. Remember she was so close to the site of the explosion. She was on sick leave a whole week. After that she wouldn't have me in her class.

LAGBAJA   Really! Wouldn't have you in her class! The very idea! As if she owned the school! Didn't you tell your old man? And didn't he come marching indignantly to school with you the next day?

BANZA   No, he didn't.

LAGBAJA   But he should have!

BANZA   Well, he didn't.

LAGBAJA   But, why didn't he?

BANZA   He was Mr Shorum.

LAGBAJA   You mean . . . *(the penny drops)* Mississ Shorum's husband?

BANZA   The one and only.

LAGBAJA   And Mississ Shorum – she was your mother?

BANZA   None other.

LAGBAJA   And you farted in her mouth? Your mother's mouth?

BANZA   She deserved it. Had it coming. Teach her to go sniffing people's arses, that's what I thought.

LAGBAJA   What a right bastard you were.

BANZA   Just her word, bastard. That's what she called me.

LAGBAJA   She did? I would too.

BANZA   She asked for it.

LAGBAJA   Naughty, naughty, naughty boy.

BANZA   Come to think of it, there never was a time when I was on good terms with her.

LAGBAJA   Never? Oh come on – not even when you were but a fetish inside her?

BANZA   A what?

LAGBAJA   You know, before you were born?

BANZA   A foetus. No, not even then. She was given to drinking, you see. Guinness, nothing but Guinness. But I hated bitter tasting drinks. So anytime she had too much Guinness I'd kick her in the stomach.

LAGBAJA   I'm sure you don't expect me to believe that fairytale?

BANZA   No, I don't.

LAGBAJA   Funnily enough, I do. It's too unbelievable to be a lie.

BANZA   For your information, it's a lie.

(The phone begins to ring)

I cooked the whole thing up.

LAGBAJA   The more reason that I should believe it.

(They listen to the phone without making any effort to attend to it. It stops)

It rained yesterday, did you know that?

BANZA   Really. I didn't know that.

LAGBAJA   You didn't know that it rained yesterday?

BANZA   I must've been too busy at my sweeping to have noticed.

LAGBAJA   You sweep –

BANZA   Streets, yes, that's my job. Always been my job. Twenty, maybe, thirty years now. A family trade actually.

LAGBAJA   Cleaning streets?

BANZA   Handed over from one generation to the next.

LAGBAJA   Well, my friend, it did rain yesterday. Cats and dogs and what have you.

LAGBAJA   Cleaning streets?

BANZA   Handed over from one generation to the next.

LAGBAJA   Well, my friend, it did rain yesterday. Cats and dogs and what have you.

BANZA   Was the ground wet?

LAGBAJA   Everywhere.

BANZA   Did folks bring out their umbrellas?

LAGBAJA   Of all colours of the rainbow.

BANZA   And those without umbrellas?

LAGBAJA   Raincoats. Mackintoshes.

BANZA   And those without raincoats, mackintoshes?

LAGBAJA   Got beaten by the rain, of course.

BANZA   And why should some have umbrellas and others none?

LAGBAJA   I'd like you to tell me. It's always been like that.

BANZA   Always?

LAGBAJA   Always. *(pause)* Who cares anyway? I'm not God. That's God's business. To give folks umbrellas.

BANZA   I met him yesterday, on the bus.

(The phone rings. It ceases on the second ring as Banza makes as if to get it)

Did I tell you?

LAGBAJA   Who?

BANZA   God. Sat right next to him on the bus yesterday.

LAGBAJA *(enthralled)* You did? You – actually met God. Oh my God! How'd he look like?

BANZA   Have you ever seen any of those sleazy Kung Fu films? *(voice change)* Ding dong ding! You killed my papa when I was a kid, now I'm gonna kill you . . . *(he assumes a Kung Fu posture, arms spread as if about to fly. He feigns at Lagbaja, who has also assumed a similar posture)* Over the rivers! Wham! Across the mountains! Ggrramm! Into the paddy-fields! Over the tree-tops! Into the temple!

(They battle each other using every detachable object in the room as weapons. Banza deals Lagbaja a 'lethal' blow)

That's how he looked, God. Like a character straight out of those meaningless gory tales. In fact, to be precise, he looked . . . like a Chinese mandarin. Long, grey beard, a garrotte in his hand. As weird as they come. And his breath stank of whisky. One swig too many, I guess. Can't grudge him that, though, not with what his world has turned into. Enough to make anyone hit the bottle. He was singing too. *(sings)* 'Sometimes I feel like a motherless child . . .'

LAGBAJA Are you, are you sure that wasn't the devil you met?

BANZA No, it wasn't. Couldn't have been, it was God. I knew it was him. What's more, he was talking dirty to the girl in the front seat.

LAGBAJA God? The Almighty? Talking dirty? No, Mensa. A joke is a joke. I'm sorry, that couldn't have been God.

BANZA Well, it was. He told me so himself.

LAGBAJA Oh, he did?

BANZA Yes, I asked him and he said to me, 'Yes my son, I am God.' And he lay a hand on my forehead and blessed me.

LAGBAJA *(excited)* He blessed you? God actually blessed you?

BANZA *(proudly)* Yes sir, he did. Placed his hand on me like this and said in his vibrant sonorous voice, 'Cursed be the day you were born, my son.'

LAGBAJA And I suppose you said 'Amen'.

BANZA Of course I did. What do you take me for? A dunce? *(he fishes out a tin of cheap untipped cigarettes from the inner pocket of his coat)* You will bore a man to death, Mensa. *(he throws a cigarette to Lagbaja, holds one himself and returns the tin very carefully to his pocket)* Every day you just sit there and yap. Does nothing ever happen in your life?

LAGBAJA Nothing. Nor in yours, come to think of it.

BANZA Every day we just sit here and yap away our lives.

LAGBAJA Our lives? I thought I once heard you say we had none.

BANZA Well, in a all honesty, do we? Our lives rolled to a stand-still a long time ago. Like that thing over there on the wall. Now we're only waiting for the rust to set in.

LAGBAJA   For the worms to fall onto the carrion?

BANZA   For the crumbling wall to cave in and bash in the wandering head of the wayfarer.

LAGBAJA   Do you realise that I hate your guts? Every time I'm with you, I'm infected by this senseless melancholy of yours. Can't you ever see anything good in anything?

BANZA   You're growing old gracefully. You are becoming senile *(pause)* Do you want to hear a story?

LAGBAJA   Not another of those crackpot stories of yours, I hope. *(he sniffs his cigarette appreciatively)* Having nothing against the good things of life – I'll say shoot on. I have nothing against – dating a fine woman – or hearing a good story. They go together, have you noticed that? Women and stories. Tall stories. And that, by the way, is the story of my life.

BANZA   Mine too. Plenty of stories but no women.

LAGBAJA   None at all?

BANZA   Not even one.

LAGBAJA   Not even your mother?

BANZA   Do I look like someone who had a mother?

LAGBAJA   No, you don't.

BANZA   I never knew my mother.

LAGBAJA   Oh God, not another sob story. Whatever happened to her?

BANZA *(grief-stricken)* She died in an accident.

LAGBAJA   An accident?

BANZA   A bicycle accident.

LAGBAJA   Oh my God. Was she riding one and got hit by a car or something?

BANZA   No. She was walking to the market and got hit by a bicycle.

LAGBAJA   And died?

BANZA   No, of course not! She wasn't killed by the bicycle. It was the cyclist did her in *(demonstrates a physical assault)* She fell into a coma and never woke up. *(pause)* It was a deadly bicycle accident.

LAGBAJA   What about the Shorums? I thought you mentioned
them . . .

BANZA   Yes, I did. The Shorums. Nice couple. Bless their
souls.

LAGBAJA   As your parents.

BANZA   No, I didn't.

LAGBAJA   Yes, you did.

BANZA   No, I didn't.

LAGBAJA   But you did. Be man enough to admit it. You did!

BANZA   Okay, okay, slip of the tongue. I had no parents.
Never knew my mother. She walked out on my old man just
before I was born. So he had to bring me up all on his own.
(pause) Before he too died shortly afterwards.

LAGBAJA *(feelingly)* Poor fellow.

BANZA   Yeah, that's what I am. A poor fellow.

LAGBAJA   Your father, not you, idiot.

BANZA   And he was too, an absolute nonentity. Woke up one
day and after watching a match on TV and decided he wanted to
be a footballer. He was sixty then. And some. Someone mistook
him for the football and kicked him into the net. That's how come
I ended up in an orphanage.

LAGBAJA   I don't like it at all. The way you talk about your
father.

BANZA   Oh, well, I'm sorry.

LAGBAJA *(suddenly angry)* Why did you do that?

BANZA   Do what?

LAGBAJA   Why did you say 'Oh'?

BANZA   Why shouldn't I?

LAGBAJA   Because it gets me down. Every time I hear someone
say 'Oh' I get the blues. It reminds me of the one woman I've
ever had in all my life. She was always saying 'Oh'.

BANZA   Oh, what?

LAGBAJA   There you go again.

BANZA   I'm sorry. But what happened to her? She leave you?
Or you left her?

LAGBAJA   Twenty years, Mensa, for twenty years we were married, this woman and I, and never had a baby.

BANZA   What was the matter with you: a faulty kick starter? Couldn't you get it up?

(Lagbaja leans over and whispers into Banza's ear)

(incredulous) She wouldn't let you! And she was your wife! For twenty years! I hope you're misquoting yourself. Why didn't you just call it quits with her?

LAGBAJA *(sheepishly)* Now that you say it . . .

BANZA   . . . it never occurred to you?

LAGBAJA   Never. But not to worry. I got her in the end.

BANZA *(eagerly)* You did? You did?

LAGBAJA   You bet I did. Would you believe that for those twenty years, for those three hundred and forty months she never let me near her, she was only pretending, and was actually dying for me!

(Banza regards him sceptically)

One day – *(he inserts the cigarette between his lips)* She came in from the market – *(he stops)*

BANZA   She came in from the market . . . ?

LAGBAJA   She made me a nice meal., the nicest in fact that I'd had in years, and knowing her man's 'fluid' tastes, topped it all with a well imprisoned beer.

BANZA   That's how I like my beer. Well imprisoned. You must've been swooning by then, I know.

LAGBAJA   Well, I wasn't. I was as calm and cool as any man whose wife decides to give him a scrumpy lunch and a . . .

BANZA   . . . scrummy . . .

LAGBAJA   . . . that's what I said. A scrumpy lunch for a treat and a mercilessly chilled beer to wit. No less. Anyway, after all this, she brought out from her bag this strange little thing that looked like a balloon and told me to wear it on my what's-it's-name.

BANZA   Your what's-it's-name?

LAGBAJA   My what's-it's-name.

BANZA   Your what's-it's-name is your what's-it's-name?

LAGBAJA   Precisely.

BANZA   Very well, go on.

LAGBAJA   She brought out this thing that looked like a balloon
and told me to wear it on my what's-it's-name.

BANZA   What was that thing that looked like a balloon?

LAGBAJA / BANZA *(together)* Something that looked like a
balloon.

BANZA   Yes. But what was it?

LAGBAJA   That's it. Something that looked like a balloon.

BANZA   In other words, this thing that looked like a balloon
was something that looked like a balloon. *(he fishes out the tin of
cigarettes. He takes back the cigarette from Lagbaja and returns
it, with his own, to the tin. He returns the tin to his pocket)*

LAGBAJA   Precisely.

BANZA   Very well, go on.

LAGBAJA   I wore this thing that looked like a balloon on my
what's-it's-name, then we got down to business. *(pause)*

BANZA   What does that mean 'down to business'?

LAGBAJA   That means we made love, idiot.

BANZA   You made love? *(giggles)* To your wife for the first
time in twenty years? *(giggles again)* And I suppose that thing
that looked like a balloon was a condom?

LAGBAJA   What?

BANZA   A condom. A raincoat. A parachute. Was it a
condom or wasn't it?

LAGBAJA   Is that what they call it? A hell lot of use it was, the
useless thing. Fell inside right in the middle of the job!

BANZA *(horrified)* Oh, God! Inside?

LAGBAJA *(sighs at the memory)* Yes. Right inside. And . . .
(brightens) . . . that's how she became a mother. You should have
seen her – so furious. Called me names too. And then the baby
came into the world. Wearing a cap.

BANZA   The baby was born with a cap on its head?

LAGBAJA   That's what I said.

BANZA   Could the cap have been the . . . ?

LAGBAJA   The very same.

BANZA   . . . that fell inside?

LAGBAJA   The very same. *(pause)*

BANZA   You lucky devil! And where are they now, your wife and kid?

LAGBAJA   I don't know.

BANZA   You bastard! You walked out on her? You're an absentee father?

LAGBAJA   She walked out on me.

BANZA   She walked out on you?

LAGBAJA   Yes.

BANZA   May I know the reason?

LAGBAJA   I called out a name while we were . . . you know, making love.

BANZA   And it wasn't her name?

LAGBAJA   It wasn't her name.

BANZA   So she walked out on you. Rightly too. Twenty years, man! Twenty years of her life, that's what you threw down the drain. My God! Some bastard you are, cheating on someone who's given twenty years of her life to you!

LAGBAJA *(miserably)* I wasn't cheating on her.

BANZA   Oh no, just having a bit of fun on the side. Whose name then did you call out in the heat of passion – yours?

LAGBAJA   As a matter of fact, yes. We were making love and I called out my name.

BANZA   Sometimes in this life, Mensa, self-love is worse than cheating on your wife. *(pause)*

LAGBAJA   My name is not Mensa. *(pause)* Do you want to know how I met her?

BANZA   Met who?

LAGBAJA   My wife. Who else? Your asthmatic father?

BANZA   Point of correction. It wasn't asthma my father had. All he ever had in all his life was an ingrowing tooth that developed into tuberculosis.

LAGBAJA   An ingrowing tooth that developed into
tuberculosis?

BANZA   Yes. *(pause)*

LAGBAJA   I met her at school.

BANZA   Your wife?

LAGBAJA   My wife.

BANZA *(bored)* I don't want to hear your story.

LAGBAJA   I'll always remember that day. It was a bitterly cold
morning. It was so hot that people were being felled at random by
sunstroke. It was evening. She was studying in an empty
classroom when I first saw her. I tried to catch her attention. She
wouldn't even spare me a look before she packed her books,
sprang up and headed for another class, a crowded one this time.
And . . .

BANZA   You followed her.

LAGBAJA   Yes . . . I followed her. After a long while she gave
me a withering look and stood up again and headed this time for
the library, which was crowded as usual. I whispered fiercely to
her: 'I love you. I'm not going to let you rest until you
acknowledge that love.' She begged me to leave her alone but I
wouldn't budge. Then suddenly, in a loud voice, she said: 'Leave
me alone! Stop disturbing me!' All eyes in the library were turned
on us. I froze. Petrified. Wishing the ground would open up – and
swallow her. Then I had a brainstorm. A brainstorm! I cleared my
throat and said in a voice as loud as hers: 'I will not leave you
alone! I will not stop disturbing you until you accept Jesus Christ
as your Lord and Saviour!'

BANZA   And that was how you ended up getting hitched?

LAGBAJA   We started quarrelling almost immediately.

BANZA   Why?

LAGBAJA   I was several hours late for the wedding. Clean
forgot that it was my wedding. *(pause)* Got a cigarette to spare?
(Banza brings out the tin and gives him a cigarette)
For three days I've been looking for a cigarette to smoke. *(he
sniffs approvingly at the cigarette then returns it wordlessly to
Banza)*

BANZA　　　For three days I've been coming out every night around this time to look at the night in all its vast meaninglessness.

(Lagbaja looks lengthily at an imaginary wristwatch)

LAGBAJA　　Is it night already?

BANZA　　　Do you have to be told?

LAGBAJA　　But I can still see the sun outside.

BANZA　　　Makes no difference one way or another.

LAGBAJA　　But, but if the sun is still out, does it not follow that it's still day?

BANZA　　　You stretch my patience. You and fools like you who go about staggering in this vast void of darkness and yet will talk about seeing the sun and the moon and the stars and all sorts of things! It's always night, do you hear that? Always one dark, starless night with the dead walking abroad and your hair standing on end, and your teeth clattering from fright, do you hear that? The sun and the moon and the stars are only illusions. They've never been there. Only the night exists, real, foreboding, with all those mega-headed monsters playing football with human skulls. Every other thing – sun, moon, star – is swallowed whole in the anger of the night.

LAGBAJA　　Pretty bleak, wouldn't you say? Yet from day to day the world continues to thrive.

BANZA　　　One day, I tell you, we'll all wake up and be covered by a sudden sweat.

LAGBAJA　　Hey, can't you look on the bright side for once? Don't you ever project into the future?

BANZA　　　Into the future? No, thanks. I'm not finished with the present yet. As to the future: when I get to that bridge . . .

LAGBAJA　　. . . you'll set on the broken planks and fall down the river, yes thank you. Ever heard of being optimistic?

BANZA　　　At the funeral of my best friend.

LAGBAJA　　I thought I was your best friend.

BANZA　　　Who said you weren't? *(pause)* It rained yesterday, did you know that?

LAGBAJA　　It's been so many years since it rained.

BANZA   Everywhere was wet.

LAGBAJA   I was a kid when last it rained.

BANZA   The parched farmlands were flooded, trees bearing fruit uprooted, animals drowned, houses swept away.

LAGBAJA   Is that what life is all about? Droughts and floods and nothing else?

BANZA   People were killed too.

LAGBAJA   Anybody I know?

BANZA   Yes. Plenty of them. But nobody of value, if you must know. Swept away every house in town except the beer-parlour. Killed everybody except, I suppose, you and me and Sidi.

LAGBAJA   Nice woman, Sidi. *(reflective pause)* A woman like her I've never come across. Is it true she used to clap very well?

BANZA   I've danced with her and seen her dance.

(They dance)

A better dancer I'm yet to come across. But I've never seen her clap.

LAGBAJA   One of these days I'm going to dance with her.

BANZA   Sidi comes very expensive, I hope you know that.

LAGBAJA   Money is not an object. I'll cut my balls and mortgage them for Sidi.

BANZA   Then you'll be pretty useless to her, I'm afraid.

LAGBAJA   Producing kids like a guinea-pig is no longer the thing in vogue.

BANZA   Then commit suicide, my friend. De-congest the human race.

LAGBAJA   I did try once. Jumped off the top of a twenty-storey building.

BANZA *(sceptically)* And what happened after that?

LAGBAJA   I woke up from the nightmare, sweating. *(pause)* It rained yesterday, did you know that?

BANZA   It's been so many years since it last rained.

LAGBAJA   Cats and dogs. Bolts of lightning like burning spears across the sky. Thunder . . .

LAGBAJA   And the ground?

LAGBAJA   Wet, so wet. And soft.

BANZA   Did it drop like pebbles?

LAGBAJA   And more. Like rocks rolling down a valley.

BANZA   And the farms? Did it fall on them and ease the thirst of their parched tongues?

LAGBAJA   They have no tongues.

BANZA   What?

LAGBAJA   The farms.

BANZA   But it fell on them, all the same?

LAGBAJA   All the same, it fell on them. The people rejoiced as well.

BANZA   The people are always rejoicing.

LAGBAJA   What's wrong with that?

BANZA   Sooner or later, they're back there crying again. *(he brings out the cigarette tin)* Did I tell you I met God yesterday?

LAGBAJA   Can you spare one? *(he receives a cigarette from Banza, who has stood up and headed for the door)* For three whole days I've been looking forward to this. A cigarette to smoke.

(he sniffs the cigarette. Banza goes out. To the nearest member of the audience)

Three whole days, oh God, and here I am, the proud possessor of one.

(The phone begins to ring. It should continue ringing until Banza returns, bursting in through the door. He is drenched to the bone. The only dry object on him is the cigarette between his lips. The phone stops ringing. Momentarily)

Gone for a swim?

(Banza is shivering. He brings out a box of wet matches and takes out one soaked matchstick after another, unsuccessfully trying to light the cigarette between his lips)

BANZA   It's started again. The rain. Street outside is totally submerged. People are having to use canoes to cross.

LAGBAJA   What do we do? Stay at home and lose our jobs?

BANZA   No street to clean, man, the street's been swept away.

LAGBAJA   Come on, let's get going.

(Banza is still rubbing one wet matchstick after another on the matchbox in his bid to light the cigarette)

BANZA   I said it's raining, didn't you hear me?

(Lagbaja is still sniffing his cigarette. He hands it back to Banza. The phone starts ringing again. Banza eyes the phone, looking worried)

It could be Sidi.

LAGBAJA *(ominously)* And then it could be not. *(he begins to leave)* I shall see you when I come back. Don't forget to make supper.

He leaves through the door. Sound of heavy rain. Banza eyes the phone, then eyes the door. He repeats this sequence of movements. He seems to panic.

BANZA   Hey you bastard, wait for me!

He runs after Lagbaja. The phone continues to ring.

Slow fade to black.

ACT TWO – Howling

The lights come up on the room. Except for an old rusty piston lying rather conspicuously on the table between Banza and Lagbaja, it is as before.

It is dead of night.

In the distance the barking and whine of a dog. The phlegmatic and abortive starting of an aged and consumptive car. A shrill protracted scream.

LAGBAJA   Did you hear that?

BANZA *(irritably)* What? I didn't hear anything. Not a sound.

LAGBAJA   A dog barking.

BANZA   Dogs are meant to bark.

LAGBAJA   It was also whining.

BANZA   That too is in the nature of a dog.

LAGBAJA   In my village it's an evil omen. A dog only whines
like that when death is lurking around the corner.

BANZA   Perhaps it's about to die

LAGBAJA *(overlapping)* Perhaps it's about to die . . . Did you hear
the car?

BANZA   What car?

LAGBAJA   There was a car out there that was trying to start.

BANZA   Did it . . . ?

LAGBAJA   . . . start? No, it didn't.

BANZA   Even the key to success doesn't always fit into your
ignition, no?

LAGBAJA   Someone out there was screaming. And I could have
sworn it was a woman.

BANZA   Perhaps she was . . .

LAGBAJA   On second thoughts, I think it was a man.

BANZA   . . . being raped?

LAGBAJA   Oh God! I hope it wasn't that.

BANZA   But supposing it was? It is perfectly in the nature of
men to rape women, and women to rape men, and women to rape
women, and men to rape men . . .

LAGBAJA   . . . sometimes they simply make love.

BANZA   . . . and sometimes it's hard to tell the difference.
(pause) You saw the sign yourself: 'You are requested not to
throw cigarette ends in the urinals as it makes them soggy and
damp, and difficult to light.' *(pained)* You saw the sign. *(pause)*

LAGBAJA   Yes. There is evil out there, Temedu.

BANZA   There is nothing out there. Nothing but this failure
that is everywhere.

LAGBAJA   There is evil out there. I tell you. Haven't we had
this conversation before?

BANZA   Before you died, yes, a long, very long time ago.

(Lagbaja looks at him strangely)

LAGBAJA   Before I died?

BANZA   ⸀You died. Don't you know that you died?

LAGBAJA   From one friend to another, I strongly suggest that you seek the help of a psychiatrist as a matter of the utmost urgency, my friend.

BANZA   But I killed you. I did kill you. Don't you remember that I killed you?

LAGBAJA   No doubt you've taken leave of your senses.

BANZA   But I tell you! You died. I killed you. You died and resurrected.

LAGBAJA   You're absolutely insane.

BANZA   I shot you in the head. With this – this!

LAGBAJA *(takes the pistol and examines it, then tosses it back on the table)* You're certified. An intellectual eunuch. Absolutely hysterical. You should be committed.

BANZA *(astounded)* Are you denying that you died? That you resurrected?

LAGBAJA   Not only that, I'd add also that every word you utter detracts from the sum total of your sanity. You're psychoschizo-phrenic. *(pause)* Uuumh, that sounded nice. Nice. The more my life falls apart, the more my vocabulary seems to improve. *(pause)* Have they set him free?

BANZA   Who?

LAGBAJA   Him.

BANZA   Him?

LAGBAJA   Him.

BANZA   Well, have they . . . ?

LAGBAJA   . . . set him free?

BANZA   No, they haven't.

LAGBAJA   They haven't?

BANZA   They haven't.

LAGBAJA   Then they must have killed him.

BANZA   Tortured him to death, yes, I worked there once, remember? The Department of Persuasion. We used tocut out their balls. Squeeze them out. Orange pips.

LAGBAJA   He couldn't be . . .

BANZA   . . . dead?

LAGBAJA   But he must be.

BANZA   But he must be.

LAGBAJA   You think he might be dead?

BANZA   I think he's dead. Hung for a heretic.

LAGBAJA   Then he must surely be dead.

BANZA   He definitely is dead. *(pause)* Not that I would exactly mourn him.

LAGBAJA   You wouldn't?

BANZA   I once caught him with my wife, the bastard.

LAGBAJA   You once caught him with your wife?

BANZA   Talking to her. The bastard. Talking to my wife.
          (pause)

LAGBAJA   I have an erection.

BANZA   Sorry, I'm a married man.

LAGBAJA *(stands up and fiddles with his zipper and makes as if to masturbate)* May I?

BANZA *(starts furiously)* Did I hear you right? Say that again!

LAGBAJA   I said, may I . . .?

BANZA *(further enraged)* Every sperm is special. Do you hear that? Every sperm is great. If one sperm is wasted. God gets quite irate. *(pause)* Have you never seen that graffito? Don't you ever read?

LAGBAJA *(genuinely contrite)* Oh, I'm sorry, very sorry. I didn't know that. I've never seen any graffito. I didn't know that. Honest to God, I didn't.

BANZA   Didn't know what?

LAGBAJA   That God was capable of emotions. *(pause)* I still have a hard-on.

BANZA   So go to town, man! Paint the town red! Get yourself a pumpkin. *(pause)*

LAGBAJA   I prefer a woman.

BANZA   There you go again, sniffing a gift horse in the mouth.

LAGBAJA   And where does he stand in this matter?

BANZA   Who?

LAGBAJA   God. Won't he get irate?

BANZA   Probably sulk for a day or two. Then he'll go minding his own business.

LAGBAJA   Give your life to him, man! Give your life to him!

BANZA   And if I do give my life to him, what will I be left with?

LAGBAJA   But he saves, you know, he saves.

BANZA   And why can't we also? We'll make it a joint account. *(pause)* Have you never seen a corpse smiling?

LAGBAJA *(uneasily)* No, I haven't.

BANZA   Sometimes, you know, sometimes I'm overcome with a paranoia: I'm the last human being left on earth and I'm surrounded by five billion corpses. Phew! Five billion. The thought makes me grin like a fool. *(pause)* Do you know that a man's beard continues to grow even after he's dead? And the nails as well. Until you begin to rot. I was once a morgue attendant, you know. Before the flood. Superb job. Made you feel like God. Sometimes after yet another of those multiple accidents involving those luxury buses, and the casualties were brought in and stacked one upon the other like so many lumps of yam in a barn, I'd stand among them, these denizens of the graves, alone, savouring the gut-smell of blood and bile and decay that filled the air like sour-sweet mango perfume. I would stand among them, smiling back at those who smiled . . . *(demonstrates)* 'Hello, baby, how're you doing? I like the way you smile. Like a bloody bitch. I like the way you smile. Honest to God I do. Like the patron saint of all bitches. If there's a hell, I'll meet you there. Buy a drink and that's a date.' *(pause)* 'Hello, old man.' *(fondles an imaginary protrusion)* 'Now, that's my man. Went and croaked with a hard-on, didn't we? I've got half a mind to give you a blow-job right now. Just to see the look on God's face. I bet you must have been some teenage idiot's sugar daddy. Were you thinking dirty when it happened? A big problem for the

undertaker, I hope you realise that, you fool. Dying with an
erection, for God's sakes, have you no decency?' *(to Lagbaja)*
The more I look at you, the more I'm reminded of those corpses.
You look – ordinary – most inordinately ordinary, have I never
told you? Every time I look at your face I have this nauseating
feeling that you could have been anyone else. You could have
been me, for instance. Or my father or even my mother. You
could have been anybody. Anybody. But . . . *(spits in disgust)* . . .
you chose to be you. I could sometimes almost mistake you for
myself when we meet in the doorway. *(he turns pointedly towards
Lagbaja who has all this while been staring passively into space,
a fatuous grin permanently installed on his face)* Have we never
met in the doorway? *(waits in vain for a response)* I suppose we
must have. Or you wouldn't have that smug look in your eyes.
You could choke a man to death with the stench of that smugness.
*(he stares furiously at Lagbaja's passive, almost idiotic,
absolutely smugness-bereft presence)* You are the smuggest
bastard I've ever met, do you hear , do you . . . *(pause)* Time is
passing. *(pause)* I wonder what else it should be doing. Every
minute of my life I've been the sole witness to the birth of
another minute. It's the most monotonous experience you could
witness. God is a rather dodgy old sod, is what I say. I wish he
would do something distantly radical one of these days. Stop the
hand of the clock, for instance. But I guess he couldn't. Might
give him an orgasm, stain the holy robe, you see. And that'd
mean a police record. Ruin his chances of re-election.

LAGBAJA *(the vacant look still on his face)* Why did you kill her?

BANZA   Who?

LAGBAJA   Why did you kill her?

BANZA   *Who?*

LAGBAJA   I said why . . .

BANZA *(overlapping)* I was framed.

LAGBAJA   Oh. *(pause. With a look – hesitant at first – of
distress at his groin, slowly)* I – I think I ought to tell you
something, Temedu.

BANZA *(sighs)* There are so many things in this life you ought to
tell me.

LAGBAJA   It's four days gone now, Temedu, and I still haven't had my period.

(In the distance the barking and whining of a dog. The phlegmatic and abortive starting of an aged and consumptive car. A shrill protracted scream)

Did you hear that?

BANZA *(irritably)* What? I didn't hear anything. Not a sound.

LAGBAJA   A dog barking.

BANZA   Dogs are meant to bark.

LAGBAJA   It was also whining.

BANZA   That too is in the nature of a dog.

LAGBAJA   In my village it's an evil omen. A dog only whines like that when death is lurking around the corner.

BANZA   Perhaps it's about to die.

LAGBAJA *(overlapping)* Perhaps it's about to die . . . Did you hear the car?

BANZA   What car?

LAGBAJA   There was a car out there that was trying to start.

BANZA   Did it . . . ?

LAGBAJA   . . . start? No. It didn't.

BANZA   Even the key to success doesn't always fit into your ignition, no?

LAGBAJA   Someone out there was screaming. And I could have sworn it was a woman.

BANZA   Perhaps she was . . .

LAGBAJA   On second thoughts, I think it was a man.

BANZA   . . . being raped? *(pause)*

LAGBAJA   Did you see the lights?

BANZA   What lights?

LAGBAJA   At the end of the tunnel.

BANZA   A train approaching, perhaps? *(pause)*

LAGBAJA   Perhaps there is evil out there, Temedu.

BANZA   There is nothing out there. Nothing but this failure that is everywhere.

LAGBAJA   There is evil out there, I tell you.

BANZA *(in exasperation)* Very well then. There is evil out there. Shall we go looking for it with a handgun?

LAGBAJA *(dejectedly)* Perhaps after all that's what we should do. Get ourselves some handguns.

BANZA   We will, we will. We'll line the whole lot of them evil-doers out there, we'll line them up at a seaside stadium with their backs to the sea and their faces to the sand. And shoot them. Every last one of them. We'll shoot them. Spill out their evil-churning guts and declare surplus for the vultures. *(facing Lagbaja)* Isn't that what we should do? We'll do it, don't you worry. So long as you don't come crying to me when you see them resurrecting three days later. A certain Jewish gentleman did that two thousand years ago if you remember and ever since it's become something of a fashion.

LAGBAJA   I'd like to see them do that. Resurrect. Really I would. You have a saying don't you? The one about trespassers.

BANZA   Which one? *(pause)* You keep intruding on my thoughts. Every time I come up with a lofty idea you spirit it out with your endless chatter. If I had my way I would've shot you ages ago.

LAGBAJA   And supposing I survived?

BANZA   I'd shoot you again.

LAGBAJA   Naturally. Don't you think that's what we should do to them out there?

BANZA   What? Shoot them down every time they come up for air?

LAGBAJA   Shoot them down every time they come up for air.

BANZA   By the time we're finished we'll probably be right there beside them – clawing out for a reed to hold on to. *(pause)*

LAGBAJA *(hesitantly)* Excuse me.

BANZA *(impatiently)* Yes?

LAGBAJA   May I wank off? *(he turns his back on Banza and proceeds to masturbate)*

BANZA   It's someone's birthday today – yours or mine. I cannot remember the last time I had a birthday. Birthdays are for howling, I always say, for letting go. Go to the highest point you can find and howl to him up there: 'Pull back the time, you cheat! You keep it all and only dole it out in trickles to us. Give us back all those centuries you've stolen from us! And what makes you think we don't know why you queue us up and kill us so? Because it's the only way you can go on being alive.' I swear to you, Temedu, the day we find the key to immortality, God will simply drop dead. *(pause)* What did you say?

(Lagbaja is not in a state to say anything. He is masturbating)
That he'll kill us all before we can? Well, I've got news for you – he can't kill us.

LAGBAJA *(as he climaxes)* He can't? Who can't?

BANZA   God. Because if he does, he'll have destroyed himself
as well.

LAGBAJA   How?

BANZA   He wouldn't exist if there wasn't you and me to think that he does.

LAGBAJA   No?

BANZA   No. The boss is only boss for as long as he has someone to boss over.

LAGBAJA   I feel – good. *(he brings out a wine glass from behind him. It is filled to the brim with a thick, milky substance)*

BANZA   What's that? *(he takes it from Lagbaja and takes a sip)* Tastes like come.

LAGBAJA   Semi-skimmed. There was that case of the celibate monk some time ago who started secreting a milky substance from his sweat glands. Turned out to be sperm. *(pause)* If you pricked my skin with a needle five minutes ago that's what would have come oozing out, not blood. I was full to bursting point.

BANZA   Have we not had this conversation before?

LAGBAJA   Not with you I haven't.

BANZA   I seem to remember it from another life a long time ago. I could have sworn that was a thousand years ago, this very minute a thousand years ago, sitting at this very spot, on another seat very much like this one and with another fool who could well have been you. *(looks at himself dejectedly)* Only thing is, I don't seem to have changed at all.

LAGBAJA   But you have. But you have.

BANZA   Really? You think so?

LAGBAJA   I know so. I should, shouldn't I? *(pause)* I'm your father after all.

BANZA *(betraying no surprise whatever)* You are my father?

LAGBAJA   To the last pint of blood, yes. To the nearest genetic hundred. I gave you birth, don't you remember?

BANZA   How could I?

LAGBAJA   You were the fastest growing kid I've ever known – started walking at age six months and turned to crawling three months later. You crawled for fifteen years to a day.

BANZA *(beaming with pride)* I did? I've always known it too. I knew there was something – something special about me. *(becoming more friendly)* So you're my father? *(he extends his hand for a shake. The hand hangs awkwardly in the air for some time then drops. Immediately it drops, Lagbaja extends his own hand, also for a shake, and is similarly rebuffed. Lagbaja's hand drops. They are both grinning from ear to ear)* So you are my father.

LAGBAJA   Yes I am.

BANZA   So you are my father.

LAGBAJA   Yes I am.

BANZA   So you are my father.

LAGBAJA   Yes I am.

(Banza erupts in happy laughter while Lagbaja looks on with a deathly grimace. The moment Banza stops laughing. Lagbaja bursts into his own convulsive laughter while Banza looks on with a puzzled grimace)

BANZA *(totally expressionless)* This must be the happiest day of my life.

LAGBAJA *(yawns)* Mine too. *(pause)*

BANZA *(sudden change of mood)* Do you know what I think of you? What I really think of you?

LAGBAJA *(cowering)* No. What do you think of me?

BANZA *(relaxes)* You are a good fellow. Beneath contempt, but a nice kind of person. I would kill you. And I will too. Such a pity. We could have visited with each other till we were both old.

LAGBAJA *(yawns)* Yeah, such a poor pity. But you have no choice, have you? You will kill me.

BANZA Unfortunately, yes, I've got no choice. I just have to.

LAGBAJA Such a pity too. Poor fellow. I wish I could help, honest to God, I wish I could. But – *(he gestures helplessly)*

BANZA Don't you sometimes wish you were dead?

LAGBAJA There are so many things I wish I were. But if horses were wishes . . .

BANZA And don't you sometimes wish you'd wake up after three days?

LAGBAJA That's called a coma.

BANZA Did I tell you about my father – how he died?

(Lagbaja nods)

I was eight years old then, or five or twenty, or five and twenty. We were on a country-wide tour, my father and I. He had this car then, a blue station-wagon. The make is irrelevant. the place insignificant. We were on this long lonesome highway, I remember, and my father, being the reckless driver he was, was making a steady twenty miles an hour. Really taking his time, you'll agree with me, considering that the car couldn't go any faster, simply taking his time. We had the road to ourselves for close to two hours when, suddenly, from behind us came this big monster of a truck. One moment he was behind us, the next it was dead level with us. We wouldn't really have noticed the bastard if he'd simply sped past us and left us in our shells. But no way; for the next half hour the idiot simply remained level with us, and of course this began to irritate my father. I mean a man can only take so much . . . Father leaned out of the car and screamed: 'Move, you bushman!' Or that was what I thought he was going to say, because that was everybody's middle name as far as my father was concerned – bushman. But he never got to saying anything: the moment his head came leaning out of the car, I saw this short devil of an axe come slashing down on his neck from the truck. The axe went right through, neatly severing the head from the body. A perfect work of art, I nearly wept, seeing my father's head that day, rolling on the highway like a stray ball. But father was a man of firm resolutions. He was. Didn't utter another word until thirty minutes later – when he brought out his handkerchief to wipe the sweat off his face and that was when, for the first time, he noticed that he hadn't got a head. And burst into tears. *(pause)* That was the only time I ever saw him cry.

LAGBAJA   Sad story. A bloody sad story. A sad and bloody story. I'll remember it any other time I feel like a bad mood. *(pause)* Temedu.

BANZA   Yes, Temedu.

LAGBAJA   I have an erection.

BANZA   You have an erection?

LAGBAJA   I have an erection.

BANZA   You have an erection?

LAGBAJA   I wish I could set him free.

BANZA   Who?

LAGBAJA   Him.

BANZA   Him?

LAGBAJA   Him.

BANZA   He called God a common thief.

LAGBAJA   No, it wasn't God he called a thief. It was one of his prophets.

BANZA   Same thing. If you ask me.

LAGBAJA   Tell me, why do these gods always turn out to be false?

(Banza picks up the pistol and begins to load it)

BANZA   I've never known one to be a god.

LAGBAJA   This one thinks he creates. Creates.

BANZA   But he does, doesn't he? And then destroys. One comes after the other, not so? Like marriage and divorce.

LAGBAJA   Mere masturbation, if you ask me.

BANZA   Sheer wastage. Totally useless. All the same, I sometimes wish they'd set him free.

LAGBAJA   God? They jailed God?

BANZA   No. Him.

LAGBAJA   But you know his crime. You're aware of the enormity.

BANZA   He said we were even more irresponsible than God. He said that. He compared us with God.

LAGBAJA   He did?

BANZA   He did. And worse.

LAGBAJA   In that case, in the light of this additional evidence, I hope he rots in jail.

BANZA   I hope he rots in jail. *(pause. Politely)* Please let me know when you're ready.

LAGBAJA   Ready for what?

(Banza waves the pistol apologetically in the air)

BANZA   There's only one bullet left . . .

LAGBAJA *(sarcastically)* . . . and it's got my name written on it? Is that what you're trying to say?

BANZA *(quiet desperation)* I can't afford to miss.

LAGBAJA   Not to worry. You just aim for my head.
(he stands up and extends his hand for a shake. Banza ignores it. Lagbaja's hand hangs awkwardly in the air for a while then drops. Immediately it drops, Banza extends his own hand also, for a shake and is in turn rebuffed. Banza's hand drops. They are both grinning from ear to ear)
Thanks for everything, my man. I'll miss you.

BANZA   I'll miss you too, father.

LAGBAJA   Is my bag packed?

BANZA   Everything.

LAGBAJA   My whisky case. If you should forget to pack my whisky case, I'll die of thirst over there. I hope you know that.

BANZA   Rest assured, father. I personally packed it myself.

LAGBAJA   And my carton of cigarettes?

BANZA   You don't smoke.

LAGBAJA   And I'm a vegetarian, and I drink decaffeinated coffee. Did you or did you not pack my carton of cigarettes, boy?

BANZA *(quietly)* Everything is packed.

LAGBAJA   Are you . . . ?

BANZA   I said, everything is packed, father. Trust me.

LAGBAJA *(musingly)* In the old days, when the king died he was accompanied by his chief Horseman. You're lucky these days if you go with a carton of cigarettes. What has the world come to?

(Banza aims the pistol carefully at Lagbaja's head)

BANZA   Goodbye, father. Say me well to mother.

LAGBAJA *(pained)* What has the world come to?

(Banza pulls the trigger. It merely clicks. There is no bullet in the pistol)

BANZA *(as Lagbaja comes crashing against the bar)* And don't you forget to resurrect!

Lagbaja falls down as if lifeless.

Banza turns slowly round, a look of fear, of terror, slowly creeping onto his face. He gingerly drops the pistol on the table – and begins to go off. At first he walks slowly, then he makes as if to break into a race. He freezes in that position.

Blackout.

In the distance the barking and whining of a dog. The phlegmatic and abortive starting of an aged and consumptive car. A shrill protracted scream. As Banza comes running back on stage, there is a new and deeper terror now on his face.

Lights up.

Lagbaja is seated by the table, an idiotic grin stuck like plaster on his face.

LAGBAJA   Did you hear that?

BANZA *(irritably)* What? I didn't hear anything. Not a sound.

LAGBAJA   A dog barking.

BANZA	Dogs are meant to bark.
LAGBAJA	It was also whining.
BANZA	That too is in the nature of a dog.

LAGBAJA   In my village it's an evil omen. A dog only whines like that when death is lurking around the corner.

BANZA   Perhaps it's about to die.

LAGBAJA *(overlapping)* Perhaps it's about to die . . . Did you hear the car?

BANZA   What car?

LAGBAJA   There was a car out there that was trying to start.

BANZA   Did it . . . ?

LAGBAJA   . . . start? No it didn't. Even the key to success doesn't always fit into your ignition, no?

LAGBAJA   Someone out there was screaming. And I could have sworn it was a woman.

BANZA   Perhaps she was . . .

LAGBAJA   On second thoughts, I think it was a man.

BANZA   . . . being raped. *(pause)*

LAGBAJA   Did you see the light?

BANZA   What light?

LAGBAJA   At the end of the tunnel.

BANZA   There was a light at the end of the tunnel?

LAGBAJA   Yes.

BANZA   Are you sure?

LAGBAJA   Yes.

BANZA   In that case. I don't think it matters whether or not I saw it. *(pause. He takes out from his pocket a tin cigarette case. He brings out cigarette after cigarette. They are all soaking wet. Angrily, to Lagbaja)* You saw the sign yourself: 'You are requested not to throw cigarette ends in the urinals as it makes them soggy and damp, and difficult to light.' You saw the sign, and yet . . . *(to himself)* I should've laid them out to dry.

LAGBAJA   There is evil out there, Temedu.

BANZA   There is nothing out there. Nothing but this failure that is everywhere. *(looking at the cigarettes sadly)* I should've laid them out to dry.

LAGBAJA   There is evil out there, I tell you. Haven't we had this conversation before?

BANZA *(to himself)* I should've . . . *(he seems to snap out of it)* . . . what? . . . Before you died, yes, a long, a very long time ago.

(Lagbaja looks at him strangely)

LAGBAJA   What's that supposed to mean – before I died?

BANZA   You died. Don't you know that you died?

LAGBAJA   From one friend to another, I strongly suggest that you seek the help of a psychiatrist as a matter of the utmost urgency, my friend.

BANZA   But I killed you. I did kill you. Don't you remember that I killed you?

LAGBAJA   No doubt you've taken leave of your senses.

BANZA   But I tell you! You died. I killed you. You died and resurrected.

LAGBAJA   You're absolutely insane.

BANZA   I shot you in the head! With this – this.

(Lagbaja takes the pistol and examines it, then tosses it back on the table)

LAGBAJA   You're certified. An intellectual eunuch. Absolutely hysterical. You should be committed.

BANZA   Are you denying that you died? That you resurrected?

LAGBAJA   Not only that. I'd add also that every word you utter detracts from the sum total of your sanity. You're psychoschizo-phrenic. *(pause)* Uuumh, that sounded nice. Nice *(pause)* Have they set him free?

BANZA   Your father?

LAGBAJA *(overlapping)* My –

BANZA   I'm your father. I'm free. On parole, at least.

LAGBAJA   You're my –

BANZA *(overlapping)* I'm your father. To the last pint of blood. To the nearest genetic hundred. You want proof? You were pregnant once – remember? Remember the abortion? I was that abortionist.

LAGBAJA   But you're dead. Aren't you dead? Your head was cut off. The baby sued, remember? She took exception to being aborted.

BANZA *(hotly protesting)* It was nothing personal . . .

LAGBAJA   . . . and convicted. You were beheaded.

BANZA   Spare Parts. I walked into the Spare Parts department one evening when no-one was watching and picked up another one.

LAGBAJA   Bullshit. *(pause)* It rained yesterday.

BANZA   It did?

LAGBAJA   The ground was wet.

BANZA   And that's new? That strikes you as unusual?

LAGBAJA   People brought out their umbrellas.

BANZA   No that's unusual. Usually they simply dash through the rain and hope for the best. And those without umbrellas?

LAGBAJA   Raincoats. Mackintoshes.

BANZA   The only argument against a raging downpour is to put on a raincoat. They put on raincoats. That's – wise. And those without raincoats, mackintoshes?

LAGBAJA   Got beaten by the rain, of course.

BANZA   And why should some have umbrellas and others none?

LAGBAJA   I'd like you to tell me. It's always been like that.

BANZA   Always?

LAGBAJA   Always.

BANZA   Are the horses ready? *(pause)*

LAGBAJA   What horses?

BANZA   I thought – I thought . . . I thought we were . . .

LAGBAJA   Horsemen?

BANZA   I thought we were horsemen.

LAGBAJA   Yes.

BANZA   There were four of us.

LAGBAJA   Yes.

BANZA *(insistently)* There were four of us!

LAGBAJA   Yes.

BANZA   What happened . . . ?

LAGBAJA   To . . .

BANZA   Yes . . .

LAGBAJA   The flood did for them. They drowned.

BANZA   They drowned?

LAGBAJA   Yes. But we survived.

BANZA   They drowned. We survived.

LAGBAJA   Yes. We survived.

BANZA   We're survivors.

LAGBAJA   Yes.

BANZA   We survived.

LAGBAJA   Yes.

BANZA   We'll always survive.

LAGBAJA   Yes.

BANZA   There'll be bad times and no-so-good times. Good times and so-so times. But we'll always survive.

LAGBAJA *(happily, like a prayer)* Yes, yes, yes, yes. Oh God, yes. *(pause)* This must be the happiest day of my life.

BANZA   Mine too.

Lagbaja erupts in happy laughter while Banza looks on with a deathly grimace. The moment Lagbaja stops laughing Banza bursts into his own convulsive laughter while Lagbaja looks on with a puzzled grimace.

Instant black.

The end.

'Biyi Bandele

Born on 13 October 1967. His plays have been produced at the Royal Court Theatre, Battersea Arts Centre, The Gate, The Bush and several other theatres in the UK.

☐

☐

He has also written for radio and TV and has just finished writing his third novel as well as a screenplay for British Screen and Skreba Films. He is currently writing a play for the Royal Shakespeare Company.

London New Play Festival Production Index

1989
TOM'S GIFT by David Ansdele
THE QUILT by Val Doulton
MILES TO GO by Richard Daugs
THE WORLD OF BRIAN LONELY by Ian Gideon
BOO TO THE MOON by Paul Slabolepsky
MEDEA: NINE NIGHT by Seth Baumrin
BODYSURFING by Max India
MARITAL AIDS by Jack Bradley
HANNAH'S PLACE by Sue Aldred
DINNER AND A MOVIE by Julie Balloo
WRITTEN IN SICKNESS by Giles Croft
EYES DOWN by Polly Churchill

1990
SOMETHING IN THE AIR by Alan P Cooke
BURIED BY BLOSSOM by Angela Lanyon
JACOB'S LADDER by Sue Aldred
CHERUB by Jan Maloney
CLAY by Julie Balloo
FRAGMENTS by Murray Woodfield
AFTER EEYORE by Nicola Davies
ROUTINE BUSINESS by Paul Hinksman
SWAG CITY by Jack Bradley
HONEYMOON IN DEALY PLAZA by Laurance Kraus
THE CASTAWAY by John Hanamy
BLOOD ON BLOOD by Rebecca Ranson

1991
WHO KILLED THE DIRTY DIGGER? by Janine Amos
TWO FACED by Sarah Woods
WHEN A ROVER RETURNS by Stephen Ferns

WHY BANANAS BEND by Duncan Gould
FREE by Barbara Lindsay
IT NEVER RAINS by Robert Peckham
SHATTERED PEACE by Claire Booker
SERINGAPATHAM by Norman King Lloyd
JOY SOLUTION by Stuart Duckworth
GABRIEL AND GABRIEL by Julie Balloo
BALLAD OF THE LIMEHOUSE RAT by Tim Newton
ASSETS by Paul Bishop
THE HEART OF SUNDAY NIGHT by Trevor Miller

1992
HOMEWORK FOR MEN by John Lazarus
NIGHT NIGHT by Louise Warren
ASKING FOR IT by Ruth Worrall
EVERLASTING ROSE by Judy Upton
STRINDBERG KNEW MY FATHER by Mark Jenkins
GONE FISHING by Claire Booker
SISTER, GIRL by Brandyn Barbara-Artis
BATTYMAN BLUES by Oscar Watson
RUBBER DOLLY by Don Hannah
STRAIGHT TAILED BILL by Tim Blackwell
THE PRISONER'S PUMPKIN by Alan McMurtrie
THE FLESH TRADER by Trevor Miller
WINTER SOLSTICE by Mark London Williams
DEVIL'S CHOICE AND EGG ETC. by Katie Campbell
THE CEZANNE SYNDROME by Normand Canac-Marquis
TOM AND JERRY by Julie Balloo
WALKING IN L.A. by Brandyn Barbara-Artis, Tim Blackwell
and Mark London Williams

1993

WILD TURKEY by Joe Penhall
THE FREEWHEEL ARMADA by Brian Devlin
JERSEY CITY by Wendy Hammond
SOUNDINGS by Andrew Rattenbury
IN THE FIELDS OF ACELDAMA by Naomi Wallace
BUTTER'S GOAT by Scott Frank
BLOOD RED by Michael Sharp
NORMALITY by Bernard Padden
MOSES NAPOLEON AND THE QUEEN OF SWEDENBERG
by Cecily Bomberg
THE RICH YOUNG RULER by Linda Marshall
FLESHING OUT by Graeme Holmes
CLOSE TO YOU by Mark Ravenhill
CRAZY QUILT by Scott Burke
A FEW WHITE BOYS TALKING by Bonnie Greer

1994

SHREADS AND FANCIES by David Bridel
ST JAMES AND THE TATOO MAN by Craig Baxter
BINARY PRIMES by Tim Latham
END OF THE ROUND by Glen Neath
THE GIRL WHO FELL THROUGH A HOLE IN HER JUMPER
by Naomi Wallace and Bruce McLeod
JULIE JOHNSON by Wendy Hammond
TWO HORSEMEN by ´Biyi Bandele
SAY ZEBRA by Sherry Coman
CARTOONS FROM A COLD CORNER by Julie Balloo
THE HISTORY OF WATER by Noelle Janaczewska
HUMMINGBIRD IN FLIGHT by Nick Sutton
ONE MAN'S MEAT by Jessica Townsend
CRASH by Neil Biswas

1995
ZERO POSITIVE by Harry Kondoleon
ME AND THE BOYS by ´Biyi Bandele
THE DARK ROOM by Sara Clifford
'OH CHRIST!' by Aiden Healy
SPARROWS SMALL BIRDS HAUNTING HOUSES
by Martyn Hesford
WHITE NOISE WHITE LIGHT by Gary Swing
JACKED by Phil Willmott
THE MOTHER KNOT by Venice Miller
THREE TIDES TURNING by Louise Warren

1996
TONGUE-TIED by Sara Clifford
HOOVER BAG by Anthony Neilson
AN AUDIENCE WITH QUEEN by Anita Sullivan
HARD SHOULDER by John Doona
SCENES FROM PARADISE by Michael Wall
THE CRICKET TEST by James Waddington
(GAY MARRIAGE IN SUBURBIA a trio of plays:)
LEIGHTON AND LEIGH by Tim Blackwell
MAISON SPLENDIDE by Laura Bridgeman
SEMPER SUBURBIA by Tom Minter

1997
DAHLIAS AND MOONSHINE by Tom Minter
TRY A PAIR OF BAGGY TROUSERS by Gillian Plowman
LINGER by John Doona
A SOMEWHAT INDECENT SITUATION and **FLOW LIKE HONEY** by Kevin MacGee
A NIGHT DIVIDED by Paloma Pedrero
THE BORGIA'S DINING ROOM by Phil Willmott

THE CONFESSION by Arnold Wesker
THE WRONG PARENTS by Sally Wainwright
STEAM BASIN by Mark Schofield

1998
THE LAST GIRL by David Bridel
EVERLASTING ROSE by Judy Upton
TV TOTS MEET BOMB BOY by Finneas Edwards
THE HOUSE OF RUBY MOON by Helen Cooper
SHIRTS AND SKINS by Tim Miller
UNDERBELLY by Dean Barker, Tamsin Hollo, Adam
Smethurst, Monica Dolan and Greg Feeman
RAINPROOF by Nick Discombe
JOSEPH by Richard Holden
TRAINER by Helen Kelley
IVAN by Stewart Permutt
EVER FALLEN IN LOVE by Julie Balloo
(additional material by Jenny Eclair)
TIRED OLD JESUS by Anthony Neilson

ARTISTIC POLICY

LNPF was founded in 1989 to develop and produce new plays and new theatrical forms. It is the purpose of the Festival to continue to define and redefine what is 'new' in theatre today and to present that variety of contemporary drama in full productions, wherever possible.

One of the primary aims of the Festival is to help young and early career writers through the step beyond the Reading of a play and onward to a full production. In addition to very new playwrights, the Festival also programmes the plays of mid-level writers who have had production experience.

The Festival aims to be a 'great equaliser', bringing together writers and theatre artists working at various levels. A variety of writing styles, in both full-length and one-act formats are chosen for the Festival by a fifteen member Literary Committee, including drama, comedy, performance art, combined art, children's plays and devised work. Extensive script selection criteria include the immediacy of the play, its originality of form, structure, language, content, message to the audiences of today and also most importantly, the play's entertainment value.

For more information contact:

LONDON NEW PLAY FESTIVAL
Diorama Arts Centre,
34 Osnaburgh St.
London NW1 3ND
Tel: 0171 209 2326
Fax: 0171 916 5282

To submit a script, please enclose a stamped self-addressed envelope and send it for the attention of the Literary Manager.

The annual script deadline is January 15th and the script submitted must be of a new play, previously unperformed in the theatre or any related media.

For further information about THE WRITING SCHOOL send an SAE to the Education Director at the above address.

FESTIVAL COMPANY

Artistic Director	Phil Setren
Literary Manager	David Prescott
Education Director	Christopher Preston
Administrative Director	Karen Gerald
Casting Director	Gary Davy
Casting Assistant	Stephanie Lister
Production Manager	Ben Ratcliffe
Asst. Production Managers	Jayne Rose Nelson
	Neil Alexander
Festival Photographer	Sean Patterson
Development Officer	Chris Cooke
Administrator	Bill Sterland
Press Representative	Marie Clements

FESTIVAL PATRONS
Edward Bond, Caryl Churchill, Alan Cubitt, Sarah Daniels, Nick Dear, David Edgar, Chris Hannan, David Hare, Dusty Hughes, Robert Holman, Gillian Plowman, Arnold Wesker.

Published wth the financial assistance of:

THE PEGGY RAMSAY FOUNDATION
STOLL MOSS THEATRES
THE CAMERON MACKINTOSH FOUNDATION

MEDITERRANEAN PLAYS BY WOMEN
ed. Marion Baraitser

A collection of astonishing plays by women from countries geographically linked but politically divided.

Twelve Women in a Cell, (trans. Marion Baraitser / Cheryl Robson) a play written after a period of captivity in Egypt by dissident writer **Nawal el Saadawi.**

The End of the Dream Season, (trans. Helen Kaye) a woman doctor outwits her friends and relations to retain her inheritance, by Israeli writer **Miriam Kainy.**

Libration, (trans. Lola Lopez Ruiz) a mysterious, intense and comic two-hander about two women who meet in a city park at night, by Catalan writer **Lluisa Cunillé.**

Mephisto, from the novel by Klaus Mann, (trans.Timberlake Wertenbaker) the story of a German actor who sells his soul to Nazi ideology by the eminent French writer/director **Ariane Mnouchkine.**

Harsh Angel, (trans. Rhea Frangofinou) a gentle Chekhovian tale of a family torn by the partition of their native land, written by Cypriot writer **Maria Avraamidou.**

Veronica Franco (trans. Sian Williams / Marion Baraitser) describes the life of a sixteenth century Venetian courtesan and poet, by Italy's foremost woman writer **Dacia Maraini.**

a great opportunity for those who don't see much live theatre by women to know what they've been missing. Everywoman Magazine

Price: £9.95   **ISBN 0-951-5877-3-0**

SIX PLAYS BY BLACK AND ASIAN WOMEN WRITERS
ed. Kadija George

A landmark collection of plays for stage, screen and radio showing the range and vitality of Black and Asian writing.

My Sister-Wife by Meera Syal, a taut thriller about two women who discover they are both married to the same man. 'A phenomenal talent.' Sunday Times.

Running Dream by Trish Cooke, tells the story of three generations of West Indian women with warmth and humour. 'the author's promise ripens.' The Times.

Song for a Sanctuary by Rukhsana Ahmad, explores the painful dilemma of an Asian woman forced to seek help from a women's refuge. 'perceptive and moving.' Morning Star.

Leonora's Dance by Zindika, four women share the house of a ballet dancer, whose contact with the supernatural lays the ghosts of the past to rest. 'a compelling show.' Caribbean Times.

Monsoon by Maya Chowdhry, is a poetic account of a young woman's sexual awakening. 'evocative and sensual.' Radio Times.

A Hero's Welcome by Winsome Pinnock, a tale of misplaced loyalty, longing for escape and early love. 'terrific new play' The Independent.

'showcases a wealth of talent amongst Black and Asian communities... often neglected by mainstream publishers.' Black Pride Magazine

Price: £7.50   **ISBN 0-9515877-2-2**

SEVEN PLAYS BY WOMEN, Female Voices, Fighting Lives
ed. Cheryl Robson

A bumper collection of award-winning plays by a new generation of women writers together with short critical essays on theatre today.

Fail/Safe by **Ayshe Raif**, 'a most disturbing lament for the way that some family ties become chains from which there will never be escape...' The Guardian

The Taking of Liberty by **Cheryl Robson**, 'the extraordinary tale of a town in the French Revolution: when the women take offence at an improvised statue, the incident escalates into savage retribution.' What's On.

Crux by **April de Angelis**, follows four women who follow their own doctrine of pleasure and hedonism in opposition to the stifling dictates of the Church. 'stimulating and humorous new play.' Time Out.

Ithaka by **Nina Rapi**, 'theatrically inventive, often surreal, witty and funny... sensitive charting of a woman's quest for love and freedom.' Bush Theatre.

Cochon Flambé by **Eva Lewin**, explores the sexual politics of waitressing in a comic, one-woman play.

Cut it Out by **Jan Ruppe**, a sharp blend of humour and pathos, tells the story of Laura, a self-lacerator.

Forced Out by **Jean Abbott**, a powerful drama of a lesbian teacher's confrontation with her community's prejudices, unleashed by a newspaper's gay witchhunt.

a testimony to the work and debate that is going on among women, artistically, theoretically and practically. It is an inspiring document. What's On

Price: £5.95   **ISBN: 0-9515877-1-4**

THE WOMEN WRITERS' HANDBOOK
eds. Robson, Georgeson, Beck

An essential guide to setting up and
running your own writing workshops.

Creative Writing Exercises

Extracts from workshop writings

New poetry and fiction

Contact Directory

Essays on writing and dramaturgy by

CARYL CHURCHILL
JILL HYEM
BRYONY LAVERY
AYSHE RAIF
CHERYL ROBSON

*A gem of a book. Everything a woman writer
might need in one slim volume.*
Everywoman Magazine

PRICE: £4.95   ISBN: 0-9515877-0-6

HOW MAXINE LEARNED TO LOVE HER LEGS
and other tales of growing-up
ed: Sarah Le Fanu

A sparkling collection of short stories exploring a host of female parts - rites of passage, revelations, strange relationships, love, loss, danger - the pleasures and pains of growing-up female in one entertaining volume.

Featuring 23 new and established authors including:

HILARY BAILEY **KATE PULLINGER**
BONNIE GREER **RAVI RANDHAWA**
KIRSTY GUNN **MICHELE ROBERTS**
GERALDINE KAYE **ELISA SEGRAVE**

'Being a clerical officer wasn't a bad job but April was a girl, who at 12 years of age had re-upholstered a 3-piece suite without a pattern.'

'she only went to school to please her mum, be-cause looking after mum was the most important thing... she felt more like her mum was her and she was her mum. A pity they coudn't swap.'

'Auntie Poonam always thought things were worse when done in broad daylight... in front of the whole world, sister. Shameless!'

'I have a young erotic mother...'

PRICE: £8.95   **ISBN: 0-9515877-4-9**

A TOUCH OF THE DUTCH, plays by women
ed. Cheryl Robson

Internationally renowned and award-winning writers.
The first ever collection in English of modern Dutch drama, demonstrating the range and sophistication of new theatre writing by women in the Netherlands.

Write me in the sand by Inez van Dullemen (trans. Anthony Akerman) is a poetic portrayal of a family where layer upon layer is removed to reveal the painful secrets within. Performed to acclaim throughout Europe, available in English for the first time.

The Caracal by Judith Herzberg, Holland's leading woman writer, (trans. Rina Vergano) is a comic one-woman show about a teacher whose complicated love-life is revealed through fragmentary telephone conversations.

A thread in the dark by Hella Haasse, internationally renowned novelist, (trans. Della Couling) is a profound retelling of the myth of Theseus and the Minotaur, from the viewpoint of Ariadne. Widely acclaimed at home and abroad, the play won the Visser Neerlandia prize.

Eat by Matin van Veldhuizen, (trans. Rina Vergano) is a darkly humorous exploration of the lives of three sisters who come together to eat, drink, reminisce and celebrate the anniversary of their mother's death.

Dossier: Ronald Akkerman by Suzanne van Lohuizen, (trans. Saskia Bosch) is a highly topical two-hander, detailing moments between a patient suffering from AIDS and his nurse.

Introduction by Mieke Kolk, senior lecturer in Theatre Studies at the University of Amsterdam, former critic and cofounder of the women's theatre group Persona.

Price £9.95   **isbn 0-9515877-7-3**

YOUNG BLOOD
plays for young performers
edited by Sally Goldsworthy

'this fascinating and varied collection of plays... with something for everyone' NPT Magazine

* large cast plays, roles for boys or girls, up-to-date material

the girl who fell through a hole in her jumper by Naomi Campbell
a young girl falls through a hole in her jumper into a brilliant fantastical world - how will she get home?

the search for odysseus by Charles Way
an angry and awkward adolescent searches for his lost father to the edge of the world.

darker the berry by J.B. Rose
a comic Caribbean Cinderella in which two sisters struggle to break free from the poverty of island life.

geraniums by Sheila Yeger
the battle of Cable Street retold and set against the political choices of young people in the '90's.

out of their heads by Marcus Romer
the friendship and betrayal of three young people who take a trip beyond anything they ever expected.

Sally Goldsworthy, editor is Head of Education at the Lyric Theatre, Hammersmith and formerly director of the London Bubble Youth Theatre.

Price: £9.95   **ISBN 0-9515877-6-5**

ORDER FORM

- THE WOMEN WRITERS HANDBOOK   £4.95
- SEVEN PLAYS BY WOMEN   £5.95
- SIX PLAYS BY BLACK AND ASIAN WOMEN   £7.50
- HOW MAXINE LEARNED TO LOVER HER LEGS   £8.95
- MEDITERRANEAN PLAYS BY WOMEN   £9.95
- A TOUCH OF THE DUTCH   £9.95
- YOUNG BLOOD   £9.95
- BEST OF THE FEST   £12.99

ADD 10% UK / 20% INTERNATIONAL POST AND PACKING

NAME_____

ADDRESS_____

_____

_____

POSTCODE_____

PAYMENT BY CHEQUE OR POSTAL ORDER IN £ STERLING TO:

AURORA METRO PRESS
4 OSIER MEWS
LONDON W4 2NT

TRADE DISTRIBUTION TO:
CENTRAL BOOKS
TEL: 0181 986 4854 FAX: 0181 533 5821